'*Salt Water and Honey* is an ⟨...⟩ us deep into the heart of gri⟨...⟩ to have a child and allowing us to have a sense of how that feels as miscarriage follows miscarriage. She wrestles, too, with her faith, with prayer and liturgy when prayers go unanswered and liturgy does not help. There are no easy answers, no obvious happy ending, but there is a shift in her vision that helps her through. And for others facing similar struggles, people of any faith or of none, there is comfort to be had in knowing they are not alone and that there may be different and gentler times ahead.'

Ruth Bender-Atik, National Director
of The Miscarriage Association

'Unpicking the fairy tale of perfection is long overdue for so many people who have been taught to believe their faith would protect them from difficulty. After hearing Lizzie speak with humility and honesty about her faith and experiences and life "in between", I was pleased to see she'd committed her story to a book that tackles with characteristic openness and vulnerability so many issues that desperately need to be brought into the open. Lizzie brings to life her own stories of heartbreak and hope, failure and friendship with an accessible, authentic voice that will resonate with and encourage many going about their everyday lives with brave faces and hidden pain and hopefully lead others to greater empathy and understanding.'

Vicky Walker, writer, speaker and radio presenter

'This book is extraordinary, and beautiful, and so, so important. Lizzie writes with a powerful and passionate honesty about the journey through the grief of infertility and loss. It's raw, but in a good way, a way which invites you in to the story and allows you to feel both the pain and the hope. And there is hope, and love, and faith, shining at all times through the darkness.'

Revd Kate Wharton, Vicar of St. Bartholomew's, Roby, and
Assistant National Leader of New Wine England

'This is one of the most powerfully honest books about the pain of infertility, miscarriage and childlessness I've ever read, and yet Lizzie never loses us in the darkness of grief. With exquisite beauty and bravery, she gives voice and dignity to the sadness and despair so many of us walk in as we navigate this silent grief. In gently dismantling the crippling "happily-ever-after" myth that healing and wholeness always means pregnancy and childbirth, Lizzie invites us into what she's discovering – that it's possible to know God's comforting presence, even in this, and that with his help we can choose a different vision for our lives, one that can even be richer and fuller than the dreams we fear we've lost.'

Rachel Gardner, Director of National Work Youthscape

'This book is a memoir by someone you've most likely never heard of, which is why it's important. It's her *story* that matters. Lizzie Lowrie takes our hand and leads us on a journey through paradox, winning our trust with her remarkable candour as we follow her through both anguish and amusement. So, grab your cup of coffee or tea and a box of tissues. It's a serious and light-hearted, heartbreaking and cheerful, spiritual and irreverent trek through the well-written pages. Gut-wrenchingly honest, funny and darkly humorous, Lizzie Lowrie writes with vivid detail from "where clichés go to die." It is a story of redemption that never denies the presence of pain. If you're the kind of person who wants to live an authentic life of faith, of hope, and of love in the face of life's struggles, we could not recommend a book more highly.'

Mary and Mike Sares, Steel Toaster Ministries and founders, Scum of the Earth Church, Denver, Colorado USA

'I used to think the best way to help someone find hope was to give them a success story – some glimpse of their dream coming true. But after a personal brush with deep pain, I discovered hope is often born through the kind of raw sharing contained in these pages – of deep loss and painful wrestling that help us know we're not alone in our own dark times. Combining gut-wrenching honesty with humour and beautiful portrayals of friendship, *Salt Water and Honey* helps us in ways simple success stories can't. Because one of our deepest fears we have about our dreams not coming true is that our lives will be over. They won't be. Read this and see what's possible instead.'

Sheridan Voysey, author

'Lizzie is one of those special storytellers who you could listen to recite a shopping list because you know it will make you laugh and make you cry. She tells her story with honesty, humour and hope. It has been a privilege to walk part of this journey with her and Dave, and we are thrilled that other people will be encouraged by the truth they will find in this book. This book is for everyone – we all face struggles; we all have doubts. We hope that *Salt Water and Honey* will remind those who can relate to Lizzie's story that they are not alone, that their grief is real and valid and that their own story truly matters.'

Sheila and Elis Matthews, co-founders of Saltwater and Honey

'This is a book about hope and one which totally blew me away in its honesty, rawness and compassion. It is a book about redefining failure in light of a much bigger perspective.

'We so often shy away from failure as people and yet the book redefines this concept by pointing instead to the redemptive opportunities in life's setbacks.

'This book made me laugh out loud, cry noisily on the tube but above all helped me, yet again, to realise why I am a Christian: not because of me, not because of what is or isn't happening in my life, but because the God we serve is so much bigger and brighter and more hopeful than all of that, and this hope shines from these pages.

'It is a book about fertility, loss, friendship and life's myriad experiences. It is a book which reminds us we are not alone and that there is always hope.'

*Anya Sizer, Regional Representative
for Fertility Network UK in London and champion for
Home for Good and Saying Goodbye*

'Opening this book is like stepping into a secret garden: a garden that is wild, untamed, unpredictable and that doesn't follow the classic order of the seasons, yet within it is such beauty and originality – a secret garden that isn't buried under the weight of the pain, but planted in it.

'Lizzie so generously, humbly and bravely invites us into the most private, intimate and sacred parts of her life, as she writes from her "messy middle" – not from the other side, where it's all neatly ordered and resolved, but from the trenches of infertility. The beautiful prose of this tender, poetic and honestly crafted book will bring a greater degree of understanding, insight, comfort and perspective to its readers. It's about time a book like this was written for all those still in the waiting. And for those alongside them.'

Andy and Sarah Lang, founders of The Rhythm of Hope

Salt Water and Honey

Lost dreams, good grief and a better story

Lizzie Lowrie

Authentic

First published 2020 by Authentic Media Limited,
PO Box 6326, Bletchley, Milton Keynes, MK1 9GG.
authenticmedia.co.uk

British Library Cataloguing in Publication Data
A catalogue record for this book is available from the British Library.
ISBN: 978-1-78893-095-6
978-1-78893-096-3 (e-book)

Cover design by Ian Barnard www.ianbarnard.net
Printed and bound by CPI Group (UK) Ltd, Croydon, CR0 4YY

Over the years I have struggled to find where my story fits. But even in the moments when I have been angry with God or wondered whether he even exists, I have not yet found something other than the Christian story that has helped me make sense of who and where I am. God is in the business of redemption, and throughout history he has taken messy, broken lives and turned them into something beautiful. When I look back, I can see these same golden threads of redemption working through my life and my losses and I am so grateful.

Contents

Foreword

Whether you consider yourself a Christian or not, if you've experienced involuntary childlessness, it's quite likely that your faith in life (let alone your faith in God) has been seriously shaken. Because not only does the blatant unfairness of involuntary childlessness bring us face to face with the inconvenient truth that life isn't actually fair, it also reveals how utterly clueless most traditional faith-based communities and wider society are at acknowledging and supporting those grieving the family they longed for.

And this is why Lizzie's earthy, frank and humane memoir is so important. It's a story of enduring multiple unexplained miscarriages whilst struggling to fit into her role as a Church of England vicar's wife; a world full of 'middle-class conversation, extravagantly fertile women and cake', and the depths of despair she plumbed before making peace with that. She recalls looking for advice on the internet about how long it might take her to get over a miscarriage, but finding nothing apart from women talking about getting pregnant again. As she writes, 'the story of the in-between has no voice on the internet.'

This is the story of that in-between. Of being in-between the hope of motherhood whilst experiencing the heartbreak of multiple miscarriages. Of being in-between joy and envy when it seems that everyone else is sailing into parenthood leaving you behind. Of being in-between pregnant and unpregnant, even whilst carrying a child, and the medical profession's cluelessness around this ambiguity. It's about living in limbo in your body, your soul, your life, your marriage, your work, your friendships, your family, your community, your Church, your faith and your identity as a woman. And of the devastating sadness of feeling lost and alone in that in-between.

Deeply moving, tragic and shot through with dark humour, this memoir charts Lizzie's years of heartbreak and desolation over her inability to keep a baby alive in her womb, her sense of alienation from the community and faith that had formerly given her life purpose, and her gradual redefinition of herself as a woman, a wife, a Christian – and as something much greater than her childlessness. It's also a moving love story of a marriage tested and not found wanting, even in the bleakest of times. About how breaking through the wall of silence around infertility, miscarriage, baby loss and childlessness can create a space for others to grieve their losses too, and in doing so can bring together a new kind of faith-based community, a grittier one built on helping others find their way through their dark nights of the soul, with the loving support of those who've been there too.

This book is a story about finding something else at the end of the rainbow other than that longed-for baby; it's about a different kind of happy ending than the one you expected. It's about redemption, but not in the way you'd imagined. And a lot of cake.

Jody Day
Founder of Gateway Women
www.gateway-women.com

Preface

When I was 8, I fell in love with a fairy tale, a happily-ever-after. As I grew, this story of a perfect family, a perfect job and the perfect life etched itself into my heart. This fairy tale was more than my first love: it was my first dream and my first plan and I surrendered my unguarded heart to this happy tale. But, unlike other childhood passions – like learning the flute or having a pet – this love was not fleeting or fickle. It grew with me, burying deeper into my heart, my thoughts and my dreams.

The fairy tale began to crumble as I emptied the premises of our failed business, and it collapsed altogether as I lay curled up on the toilet floor of a train, travelling home to Chester. My concerned husband scooped me up at the station and drove me to the hospital where the doctor confirmed my miscarriage. I sat silently cradling a hot-water bottle, slowly realizing that the story I had fallen for was not coming true.

As the failures and losses continued, my fairy tale became even more warped and twisted – no longer full of hope and new life, but dark with defeat and depression. Instead of bringing joy, the story I had fallen in love with left me feeling empty, lacking. It defined me and isolated me as I retreated from those who were living out the happily-ever-after I had given my heart to. Eventually I decided it was time to let my first love go. I had to put the book down and leave the fairy tale behind. As I searched for a different story, I found that people were only willing to share their happily-ever-afters. So I wrote the book I longed for; the book for those who are lost in the wreckage of their dreams, the ones whose story doesn't look anything like they hoped it would and are struggling to find their place in the world. Because now I realize that fairy tales are for kids but the greatest stories are found within the ruins of lost dreams.

Acknowledgements

Writing a memoir sounds like a very solitary task, but the hours I have spent alone writing have served as a powerful reminder that our stories were never meant to be lived out in isolation. I am so grateful for the people around me: for those included in this book and the many who aren't, including all my wonderful new friends at StoryHouse. Thank you for all your support and prayers over the years and for encouraging me to write this book – you will always make my story better.

Thank you to everyone at Authentic Media for giving me this opportunity and for editing and publishing the book I longed for. Thank you to all the people who have given time to read many drafts of my work including Damien Barr, Morag and Dave – your input definitely made this book way better than it was. Thank you to Ian Barnard for the amazing book cover you designed for me. Thank you to Jody Day for writing the foreword and for my friends who endorsed this book. Thank you to Alec – your generosity gave me the confidence and the skills to start writing.

Thank you to the churches and church leaders who showed me what church should look like. Andrew Buchanan, Mike and Mary Sares – your love for Jesus, your faithfulness to the gospel and your compassion for the left-out and the messed-up, showed me what God is like and also kept me in church.

Thank you to all the students, spouses and staff at Dave's training college – for the loving support you gave to Dave and

I, even after we tried to run away! Thanks especially to Bee, Laura, Cath, tiny Rach, Becci, Hannah, Sheila, Rach, Esther, Erin, Kathryn, Jenny, Julie, Katie and Kaf – I couldn't fit all of you in the book, but thank you for being my friend! Thank you also to Petals: the Baby Loss Counselling Charity and all the support and advice you offered me and Dave.

Thank you to the two special groups of women in Weigh and Pray and Red Tent, who I shared so much food, laughter and tears with. There is something so precious and beautiful about a group of women sharing their lives with each other; thank you for loving me and for helping me share my story.

Thank you to Rach and Jane – your courage and compassion transformed my life and showed me what Jesus is like. Thank you for your advocacy as you represented those of us struggling with infertility, miscarriage and childlessness in our small community. Your decision to enter into our suffering with us has empowered us to do the same for others.

Thank you to the Saltwater and Honey community. What a privilege it's been to meet so many people who share similar stories. May you always know that you're not alone, it's OK to grieve and your story matters.

Thank you to Sheila and Elis, I'm so grateful we found each other! It's been so much fun to create something new together. I never imagined our blog would turn into a ministry for those struggling with infertility, miscarriage and faith, especially because we're not strategic or professional in any way! What a privilege it has been to watch God redeem our stories and use our pain for something so good.

Sheila, I know you're married to Elis and I'm married to Dave, but we really were meant to be together! You have brought so much joy into my life – thanks for going on this vulnerability journey with me. One day we will meet St Brené and we will tell her how her work gave us the words to articulate what we were learning and how it was changing us.

Thank you to the Rowland-Smiths and the Lowries for walking with Dave and I through both the salt water and the honey.

Thank you to Dave, my husband, who not only encouraged me to share my story but also lived it. Thank you for the hours you willingly gave to read my drafts, make me coffee and repeatedly tell me 'you can do this'. You are my best friend and I'm so grateful for how you constantly encourage and challenge me to tell a better story.

1

Dearly Beloved . . .

I cup my hands and bring them up to my mouth trying to breathe life into them, but it makes little difference. I check my watch again under the light provided by a street lamp as we wait for the winter sun to rise.

'It's almost five,' I tell Dave.

'It's fine,' he mumbles. 'They know we need to clear everything out first thing, they'll be here soon.' He pulls his beanie hat further over his ears, then goes back to kicking stones down a drain. Hands tucked into the pockets of his jeans, his breath curls up into the frozen December air. He's still not wearing a coat. I don't even know if he has a coat. I can't believe I'm going to marry him and I don't know if he owns a coat or not.

'Here they are!' The headlights from Rob's white transit van feel like spotlights, illuminating the secrecy of what's about to happen. Rob skilfully manoeuvres the van and trailer outside the grey back doors of the café, before Joy jumps out the front seat and gives us both a big hug. Her tall frame feels larger than normal, holding the broken pieces of me together. Things must be really bad because Rob hugs me as well. Few words are spoken as we walk towards the back doors; we've got a job to do and the sooner it's done, the better.

Dave unlocks the doors and we walk down the brick corridor, past our office, through the double doors and into the café. I flick the panel of light switches on, as I have done every morning for the past ten months, Rob starts tearing bin bags off a big black roll and we silently blackout the glass front of the café. When the café opened, we invited everyone to celebrate, but now we're hiding; the shame of failure obscured by black bin-liners.

'Show me everything you want to take first, then I'll tell you what order to bring it out in, so we can pack the van properly,' Rob says.

We point to the large, brown leather sofas that were just starting to relax, their fabric softened by the many coffee dates they had entertained; the mismatched wooden chairs and tables we'd bought at an auction; the pool table and the coffee machine that Dave spent months researching and promptly fell in love with as soon as it arrived. I wasn't jealous. I was pretty certain that he loved me more, but I'm worried now about how sad he'll be when we drop her off at her new home in an arts café in the basement of a church in Manchester.

'Right, let's take this table first,' Rob tells us. The four of us gather round the big, long table at the front of the shop, hands under the table top. 'One, two, three, lift.' We slowly shuffle it out of the building, Joy and I walking backwards without tripping up – quite an achievement – through the corridor and outside into the promising light of a new day, the wintry sun resting on the rooftops of the city taking its Sunday morning lie-in.

'It's quite pretty, isn't it?' declares Joy, looking up to the pinky-yellow sky.

'Still not pretty enough to make me get up this early more often,' adds Rob, as he grabs the chairs Dave hands to him and stacks them in the back of his van.

We silently travel between the van and café. My body moves with an energy that should not be there. Each object is carefully carried out of the building with the honour afforded to our meticulously constructed dream; the silence of the empty café space following us out like the silence following an explosion in a film, the impact of the blast expanding with a force so loud, it almost can't be heard.

As soon as we load the last sofa onto the trailer, Joy jumps onto it, arms and legs sprawled over the soft, red cushions. 'Can we rest now?'

'No,' Rob tells her, carrying blue tarpaulin over to the trailer. 'If you don't get up soon, you're going to be strapped in!'

'That sounds like fun!'

'OK, then.' Rob hands Dave one end of the tarpaulin and they throw it over her. She lies still underneath for a few seconds.

Ripples appear under the blue sheet. Her head appears. 'Pah! That stinks! I'm getting out!' She clumsily picks her way through the chairs and coffee tables, jumping off the trailer. The boys rope down the tarpaulin, then drive off to distribute its contents to some of the local churches in Chester. Joy and I drive back to hers with the boot of my Peugeot 206 filled with paperwork, failure written through each page.

There was so much more I wanted to pack up into Rob's van, like the orange and brown retro wallpaper and a wall mural of an angel, surrounded by a Bible verse that said, 'See, I am sending an angel ahead of you to guard you along the way and to bring you to the place I have prepared' (Exod. 23:20). I wanted to take the poems and words written on the walls in the prayer room. I wanted to relive moments again – Rob moaning about how much time it took to paint the ceiling. Our coffee taste-testing session – downing shots with Dave's friend from a local coffee house, chatting and laughing past midnight. Our opening party when we announced we were dating and Dave's mum hugged me. Our music nights, the wedding reception we gave for a couple from AA – Alcoholics Anonymous – the time when two guys just walked in and started playing flamenco guitar. The games of pool with the staff from the Pakistani restaurant next door. I wish I could pack all this up in the back of Rob's van or at least bottle it and take it on the train back to Sussex with me to help make the news I had to break to my parents a bit easier to swallow.

I tell Mum and Dad about the café on Christmas Eve and spend the following week avoiding eye contact and silencing hushed conversations when I enter a room. I'm just as worried as they are about me, but I'm middle class and a Christian, so unravelling is not an option. At least we've got a wedding to talk about. In four months Dave and I will be married, so I just keep steering the conversation round to weddings because everyone knows what to do with that. During my week at home, I give out Christmas presents bought with someone else's money, pull crackers, play games, sing at the flaming Christmas pudding and say goodbye to my parents in the same way I greeted them – tired and unable to look them in the eye.

My return, back to the familiarity of Chester and Dave, hasn't stopped the dark thoughts that keep claiming my head and my heart. The mornings are worse – my mind opens up before my eyes open, and that's the bit I don't like. For a moment there is peace, and then I remember. I turn over. I'm not ready to face what lies beyond the daylight falling through the floral curtains. The dark-green carpet surrounding my bed absorbs the light, enabling me to fall back into the ignorant peace of sleep for a little bit longer. My routine has changed, defined by what I've stopped doing. I don't set my alarm. I don't work.

We've decided to wait until after the wedding to give us time to close the business and recover.

I no longer read my Bible and I'm definitely not praying. Reconciling my faith with what's happened hangs too heavy over me, and for now I feel I've earned a break from God. I thought it would be easy, but this conscious avoidance keeps catching me, as though God is trying to squeeze through the crack in a door and I'm having to repeatedly slam it shut in his face.

I really should get up. My head is desperate for coffee. I tread along the dark-green carpet and into the green bathroom, with its matching avocado bathroom suite. I splash water on my face. Although I know the water's clean, I still close my mouth, just in case the green ceramic has finally penetrated the water flowing from it and turned it into dark-green sludge. I grab the jumper and jeans I'd thrown onto the swamp-like carpet late last night and descend into the darkness of the lounge-diner below.

The house I'm renting is owned by a missionary and it's cheap. I've never met my landlady but I feel just as blessed by her life as the families she works with in India, because I know that without her generosity I would probably be homeless right now. As well as her life of service to the poor, the only other thing I know about her is that she likes earthy colours – well, basically, green; in particular, a kind of greeny-brown. When you walk through the front door and into the lounge-diner, the green walls, carpet and matching furniture envelop you, leaving you wondering if any other colour even exists. The walls and furnishings absorb most of the daylight travelling through the net curtains. The remaining light is enough to remind you that there was life outside, but not enough to make you feel as though you should be joining in.

The long, dark-brown kitchen boasts two kettles, five cafetières and cupboards crammed full of crockery. There's the obligatory greeny-brown dinner plates with matching coffee cups, then next to them a cupboard crammed with just frying pans. There's also a cupboard full of repurposed food containers spanning several decades; ice-cream tubs from the eighties, sunflower-spread tubs from the nineties: the history of UK plastics. The shelves are so full of recycled Tupperware that every time you venture inside for even the smallest of pots you have to quickly shut the cupboard doors again, for fear of the entire contents spilling out onto the green-patterned lino floor, crashing into the dark-green silence of the house.

Although I'm sleeping in the green house, I'm basically living at Joy and Rob's. Dave's staying in their spare room until we get married. I don't think having Dave and I around the house has helped Rob's motivation to find jobs for his handyman business. We all watch quite a lot of telly, drink coffee and eat cake and then Dave and I try to do some café admin, but mostly I just want to do wedding planning.

Working together is easy; we've always been good at that. That's why I moved up north, to work with Dave. It was just over two years ago now when I received an email from a friend, forwarding a message from some guy called Dave who wanted to set up a café in Chester. I'd just moved back in with my parents after my fourth gap year and had got a temp job that involved a lot of photocopying, so reading an email describing a dream I'd also been carrying for years got me very excited. I emailed back straight away and a couple of months later travelled up to Chester to meet Dave and talk about coffee shops.

When Dave and I first met, I didn't think of him in 'that way'. Well, he was taller than me, and that's rare, so I can't say the thought hadn't crossed my mind – I was six foot and finding a tall guy who was 'normal' wasn't easy. So, he was tall, but he had no hair. He wasn't bald, he'd just forgotten to put the attachment on his clippers that morning and had given himself a '0' haircut. I also thought he had a small mouth. I can't say why I saw this as a negative, but in that moment it felt significant.

We spent the day walking round the city, drinking coffee and talking about what our café would be like, and rather than stay in Sussex photocopying my life away, I decided to move up to Chester to open a café with Dave. We'd agreed that working and dating was a bad idea, but Dave grew his hair back and I stopped worrying about the size of his mouth and now we're getting married.

'Have either of you had any thoughts about the wedding service and what readings you'd like?' asks Andrew, our vicar. We're sat in his small study, surrounded by stacks of books and papers, our mugs empty as the conversation ebbs and flows, with him skilfully leading us from the excitement of the wedding to the sobering reality of what we've lost. He's one of the few brave enough to enter this unknown, willing to sit with the unanswered questions. But I'm just not ready to let him take me there yet.

'Actually,' Dave replies, 'I was wondering if the readings and the sermon could be based on Genesis. I've just read this great book and in it there's a chapter about Adam and Eve. I've got the book here.' He leans forward, passing the book to Andrew who's sat opposite.

'Which chapter is it?' Andrew starts flicking through the pages.

'It's the one about nudity.'

'Ah! I see it!'

Dave explains: 'Basically, the chapter talks about when Adam and Eve first met in the Garden of Eden and how important it was that they were naked; they had nothing to hide, they didn't need to pretend, they were completely comfortable with one another. When I read that, I thought it would be great for our wedding day.' We both look to Andrew, flicking through the pages of the chapter, trying to gauge how he's going to respond. He puts the book down on the small coffee table next to him.

'I think it sounds like a great idea,' he replies eventually. 'I mean, no one's going to forget the wedding where the vicar talked about nudity, are they?'

It's 5 April 2008. I leave the quiet of the green house to get ready for my wedding at the hotel where the reception is taking place later. Many of those coming to the wedding haven't seen me since the café closed, and I'm glad. I'm ready to get dressed up and show people how happy I am.

I love my wedding dress. It's beautiful. I love wearing it. The antique pink silk stretches in folds across my chest, falling down to the floor and collecting in a bustle at the back, all held together with pink and ivory flowers. Sequins sparkle over the fabric, nestling under the long veil hanging over the curls of my hair, down over my bare shoulders and falling to the floor. The silver necklace and matching earrings, designed by a friend, shine in the early spring light as I step out the car. Andrew hugs me.

Lesley, one of my bridesmaids, passes me my posy of dusty pink ranunculi, sage and rosemary and we walk into the church. The music starts and one of our regulars from the café who always ordered a peppermint tea joins in with his guitar, and my dad and I move forward as one of the other regulars from our café open mic nights starts to sing. Everyone's looking at me, watching as I walk towards Dave. I haven't felt this good in months. My hand holding my posy rests on my tummy, miraculously flattened by the power of my beautiful wedding dress. I reach Dave.

'You look amazing!' he whispers.

I try to listen to the sermon, but the excitement of the day, along with the fact I was wearing a really pretty dress and was sitting next to a man now about to be called my husband, was all a bit too much. I smile and nod, knowing the words Andrew's sharing have been crafted for us as well as for the rest of the congregation. Next to me sits Dave, looking handsome in his grey three-piece suit, with his hair and his small mouth. I hold his hand. His hand that had daily touched my face to wipe away the tears whenever I thought about what we'd lost. Our fingers locked together, sharing the heavy guilt of losing money we knew we could never repay. We are bankrupt, both relying on parents bailing us out and food from friends. I had often heard Dave's late-night confessions to failing those who'd relied on us, whose wages we'd paid. I know the shame he feels whenever he sees my dad, reminding him of the money invested and lost. I know the ways in which stress still tortures his body. We've both been stripped bare, left with nothing, naked.

Andrew finishes his sermon and asks us to stand for the marriage bit. Stood at the front of the church ready to say our vows, I look up to the gilded statue of Jesus on the cross suspended above me. Yes, he has a cloth covering his modesty on this statue, but I imagine he was naked when it happened; exposed, humiliated and weak. Standing under that cross wearing my expensive dress scattered in sequins, I feel so distant from the raw humanity displayed above me. The congregation stands with us. The dimly lit Gothic church is full, friends filling the pews that are normally stacked in a corner, quickly separated into rows by the ushers. Church leaders who'd prayed for the cafe, students who'd hung out on the sofas, the guys from AA, local business owners and a friend who used to sneak out the house to have a banoffee waffle without telling his wife. All had given time and love and money to the café. They're all here. Regular customers like the guy who always ordered a large cappuccino with an extra shot, who drove me and my dad to church this morning in his classic red Jaguar Mark Two. Then there are the two media students obsessed by our white chocolate cheesecake, who are filming the wedding, and a talented young couple from our open mic nights who will be performing at the reception this evening with their swing band.

Although the café doors have closed, everyone's here, and I'm so glad. This is how I want them to see me – as the beautiful bride, not the girl who tried something and failed.

2

Caffeine Withdrawal

~~~~~

This is the only time in my life when I can legitimately say that the honeymoon is over. Our marriage has begun and it is wonderful. I especially loved sipping Mojitos and exploring Cuba, a country I'd studied at university and always longed to visit. But now we're back and every morning the brief moment of peace I feel upon waking is quickly consumed by the shame of failure as the pain of caffeine withdrawal creeps across my forehead.

I've never really failed before, not in such a spectacular and public way, and I don't know what to do with it. I hadn't really thought about this bit – I believed the moment we closed the café would be the most painful, but it's not; life in the aftermath is so much worse. I wish there was some kind of guidebook to navigating failure, but books about marriage after bankruptcy aren't the kind of stories people want to read.

Four banks have refused our request to set up a joint account. It began with a nice lady with neat blonde hair and a red blouse in a bank in Chester city centre. We arrived with cheques written out to us in our married name and the request to set up an account. We sat sipping chilled water from clear plastic cups whilst she tapped away on her keyboard asking questions about our banking history, my wedding dress and our honeymoon in Cuba. Then she suddenly stopped typing, looked up from her screen and just said, 'No.' The silence left behind by the still-ness of her fingers on the keyboard and the abruptness of her answer interrupted Dave's description of the cigar factory. 'No, you can't open an account with us,' she repeated.

We took our cheques to three more banks and three more clerks with neat hair and colour-coordinated blouses and ties, all of whom agreed with her assessment of our future. Our credit rating after the failure of our business meant they didn't want anything to do with us. We stepped out onto the street after our fourth rejection dazed and disorientated, surrounded by shoppers discussing where to have lunch and tourists study-ing thin paper maps flapping about in the spring breeze.

It's fairly easy to fill the day with distractions, and when I'm alone I turn on the telly and lose myself in sitcoms, but when the lights go out, we talk. Lying next to each other in the dark, our fingers wrapped together, we share confessions of regret, of guilt over the debt we owe to so many of the most loved people in our lives, and wishing the memories and the pain would all go away.

The morning after our day of rejections I was once again woken up by my need for caffeine. Unable to remain lying in bed with my thoughts, waiting for Dave to wake up, I headed downstairs to make a cup of tea. The ancient brown and cream kettle was taking an eternity to boil, so I searched through the pile of post on the worktop to see if there was anything to open that didn't look like a bill whilst I waited.

I tore open a brown envelope with just our names written on the front and pulled out cash – a lot of cash. I searched for a note or a name and nothing, just one – no, *two* hundred pounds in cash. The exact amount we needed for our rent.

Dave's response confused me. 'What an answer to prayer!'

Yes, I suppose he was right, but I hadn't been praying. Had he been praying? He didn't tell me he'd prayed. Overwhelmed someone had shown us such generosity, I decided to say a small 'thank you' in my head to God. But Dave's enthusiasm for God's prayer-answering skills continued after he receive an email from a guy he knew, offering him a job as a web designer. 'This is amazing! I can't believe it – first the money, now the job. God's looking after us, Lizzie! It's going to be OK.'

Oh, how I wish the only withdrawal I was struggling with was from a lack of caffeine, but the angry pain filling my head is not the only thought I have each morning; it's always quickly followed by my conscious decision to ignore God. For years my life has been defined by my faith and by the God I have/had faith in. My daily morning routine, shortly after boiling the kettle, was always to remember my creator and chat to him about what was going on in my life. But right now, I barely have the courage to ring my parents, let alone speak to God. I am angry, I am ashamed and I am embarrassed that I trusted God with my dreams. I used to be a person who enjoyed God's company, and now I'm the person who wonders whether the life I knew before was even real, whether I made God up.

Despite my efforts to ignore God, we're still going to church. We arrive each Sunday morning, welcomed by croissants and fresh coffee served up in the café mugs we donated. Music, prayers, Bible readings and a sermon drift over me, my heart hard like the wooden pew I'm sat on. Each Sunday I sit with Dave on my left and my friend Becky on my right. Sometimes I look around at the congregation but their faces carry too many memories – people we once employed, who prayed, volunteered and gave money, reminding me of a time when I was excited and inspired and confident that God would make our vision a success. It's like doing the walk of shame every time I step through the church doors, but instead of being shown pictures of me snogging some random guy, I'm simply reminded of how my prayers weren't answered.

I'm currently lying on the sofa at home, my legs covered in the blue chenille throw that's been slowly slipping down the sofa, draping itself over me and exposing the muddy green cushion beneath. Sat to the right of me on the olive-green wing-back chair is Rob, with a mug of coffee and a bag of sausage rolls, watching *West Wing*. It's been almost two weeks since the first time I lost my memory and I'm still on the sofa watching *West Wing* with Rob, or *Friends* when Rob's not here. The doctor has no idea what to do with me so I'm waiting for an appointment with a consultant.

The first time it happened I was sat in the staff room of a language school on my first day back at work. I'd taught my first English lesson to a room full of Spanish students and was having a coffee in the staff room, explaining to a couple of my colleagues why I'm back a year after I left to set up my own business, and then suddenly my mind went blank. I lost my memory. I didn't know where I was or what day it was. I felt sick and really sleepy and scared.

I've lost my memory every day since, sometimes up to four or five times, and I've not been back to work since. I've been lying here all day in and out of consciousness, putting off making another call to the school. I check my watch again; it's almost four. I need to ring the course director, before the school closes, so I leave Rob watching President Jed Bartlet save America for the fourth time today and head into the kitchen.

'I'm really sorry but I can't come in again tomorrow.'

'Oh, OK. Well, thanks for letting me know.' She pauses. 'Lizzie, do you think it would be better if we just acknowledge that it could be a while until you can work again? We need to ensure we have enough teachers for our classes and it doesn't sound like you're well enough to work at the moment.'

'Ummm.' A huge lump rises in my throat, my face flushes and warm tears begin to form in the corners of my eyes. 'I suppose you're right. I don't want to make it difficult for you.'

'Don't worry about us, but I think you need to acknowledge that you're just not very well at the moment and that you need to look after yourself. Your health should be your main priority.'

'Yes,' I reply weakly. 'Yes, you're right. I think maybe you should find someone else to take my place.'

'OK, I will. But do get in touch when you're feeling better. We'd love to have you work with us again in the future.'

'Yes, I will. Thank you.'

'You just concentrate on getting better and hopefully we'll speak soon.'

'OK, thanks. Goodbye.' I hear the click of the phone hanging up and know I'll never work there again.

Dave's back from work a bit early today because we've got Bob coming over to see us. Bob is Rob's dad. He and his wife have supported us from the beginning and he's one of the remaining few people brave enough to still talk to us since everything went wrong. A social worker turned vicar, Bob's one of those people you want to spend time with because you know you'll always feel better afterwards.

We sit and drink coffee, Bob's tall, thin frame extending beyond the olive-green wing-back chair he's sat in, his long legs crossed by swinging one right over the other as only vicars seem able to do. 'So, how are you both doing?' he asks, leaning back into his chair, his mug resting on his knee. I look over to Dave, willing him to answer, and thankfully he obliges.

I don't know whether he's tired or hasn't had enough caffeine, but Dave's response is different to normal. It's honest – really, brutally honest – leaving the bare facts of bankruptcy, failure and my memory loss, which according to the doctors is caused by stress, just hanging there. I look to Bob, waiting for him to awkwardly change the subject or tell us that everything's part of God's plan, but he doesn't.

'I'm sad the café's closed too. But it's you guys I'm worried about,' he says. 'Firstly, you shouldn't feel guilty about the money people gave to the café; their decisions to give financially weren't and aren't your responsibility. The money was a gift and gifts aren't given with the expectation of something in return. Plus, it was God's money in the first place anyway.'

I nod, his words soothing my shame. I wish I'd recorded what he's said so I could keep playing it over on repeat.

'Do you know how I see failure?' he continues. 'It's manure. I've been part of so many failed projects over the years; I've been in charge of asking people to give money to initiatives that never really bore any visible fruit. But I believe all these failures are manure; ugly, stinking messes that no one knew what to do with. But eventually I've seen each one of those failures go on to feed the growth of new ideas, new projects and new beginnings. So right now you're right in the middle of a lot of manure, but I believe one day this mess will feed the growth of something even better.'

The next afternoon I decide to walk into town to celebrate keeping my memory all day by having a decaf cappuccino – because that's how rock and roll my life is right now. Waiting in the queue to order my drink, a lady approaches me. 'Excuse me, did you used to run that café thing?'

'Yes,' I respond reluctantly, knowing what would come next.

'I thought it was you. It's such a shame it closed. I thought it was a great idea. I guess you must have heard God wrong, then. I mean, if he'd really told you to open a café then it wouldn't have closed.'

I think for a while, trying to work out if I want to get into a really intense conversation with this lady, or if I'd prefer her to just leave me alone. I turn my body to face her square on, my eyes looking right at her. 'Well, maybe God just needed some more manure.' She looks at me confused, wondering whether she heard me right or whether I've actually gone mad.

'Oh, right, yes, err, maybe he did. Well, all the best for the future.'

'Thanks,' I respond. She turns to leave, and I order my cappuccino.

3

Weigh and Pray

~

Like most women, I've always been thinking about dieting, or trying to diet, for as long as I can remember. I don't really recall a time when I've felt skinny. I've had a few thin days, but they never last. Forced to listen to my regular laments about how uncomfortable I feel and how I shouldn't have eaten that bag of crisps, Dave is always trying to convince me I'm not fat. The problem is, I'm tall, or 'big-boned' as my mum would say, and as a result have spent most of my life feeling out of proportion with the rest of the world. I remember school photos with me on the back row in the middle, towering over all the boys. As a teenager I struggled to find clothes that fitted, forced to clothe my growing body in men's jeans and Doc Martens. This, accompanied by very short hair, marks a dark period in my life, reaching crisis point when, at 13, I was asked out by a girl at a roller disco. That was when I started my first diet and decided to grow my hair.

Some diets have been more successful than others, a high-point being my post-year-abroad diet. Rather than fall in love with learning about Italian politics or a hot Italian guy, I fell in love with the food and the coffee. I only went to one lecture, choosing to spend my EU grant on eating my way around the country. Once home my mum took me to Weight Watchers and I slowly shed the pasta, pizza, ice cream, cakes and cappuccinos, only to regain the weight after returning for my final year at uni. As I've said – being skinny is not an experience I'm used to. Eating too much, then lying in bed vowing to never eat again is more the way I roll.

Tonight I'm on my way to Steph's to watch *Strictly*. My furry, grey slippers are padding along the pavement, my pyjama bottoms trailing along the ground behind me, a large bag of Doritos in my right hand and my left hand wrapped around the neck of a bottle of rosé, the one with the biggest reduction in the supermarket and the nicest label – always the best way to choose wine, in my opinion. I step between the parked cars lining each side of the narrow street where we now live.

Four months ago, my missionary landlady and owner of the green house, returned from her post, offering us an opportunity to find somewhere smaller and more expensive but less green, and we're now living in a two-bedroom terrace on a street that to my southern eyes looks just like *Coronation Street*. I actually feel like I'm in *Coronation Street*, crossing the road in my pyjama bottoms and slippers with wine and crisps to hang out with my friend Steph at number 58; all I need now are some rollers to complete the look. I probably shouldn't be drinking; the fear of losing my memory, although less of a danger now, is still resting there at the back of my mind. But thanks to the prescription of antidepressants and medication for what the consultant diagnosed as migraines, life has become a bit more stable. I've also just started a temp job at the University of Chester, an achievement, I believe, that calls for a bit of a celebration.

On the short walk to Steph's I try to sneak nosy peeks into the living rooms of the terraced houses sitting on the pavement, each one laid out differently, the light from their homes spilling out onto the road, illuminating my path. I rush past Betty's house before the net curtain starts twitching and the door opens asking me what I'm doing and whether I think the two guys that just moved in over the road are gay, and knock on Steph's door.

'Hello, babes!'

'Hey, hon.' I step straight into the living room and give Steph a big hug.

'Right, we've got five minutes until *Strictly* starts. Let's get ourselves sorted.'

'Oh, great, it's started again,' shouts Steph's husband, Jamie, from the kitchen.

'Jamie! Shouldn't you be somewhere else?'

'Yeah, alright. I'm just about to go. I just need to grab a few DVDs.'

I love this arrangement. This way everyone's happy. Dave and Jamie get to watch zombie films and we get to watch *Strictly* in peace. Jamie leaves to walk across to our house in his slippers with DVDs and beers under his arms.

We're buried under Steph's big tartan blanket in our pyjamas. I always think an elasticated waist is necessary for nights like this. There are two bags of Doritos scrunched up on the coffee table, a box of chocolates on our laps and big glasses of wine in our hands. Steph is shouting at Bruce Forsyth on the telly: 'You're not funny any more!' Watching the toned, perma-tanned dancers on *Strictly Come Dancing* is not helping the food-guilt I am currently experiencing.

'I've decided I'm goin' on a diet, babes,' says Steph.

Sat in my PJs, faced with a dance troupe of women in bikinis, I feel I have no choice. 'I think I might need to join you.'

A dancer wearing a napkin spins around in front of a crooning Michael Bublé as Steph and I devise a plan to help each other lose weight. We'll have our own weigh-in – kind of like Weight Watchers, but free and without the pep talks. We reckon Becky and Joy will be up for doing it with us, so we decide we'll start next week with a weigh-in on Monday.

'If we're going to start next week, we should make the most of tonight, then.'

'Good idea! More rosé, babes?' She fills my glass with more of 'the cheapest rosé money can buy' – this is how Steph always orders her wine.

The following Monday evening we meet at Becky's. We decide to meet at hers because she has the nicest house and she owns a pair of scales. Joy and Becky have created a graph in their lunch hour to chart our progress – it looks complicated but they're accountants so they know what they're doing. Becky offered to cook us dinner as well – Becky's amazing. We decide to weigh ourselves before eating, apart from this first week. Weighing ourselves after eating would make us heavier, but it does mean there's more chance we'll have lost weight next week.

The four of us sit round the table. Steph's inappropriate, Becky fusses over us, bringing out dishes, topping up glasses and washing-up without us noticing, and Joy laughs loudly. We talk about work, about the weekend, about food, about men and about dieting.

It gets to 9:30 and we realize we can't put it off any longer. Becky brings the scales down and we take it in turns to weigh ourselves. We find that we're all lighter when we weigh ourselves on Becky's living-room carpet rather than the tiled kitchen floor. Steph wants to find out which room she's the thinnest in, so we take the scales into every room of Becky's house. I was really light in Becky's bedroom, Steph was lighter on the landing, Becky preferred her weight in the living room;

Joy actually tried weighing herself on Becky's bed, jumping up and down screaming out how she'd lost over a stone by just walking up the stairs. After much debate we decide to take the measurements from the scales on the kitchen floor as they're probably more accurate, if a bit mean. Joy does her accountant thing and enters all our weights into a spreadsheet; we vow to eat healthily and agree to meet at mine next Monday for the weigh-in and a healthy dinner.

It's Monday evening and the girls are here. Steph arrives first, crossing the road to our house in her slippers, Joy and Becky in suits straight from work – it's month end. Dave is sent to the living room. Door shut. Weigh-in begins. It wasn't bad for the first week – a couple of us lost, a couple stayed the same. Entries made on the spreadsheet, time for food. The large oak table fills the dining room of our tiny terraced house; it's the centre of attention, inviting us to gather round it, sharing food and stories. I dish up my mum's healthy Spanish chicken – although I sincerely doubt its authenticity as a celebrated Spanish dish, especially when accompanied by mashed potato. We eat and we talk. Steph's applying for a new job. The anniversary of when Becky should have got married is next week. Joy is struggling with praying. I told her I was too, that I still had trust issues with God. Steph hasn't prayed for months. Becky has stopped asking God for stuff since she called the engagement off. So we decide to pray for each other this week, for the job application, the non-wedding anniversary, the desire to talk to God and the struggle to sit down and actually do it.

The next Monday we're at Steph's and we have a new member – Gommie, one of Steph's friends from uni. We reluctantly weigh in – the less said about that the better – then Steph serves up dinner. Sat round the table the conversation is only briefly interrupted by mouthfuls of spaghetti Bolognese and cups of tea. Steph shares uni stories and Gommie cringes with embarrassment. Becky secretly clears the empty plates away and Joy plays around with our weight loss graph. The laptop splattered with tomato sauce, Becky rushes to wipe it off. Then Steph says something none of us expected to hear.

'I've been thinking. You know we prayed last week? Well . . . I actually found that really helpful. I mean, it's not easy but it was good to talk about stuff. I was thinking we should also say how we're doing each week and pray about it as well as doing a weigh-in.'

Silence. We look round the table, gauging each other's reaction, slowly offering murmurs of agreement once we'd established no one was against the idea. It was a good idea. Good, but scary. Steph's suggestions normally involved multiple bottles of cheap rosé and talking about sex, so this was a bit unexpected. The challenge to pray together felt like a good one: hard, but good – it meant I couldn't ignore God any more.

'I know!' shouts Joy. 'We could call it Weigh and Pray!'

We all start laughing – 'Weigh and Pray! That's a terrible name!' – but somehow it stuck. That evening we named this weird weight-loss dinner party we'd started having every Monday night. The husbands make fun of it, they've renamed it 'Get Fat and Chat' – they don't believe we'll keep up the weight loss or the praying.

The days between each Monday drift past in a perfectly non-eventful way. I'm three months into my job at Chester university now, and I'm loving the fact that someone else is in charge, someone else pays me and if something goes wrong it's not my responsibility to sort it out. If I leave my desk on time and walk fast, I can be home by ten-past five – ten-past four on a Friday. Arriving home, I let Professor Hopalong, our new house rabbit, out of his cage, feed him a carrot and put the kettle on. I sit on the floor watching the Professor jump around the dining room; running up to me, he gives a few sniffs and lowers his head, inviting me to stroke his soft, grey fur with my right hand and sip my tea with my left.

Dave arrives back about six, we cook dinner, and move into the lounge, the Prof hopping along behind us. Most evenings are like this, watching telly, water pistol ready to squirt the Prof when he starts chewing the furniture. When it's time for bed, the Professor hops into his home and we head upstairs, weary but peaceful. I know that a very ordinary life is not something you're supposed to pursue when you're in your late twenties, but when you've lost something, then trust me, 'normal' feels amazing. I have no ambition and I am happy that way, rejecting the middle-class world I grew up in, the teaching that I could do anything. Liars.

The choice to drift leaves little space for questions. Especially the hard ones. When we pop into town, we're rarely recognized now as the couple who ran 'That Café Thing', or if we are, people must have given up asking us what went wrong. We go to church, where I'm still enjoying sitting at the back. My choice to not engage with God says more than I'd like it to, but I'm still holding on to that childish belief that not thinking about something will make it go away, or at least not scare me any more.

Andrew, our vicar, advised us to not get involved in anything 'churchy' for at least six months and that suits me fine. I haven't told him I can't even imagine a time when I would ever want to be doing 'churchy' stuff again. But there's plenty of time to worry about that; right now I'm enjoying not being challenged. I don't have any dreams or plans for the future. I don't want to be disappointed again.

This Monday we're meeting at Becky's once more. I'm dreading it as the diet isn't exactly going very well, plus I'm hormonal, which definitely doesn't help. If the scales bring bad news, I'm blaming my period. Everyone's here, we're standing around the scales looking at them, each one of us as reluctant as the next to start the weigh-in.

Steph starts. 'I've not had a good week. It was Janet's birthday in the office and I ate two slices of chocolate cake.' Joy confesses she and Rob had three nights of takeaways because she had to work late. Gommie, Becky and I all blame our hormones.

'I'd be so much lighter if I had smaller boobs.' Becky does have a point.

'It's alright for you lot, blaming your boobs. I've only got these tiny bee stings. What about me?' Poor Steph, she's the odd one out.

'I have an idea!' shouts Joy. 'Why don't we weigh them? Why don't we weigh our boobs?'

Becky Googles it on her laptop and we all gather around her to read the different suggestions. We dismiss the first method because we don't want to handle each other's boobs. That's not strictly true: Steph was happy to handle our boobs, but we weren't. She's always been a bit obsessed with them. Whenever we're on a night out she grabs them – as though by touching them she would receive their magical powers and loose the curse of being flat-chested. Weakened with laughter, we decide to weigh ourselves normally, then weigh ourselves a second time, kneeling on the scales then lifting our boobs up and resting them on a chair in front of us and recording the difference. Joy goes first, then Becky, then me. Now it's Steph's turn.

'Mine don't register! Why aren't mine registering?'

Becky resets the scales and Steph tries again but still nothing. We all look at her, unsure whether to apologize or feel jealous before we all start laughing, watching Steph repeatedly reset the scales and lean over them, desperate to get some sort of reading. Buoyed by the hilarity of this activity, Gommie finally caves in and records her weight as well, with Steph watching on, still traumatized by her feather-light chest.

Those with more scientific minds may question our methods, but it did work, and it turns out boobs can be quite heavy. We discussed whether Joy should record our 'boobless' weight on the graph or our weight 'with boobs'. Acknowledging that our boobs aren't going anywhere, we settle on the 'with boobs' weight. Closing the laptop down, we gather around the table and start eating – fajitas. I love fajitas.

This week Gommie had brought us all a present, beautifully wrapped – Gommie loves wrapping things. Each of us has a notepad with a different design on it that she'd chosen personally. Mine is turquoise, my favourite colour – like the sea on summer holidays. She explains that the notepads are to write down what's going on in each other's lives so that we remember to pray for each other in the week. We start tonight, notepad opened, first crease made down the spine. We write – '8th November, Becky's house, fajitas'. We then go round the table, each of us taking turns to share, the rest of us recording worries, doubts, difficult situations and good news. Due to the excitement of the boob weigh-in, we run out of time to pray, but leave Becky's nourished on every level.

4

Sorry for Your Loss

'I'm pregnant!' I whisper to my brother. His eyes respond with wide-eyed excitement, congratulating me with a silent 'Yay!'. The vicar stands to start the service and all eyes are forced forward, resting on the coffin at the front of the crowded chapel. Even in death, my grandmother can still unite the family.

My brother nudges me. 'How long?' he mouths.

'Six weeks,' I whisper to him. He puts his arm around me, squeezing me closer. My aunt stands to read from the Bible, but I struggle to focus on the words that speak of a life beyond this one when my body's preparing for new life right now. She returns to her seat and the vicar guides us through some prayers. The family fills the chapel, blonde and ginger heads bowing forward, shoulders clothed in black carrying the loss of their beloved mother and grandmother.

It was a day loaded with meaning – travelling back down south for my grandmother's funeral bringing with me the good news of new life. It felt as though I'd been chosen to represent new hope to my family in their grief, my thoughts jumping back and forth between the life we were mourning and the new one that was growing inside me. I had plans; turning the spare room into a nursery, cute baby names, how having a baby wasn't going to stop us from being adventurous. Of course, I had questions too, like: how are we going to afford it? Is child-birth as painful as people say? Who do I tell? What about work? What if the baby has my pinhead and Dave's big nose?

My uncle stands to share some memories of my grandmother, his voice crumbling when he recounts the sacrifices she made to feed and clothe a family of four. My cousin joins him and talks about the plum tree at the bottom of my grandmother's garden and the sherry-drenched trifle she would serve at family parties. My brother and I both smile, remembering our first ex-perience of real alcohol from the sherry-soaked sponge, lining the big cut-glass bowl filled with fruit, jelly and mountains of whipped cream. It was always the crowning glory of every meal at her house, placed with pride in the centre of the dining table on the lace-patterned tablecloth.

As my cousin continues to share his stories of visits to Grandma's house, the recent memories of her absent conver-sations and deep confusion are quickly replaced with images of summers spent in her garden, early autumn picking plums from the tree and the dining table heavy with food. This is how I want to remember her, not the lady whose mind had been claimed by dementia. The final goodbyes are made, and I look down at my lap as the coffin disappears through the plush red curtains at the front of the chapel – I hate that bit. I can never look. It's so final.

Standing in the low-ceilinged church hall after the service, I feel distant from those around me. They are here to say good-bye, to grieve, to remember, but I hold a secret. A secret that's the size of a pea at the moment, but one that's life-changing. I accept condolences and make small talk with distant rela-tives I barely know, but who seem to know an uncomfortable amount of detail about me. The food is laid out, and a swarm of silver-haired women all 5ft and below gather around the buffet table, blocking the beige banquet of sausage rolls and egg sandwiches from the rest of the funeral party. The sherry is then poured and the women move in unison to grab their free drink, skilfully balancing a paper plate laden with cold pastries in one hand and a small glass of sherry in the other. Spotting my opportunity, I quickly break off my conversation, grab a paper plate and fill it with sausage rolls, crisps and a token cherry tomato before the silver army of tiny yet determined ladies return for second helpings. I'm eating for two now! I grab another sausage roll just to be on the safe side and leave the buffet table to make small talk with more relatives.

I move in and out of conversations, but struggle to concentrate. It's only been forty-eight hours since I found out, and my mind is occupied with thoughts of motherhood. The contrast between the new life within me and the death of my grandmother doesn't clash, though; we're celebrating the end of a long life. A life that had been lived, one that had brought new life into this world, reminding us of life's resilience, its longevity and productivity.

At this point, I have to confess this baby was not planned; we hadn't even been married a year, as my mum pointed out as soon as I told her the news. The previous week I'd been lying in bed telling Dave how strange my body felt and that I was really worried I could be pregnant. I didn't feel ready to be a mother. I was enjoying being married and wasn't sure I really wanted to share this life with a small person quite yet, but something has changed over the last forty-eight hours. I've fallen in love with the life inside me and the person I'm becoming. Mother Nature is now running through my veins, transforming me, making me feel more feminine, more alive. It's like I've jumped into a film script where I'm playing the lead, for once in my life. I've no idea how we'll afford it – this was the second thing my mum pointed out to me – but it doesn't matter, we'll work something out. We'll be that young couple with a baby who are romantically poor, wearing scruffy clothes and hairstyles that look like we don't care but actually make us look cool and really attractive. We'll go camping for our holidays and spend afternoons making things rather than spending a fortune on going to theme parks and National Trust properties. We'll become an inspiration to those parents who waited until they had savings, a family car and a home near a good school.

I saw blood before we left for the station. But told no one. I was trying to enjoy my moment, the excited voices talking about plans for the next nine months and beyond. My dad turns off the engine in the station car park, and he and mum step out the car for hugs and goodbyes, both of them tired from the emotion of the day but excited about the news I'd shared with them. I pass through the ticket gate with instructions ringing round my head – telling me to look after myself, get Dave to do more housework, eat well and get lots of rest.

I step onto the busy train, squeezing past passengers trying to force their cases into the remaining empty spaces on the overhead luggage rack, managing to find my seat just before the train pulls away from the station. Pain slowly begins to creep through my body, clawing at my stomach, forcing me to sit bent forward until eventually I'm doubled over, my forehead pressed into the back of the seat in front of me, bringing with it a single focus – I have to get home. Nothing else matters – the funeral, my family, the day that's passed have all disappeared, the disinterested passengers on the train blurring into the Sussex countryside.

Somehow I'm at Euston. I don't know how, but I'm here and I'm focused. Boarding the train for Chester, my eyes spot the first available seat and I collapse into it. The other passengers are bustling around me, coats and bags brushing past me, as I sit, curled up in my own tiny world. The train lunges forward and we're on our way, my chosen posture once again bent forward with my head pressing into the back of the seat in front to ease the pain that is now dragging itself through my body. I want to lie down, I want to curl up, I want to cry out, but I know this is not the place to do it. I glance over to the toilet cubicle. If I can just get to it, maybe I will feel better.

I couldn't make it to the toilet; instead I'm curled up on the floor, incredibly thankful that the cubicle has just been cleaned. I've never seen the toilet floor of a train as clean as this one, although I can't imagine a dirty floor would have made any difference. Lying there, my right cheek pressed against the floor, my arms pulling my knees into my body, eyes fixed on the door, willing people to stay away. I call Dave. I tell him there's blood, I'm in pain and I need him to meet me at the station. He has questions but I can't answer them, fearful that providing him with too much information will force us to acknowledge what's happening.

I lie there for the rest of the journey – an hour and a half on the toilet floor trying not to think until I eventually feel the train slowing down in its approach to the station, accompanied by a voice over the Tannoy announcing our arrival at Chester.

Grabbing onto the sink next to me I pull myself up, catching my reflection in the mirror, my right cheek burning red from pressing into the floor for so long. I lean on walls and hold onto headrests until I find my bags and am finally off the train. I walk slowly, shuffling along the platform, eyes fixed on the pavement with no care for what I must look like. The passengers walking past dissolve into the fog surrounding me as I slowly progress towards my goal . . . Through the ticket barrier that was thankfully left open, my feet moving slowly, pain rising into my throat. I see Dave. Relief. I let him rush towards me. He's talking at me, taking my bags with ease, his body full of life and strength. He places his hand on the base of my back, gently guiding me towards the car. We drive past our house and straight to the out-of-hours doctor who confirms I'm miscarrying, forcing us into a world we know nothing about and slamming the door behind us, leaving us alone with a box of ibuprofen and the news that what's just happened is very common.

Before the sun set on the day of my grandmother's funeral, another life had ended, another heartbeat had stopped. But the doctor confirming this death did not share his condolences; people did not gather to acknowledge the life that had existed. We returned home from the doctor's surgery alone. After what felt like hours on the toilet, I flushed the remains of the life that was inside me away. I couldn't look; it was too final.

That night we sat on the sofa in our pyjamas and ate cheese on toast, eventually taking ourselves upstairs to bed, lying on our backs holding hands with the hope that sleep might fill the void created by today's events. The next day we got up and went to work. On the outside nothing was different, but on the inside we were changed.

5

She Will Be Remembered

'We'd do it all over again. Yeah, we took a risk, but it was so much fun! To have the freedom to dream, to imagine and to see those ideas in real life was amazing! I don't regret what we did.'

Standing next to Dave I move my gaze from the pews of people in front of me towards him, glaring. We hadn't planned he would say this; we'd talked through what we would both share and this wasn't mentioned. He's making it sound like the café was a good thing. Dave looks over to me; it's my turn to finish off our bit before Andrew carries on with the rest of the service. I look back to the faces in front of us, faces of people who believed in our vision and prayed for us. I look down at my notes on the folded piece of A4 paper in my hand.

'Umm, I've read a lot of books about success. When people took risks and they paid off, with God blessing their ventures. Those are the stories everyone loves to share; they're the books that sell well and inspire. But I've not read many books about failure. In fact, I've not really seen many people stand up in church and talk about how their plans didn't work out as they hoped. I know that, until the café closed, I didn't really have many stories to tell about failure. I'd just kind of sailed through life. I don't know why the café closed. I mean, I know we ran out of money, but I've always believed that God is bigger than finances.'

Dave leans over and whispers to me, 'Tell them about your mum's dream.'

'Oh. Yeah. Well, after the café closed, my mum had a dream. It was of the woman who anointed Jesus' feet. Jesus was having dinner when Mary came in and started washing Jesus' feet with this really expensive perfume and wiping them with her hair. Everyone was shocked because this woman was wasting this perfume on Jesus. But Jesus used this woman as an example. To him her actions were not wasteful, but they were worshipful, because he knew her heart. He wasn't shocked by the waste of money, he was more bothered about why she did it.[1] My mum thinks that's how God sees what happened with the café – not as a waste of money, but as an act of worship.'

At the end of church, Dave is surrounded by people telling him what a great speaker he is and sharing ideas of what he could do in the future. I just want to go home. After Andrew thanks us both and asks Dave if he'd like to preach in a few weeks, we're finally able to leave. I can tell Dave's on a high, which is even more annoying.

Once we're home, Dave puts the kettle on and I go upstairs and grab the pretty journal I'd bought the other day. My plan is to write down what I'm feeling and what I want to say to God. I open the hand-stitched front cover and stare at the blank page. Nothing; I have nothing to say.

Today is the day of my scan. Dave can't get the time off work so Becky has offered to come with me. I thought I'd be fine going by myself, but now we're driving to the hospital I'm so glad she's with me. We park up, consult the hospital map and head towards the women's and children's building, walking past a group of heavily pregnant mums in dressing gowns, smoking; we go through the automatic doors and navigate our way to the right floor.

'I think this is where we're meant to go,' says Becky, pointing at the sign.

'Oh, yeah, I think you're right,' I reply, confused because this is the waiting room where all the pregnant women are. Maybe the lady at the reception desk will tell us the right place to go.

'Name?'

'Elizabeth Lowrie.'

'Address?'

I give it.

'Take a seat.'

'Erm, is this the right place? I'm here for a scan because I've had a miscarriage,' I whisper over the counter.

'Yes, this is the right place. Wait here and someone will call you through soon.'

'Oh, OK. Thanks.' Becky and I navigate through the play area with toddlers throwing bricks on the floor and I find a seat as far away from any pregnant woman as I can.

'I didn't think they'd put me in the same waiting room as people with babies,' I whisper to Becky.

'I know,' she replies. 'It's not very sensitive.' I pick up a six-month-old copy of a magazine and Becky and I flick through some of the far-fetched stories, until my name is called.

'Elizabeth Lowrie.'

I start to stand up, turning to look at Becky. 'Would you like me to come with you?' she asks.

'Is that OK?'

'Of course!' she replies, putting the magazine on the seat next to her and standing to join me as we walk towards the nurse.

After being calmly guided through what's going to happen and why, I'm sent behind a screen to change into a backless gown and told to lie down on the bed next to all the machines.

'Can you bend your knees, please?' The nurse turns and lifts this long plastic stick thing attached to loads of wires.

'What is that?'

'Have you ever had an internal scan before?' I stare at the long stick the nurse is holding. Is she actually going to put that inside me? What about those scans you see on the telly when the woman just lies back really relaxed and they rub some gel on their tummy, casually chatting with the nurse as she records the images? That's what I thought a scan was!

'Um . . . no . . .'

'You'll be fine. You may feel some minor discomfort, that's all,' she continues to tell me, pulling a condom over the long stick. 'The more you relax the easier it will be,' she says, slathering lube over the condom. I still can't believe this is going inside me; surely no amount of lube is going to make this a comfortable experience.

'Now, it will feel a bit cold at first.' I look over to Becky, whose face looks as shocked as mine. She takes my hand and keeps telling me how well I'm doing.

The nurse talks about cysts and fertility, and something called endometriosis, and I just keep thinking how I wish Dave was here as well because I can't take it all in. Why have they just dragged me through a waiting room full of pregnant women to then put a massive stick up me and tell me I've got stuff growing on my ovaries? I've just had a miscarriage. I thought they would make me feel better. Instead, I'm lying here with my legs open being told I might need an operation.

'The café downstairs does really good buttered toast,' the nurse tells me. 'I suggest you go there, have some toast and a cup of tea; that should help you feel better.'

Becky thanks the nurse, takes my arm and guides me downstairs to the café, where she sits me down before going to buy the tea and toast. I look around the café, a space once again filled with mums, mums-to-be, mums playing with kids, feeding kids. It's only today that I feel the miscarriage is complete, surrounded by examples of what could have been. I am more aware of my loss sat here in a hospital cafeteria than when the doctor told me I was miscarrying.

Becky brings over the tea and toast. The nurse was right, the toast tastes good. In between bites of hot, white, buttery bread and sips of tea, we joke about the shock of seeing the big stick covered in lube, discuss the trials of having medical investigations when you're a woman, and try to rationalize the medical diagnoses that were thrown at me before Becky drops me back home.

The house is quiet, unsure whether to welcome me because I'm not normally here at this time in the day. I'm crying. I know I'm sad, but I'm not sure exactly why. I've never known anyone cry over a miscarriage. In fact, I don't really know any people who've had miscarriages. Should I be crying? Is this right? I think about how happy I was when I found out I was pregnant, then I think about the café and what we lost, I think about Dave and all these amazing skills everyone says he has, and I keep crying.

I was Mary, once. I would have gladly sat with Jesus and smashed the jar of perfume over his feet with no thought to hold any back. I would have given him the best of me; well, I did give the best. The love I felt for the God who told me I was loved led me here to Chester, where I gave everything I had. I gave my inheritance to the café; I gave my time and my health to it until the last drop had fallen. I gave until there was nothing left, and I did it out of obedience. I did it in response to Jesus' demand to give up your old life and follow him; to lay down your desires for him.[2] I didn't do it because I was brainwashed, or indoctrinated, or made to. I did it because I wanted to.

I fell in love with Jesus on my gap year before University – I spent 6 months at the foot of the Andes, caring for the many Bolivian kids who lived in the prisons with their parents and returned home a different person, not because of the work I did, but because of the people I worked with. There was a freedom in the way they loved and served the families in the prisons, not because they felt they had a lot to give, but because they knew they were loved by God which gave them the compassion and the courage to love others. That's when I stopped wishing I was someone else because I'd discovered I was loved by God just as I was. That was when the shyness fell off me and I discovered a new kind of confidence, not in myself, but in the God who loved me. It was this new God-confidence within me that inspired me to dream, to stretch my imagination and believe that I could have a role in changing the world. That's when the God-dreams started, and the limitless prayers and the heart that melted when I sang to him.

But now there's no perfume left to spill, no jar left to break. All that remains now are the tears. I brush them away with my hand and watch them soak into my skin, and I know these are not the same tears Mary cried. These tears are because of the distance, not the closeness to Jesus. They aren't tears of joy or worship, they are ones of abandonment.

6

Secrecy

~

The door slams shut. His feet are pounding on the pavement, each step runs like a shock through his body. His heart beating in his throat. He must be quick, he doesn't want to leave the house, but someone's got to tell Andrew before the service starts. He sprints through the narrow alleys that break up the rows of terraced houses – Walter Street, Cornwall Street, Church Street. He quickly knocks on the vicarage door. Andrew opens it.

'Dave, why are you here? The service doesn't start for another hour and a half.'

'It's . . . it's Lizzie . . . she . . .' His throat dries up, his chest tight, unable to release the words. His broad shoulders start to shake. He lifts his hand to cover his eyes, hoping to push the tears back, to somehow stop them.

'What is it? What's happened?'

'Lizzie's had another miscarriage.'

'Oh Dave, I'm so sorry.' Andrew steps out onto the doorstep and puts his arms around Dave. Surprised by the force of emotion rising within him, Dave has no choice but to cry; he has no control over it. Andrew's words speak comfort over Dave as he expresses his sadness.

Words stumble out of Dave's mouth as he wipes his face repeatedly to remove the tears that won't stop falling. 'She woke up early in pain and it just got worse. She started bleeding about an hour ago, so we're pretty sure it's another miscarriage. She said it feels like the last time.'

'Don't worry about the service. I'll take care of Lizzie's bit.'

'Thank you, Andrew.' He steps back, embarrassed by his damp face, surprised by his emotional response, yet somehow relieved. His shoulders are more relaxed, his throat feels open, his heart has moved from his mouth back to his chest.

'Go back to Lizzie.'

Dave turns and leaves, his long legs stretching, covering the maximum distance possible with each stride. Briskly walking back, he wipes his face with his jumper sleeve, sniffs, clears his throat and steps into the house. He rushes to the kitchen, splashes his face with water, blotting it dry with a towel. He doesn't want it to look like he's been crying. It's not about him. He has to be strong.

There are so many stories I'd happily sit down and share with you: reaching the top of Machu Picchu and gazing down below at the lost city; eating my way around Italy; working in Bolivian prisons; tapas in Granada, the Alhambra illuminated, exalted above us; the dusky pink silk flowers cascading down the back of my wedding dress; swimming in the crystal-clear Aegean Sea; waves crashing against the Cornish coastline, deep turquoise against the slate-grey cliffs; good coffee in little independent coffee shops; Becky's lasagne; Joy's apple crumble; my mum's Christmas dinner; my love of cinnamon; household items I've now painted with chalkboard paint. I can talk about these things for days, fully embraced fragments of my life that I review and polish and present to others. These are the stories people love to hear; they spark interest, initiate conversations and build connections. These are the stories I happily lay out before people like open books, the pages well-thumbed with each retelling, but I now seem to be gathering stories that have no home, moments that no one would ever want to hear, and I don't know what to do with them because they won't go away.

I'm lying across the sofa, my head resting on a cushion, my arms wrapped around my pink spotty-covered hot-water bottle and my feet resting on Dave's lap where he's sat at the other end of the sofa. I listen to him repeat the same gruesome message over the phone to both our parents. He dutifully answers questions on my behalf, reassures them we'll be fine and that no, we really don't need anything. The worst thing about breaking the news is that no one knew I was pregnant in the first place. Embarrassed by the naivety with which we embraced our first pregnancy, we wanted to protect our secret from further pain, but loss does not respect what we chose to protect and Dave is forced to retell a story that moves from expectancy to loss in one breath.

We're watching another box set and eating cheese on toast when there's a knock at the door. Standing on the pavement are Joy and Jamie – apparently Steph is out this afternoon with friends, so she sent her husband to check up on me instead. He's looking pretty uncomfortable, but he's here nonetheless, bless him. After some awkward hugs and stilted conversations filled with the word 'sorry', Joy bravely confesses a truth we're all thinking: 'I'm not very good in these situations. I never know what to say.'

'I don't know what to say either,' I reassure her. Jamie then agrees he feels the same way and asks if he could make us a cup of tea. Joy thinks that's a great idea and joins Jamie in the kitchen. A couple of minutes later she's back, placing two mugs of tea on the oak coffee table. 'So we've decided we thought we'd do your washing-up for you. Is that OK?' She looks at us both, waiting for approval.

'Yeah, thanks,' answers Dave, and Joy rushes back through the dining room and into the kitchen. The noise of dishes clunking, hushed conversation and cupboards opening and closing to find homes for clean crockery, drifts through into the lounge where Dave and I are sat, staring at the telly. Once all the dishes are washed, dried and put away without Joy breaking any of them, we have another conversation filled with the word 'sorry', a couple of hugs and we're left in the house watching another box set.

Before going to sleep that night, I promise Dave I'll follow the advice of the out-of-hours surgery and ring the doctor's first thing in the morning for a check-up. I lean over to turn off the bedside light, glancing at my notebook before flicking the switch. Dave once again reaches out for my hand, our fingers locked between each other's. 'Do you think I miscarried because I had to carry those heavy boxes at work?' My words fill the dark silence of our bedroom.

'No, of course not, honey. It wasn't your fault,' he replies, before kissing me.

'But it could've been. I could have done something wrong.'

'You did nothing wrong. I promise.' He squeezes my hand and leans over to kiss me again.

''Night,' I reply, my voice cut short by the lump in my throat.

''Night.'

I've only been at work for ten minutes and already I really want to punch Caroline, or at least find a way to shut her up. She's just created her account on the BabyCentre[1] website, and it's now telling her what sized piece of fruit her baby is; apparently, it's the size of a grapefruit. I've never really liked grapefruit. After asking round the office if anyone has a grapefruit she could borrow, and outwardly musing whether she should quickly pop to the shops to buy one so that she can feel closer to the baby, she then Googles grapefruit diameters and, using a ruler, tries to create an exact grapefruit size with her hands. But she's having trouble maintaining the exact size of the grapefruit when she moves her hand from the ruler, so she gets Cat, the temp who's sat next to her, to hold the ruler up for her to achieve a better accuracy. She then stands up, placing her hands in their grapefruit formation on her stomach, slowly turning to face each one of us working at the four-desk cluster in the middle of the office, just in case we hadn't quite appreciated the grapefruit was inside her.

Once the three of us sat round the cluster of four desks have eventually acknowledged the grapefruit, she finally sits down. I can then hear her texting, no doubt telling people about the fruit growing in her tummy. Sat diagonally opposite me, I can't see what she's doing but she should really turn the keypad sounds off her phone instead of loudly demonstrating how little work she's actually doing. 'Apparently I should be starting to have unusual cravings,' she announces to us. 'I can't think of anything yet, but I really do fancy a bacon sandwich.'

'I'm not pregnant but I could do with a bacon sandwich as well,' replies Rebecca, who's sat next to me. I turn to look at her and we share a little smile. I want to join in and tell Caroline about the cravings I've had for egg fried rice and prawn crackers, but I know that the story of pregnancy is not mine to tell. I can't write about it, or retell it, because it doesn't feel like mine. My body rejects it and so does my voice. It's a privilege I have been denied.

'Oh, I feel a bit sick now. Maybe I shouldn't be thinking about bacon sandwiches,' replies Caroline. I hear her clearing her throat and making a nasty kind of yakking noise before going quiet and potentially deciding to finally do some work.

I felt sick too, you know, I tell her inside my head. I felt really sick; every day I'd come to work with nausea, snacking on salt and pepper pretzels throughout the day, but no one gave me sympathy, no one knew, and I can't say anything now. 'Oh, this is so great!' Caroline announces to the whole office. 'BabyCentre send you updates each week about your baby's development with little pictures.' I quickly find the BabyCentre website, cancel my account and get back to work.

That afternoon I go to the doctor's, hoping for some answers and some guidance on how to deal with a miscarriage. I didn't announce I was going out because I didn't want Caroline to send me on an errand to buy a bacon sandwich or, worse still, a grapefruit. I decide to tell the doctor about the box carrying, but she doesn't seem to think that was anything to worry about.

'Are there any other reasons why you think I could have miscarried again?' I ask her.

'Miscarriage is very common. Two losses in a row is very bad luck, but the great news is that you can get pregnant,' she replies.

'Do you know how long I should be sad for?'

'I'm sorry, I can't answer that. You just need to be kind to yourself and hopefully you'll begin to feel better over time.' She pauses, then: 'Is it OK if I examine you before you go?'

'Yeah, OK.'

'Can you take your trousers and underwear off and lie on the bed with this cloth over you? I'll wait on the other side of the curtain until you're ready.' What happened next is another story; I've simply added it to my growing collection of secrets. All I can say is there was a lamp and a latex-covered hand.

The examination doesn't go well because, apparently, I wasn't relaxed enough! The doctor tells me to return if I am still in pain a week later, before recommending I 'make sure I do something fun at the weekend'. I leave the surgery with no new knowledge on miscarriage, carrying another secret, and go back to work.

At 2 p.m. I return to my desk, the shock of what just happened still pulsing through me. My hand shaking, I turn on my computer again and try to focus on my emails. The office is quiet, Caroline's gone to her antenatal appointment and another four team members are at a meeting.

I'm looking at my computer screen, but my sight is blurred by the tears running down my face. I keep wiping my eyes with my hands, but now my nose has started running too, and I have nothing on me to absorb the amount of liquid streaming from my face. I look down at my desk, watching tears drip onto my keyboard. Then out of nowhere I start to make that guttural sound from a place I know I have no control over, and the tears begin to flow even faster. I'm trying to stay as quiet as I can so as not to disrupt the rhythm of tapping keyboards and the occasional phone call, but I know I can't hold this in for much longer, sniffing and wiping and occasionally letting out this weird hiccupy sound.

I look across the room to the door, but with my desk situated right in the middle of an open-plan office, even with it half empty I still can't risk getting to the door without being noticed; so I stay sitting, with my head hidden by my computer screen, quietly weeping. A few minutes later I hear Cat, the temp, get up and walk past me towards Anne's desk behind me. I lower my head further and look away from her, pretending to read some papers, then I feel a hand on my shoulder.

'Lizzie, are you OK?' I can hear its Anne's voice. I turn my snotty, damp, red face to look at her. 'Shall we go somewhere else for a minute?' She takes my hand and leads me out of the office and downstairs to the empty principal's common room. 'What's wrong?'

I look at her, but I can't talk, my breathing stunted by the pressure of trying to contain my emotions. Anne waits patiently, holding my hand, until eventually I speak.

'I . . . I had a miscarriage,' I tell her, choosing to stare at the carpet tiles rather than Anne's face.

'Oh no. I'm so sorry. When did it happen?'

'Yesterday.' I pause. 'It's my second,' I tell her, spotting some cake crumbs trodden into the wiry hairs of the dark-blue flooring beneath our feet. I think I'm just as upset about the latex hand but there's no way I'm telling Anne that.

'Oh, I'm so sorry. You shouldn't have come in today. I really think you need to be at home. Why don't you go home now? I can clear it with your line manager when she's back from her meeting. You stay here and I'll bring your stuff down. Is there anyone you can ring for a lift home?'

'I could try Dave.' I finally look up.

'OK, well, you stay here and I'll bring your bag and your coat down to you.'

'Thanks,' I mumble, choosing to spend a few more minutes studying the cheap flooring that adorns what was probably once a very impressive room. A couple of minutes later Anne arrives back, placing my bag and my coat next to me. Keen to leave before anyone else sees what I mess I am, I stand and start putting on my coat.

'Now, don't rush back to work. Why don't you just take the week off work?'

'But isn't that a bit long?' I look at her, longing to just be told what to do.

'No! Of course it isn't! You need time to recover.' She pats the top of my hand.

'But I'm not sick.'

'It doesn't matter. You've been through a lot and you need some space.'

'Yeah, maybe it would be good to have some time off.' I'm surprised by how welcome her advice feels.

'That's right, so I'll see you next week, then?' She looks at me.

'OK. Thanks,' I respond, feeling lighter with the thought of a few days off and encouraged by Anne's response and her kindness, especially because she's not normally someone I really speak to that much.

Andrew arrives just after 7 p.m., with bear hugs and sympathy. I do love seeing him: he just has this way of making you feel better. We sit down with cups of tea in the lounge, and he presents us with a little booklet with some Bible readings, some words for him to say, some for us to say and a couple of prayers. This was Andrew's idea – to do a little service to say goodbye to the baby, kind of like a funeral, I suppose, which is weird because we'd never met our baby, and to be honest sometimes I wonder whether he or she ever existed.

The words in the booklet spoke of the human story woven into God's story. They are beautiful in parts; they talk of grief and despair and hope and new life, but I'm struggling to let them lift my heart like they should. I do want to include God in this. I'd love to leave this story with him and move forward, but I'm unsure whether the story of miscarriage belongs in a funeral service. Surely these are words for the loss of flesh and bones and personality and stories of life and adventure, not a secret death.

7

Strong

~

It wasn't until I actually got married that I realized guys don't always naturally know how to do manly tasks. They aren't born with a sixth sense of how to carve a turkey or change a tyre. According to Dave, guys often carry out these tasks not because they are skilled at slicing roast meat and unscrewing wheel nuts; they do it because that's what's expected of them. I remember having a hushed argument with Dave in the kitchen the first time we cooked a roast dinner. I'd just presented him with the golden, crispy chicken on a board, handed him a knife and expected him to get carving. He looked back at me blankly and told me he didn't know what he was doing. I was shocked. So we Googled it, then Dave proudly carved our roast chicken at the head of the table in front of our hungry guests, and faith in my husband was restored.

I relied on Dave's strength before we even started going out. When we were working in the café and he saw how tired I was, he would send me home to rest. At the end of the day, he would do the majority of the clearing up, effortlessly lifting chairs onto tables to sweep underneath them. He would arrive early to allow me time to lie-in. He hid the stress. He bore the stress. He carried the stress. When cash flow was going in the wrong direction, he waited and worked to find a plan before giving me too much information about the gravity of our situation. When we returned from honeymoon, he started working almost straight away, giving me time to recover from the migraine attacks that kept wiping my memory clear. Dave is strong and he's carried me, and I let him, and I love him for it. That has been his role from the beginning and he does it well.

He's driving, focusing on getting there quickly. I can feel him trying to drive as smoothly as possible to minimize the pain. Nothing, apart from a lot of drugs, could minimize the pain right now, but his desire to try to make me feel better comforts me. My breathing is fast, panicked, its rhythm occasionally broken by me yelling, 'I can't do this! I can't do this again!' 'Help me, God! Please stop this! I can't do this again, please!' It's been just over a year since the first time this happened. I thought it was a one-off, but then it happened again and now, here we are for the third time.

We park up, but I can't walk; it hurts too much. Dave runs to the A&E reception and asks for a wheelchair. He wheels me into the waiting room, pain clouding my view. I have no awareness of what's around me.

Dave is speaking calmly, comforting me, his eyes focused, willing me to feel better. I realize sound is coming from my mouth. I'm groaning, the pain overflowing into audible cries and filling the waiting room. I've never groaned out loud before; I've never dared do it, but I have no choice; the sound coming out of me is beyond my control – it's wild.

I don't know whether the groaning and heavy breathing helped me get seen any faster, but I'm pretty certain the others in the waiting room are glad I've finally been called in. I'm wheeled through into the ward and helped onto a bed. I vomit. The nurse gives me two paracetamols; I'm pretty sure there's no way that's going to make any difference. My breathing becoming quicker, faster, shallow, my head light, faint. Dave is trying to help me breathe, trying to calm me with his voice, to slow my sharp gasps down, 'Oh no! Oh no! I can't do this again! I can't do this!' A mask is quickly placed on my face and slowly I start to calm. But then I feel the pain dragging itself through me again, and my breathing becomes more panicked: short, sharp, shallow breaths. I vomit. I panic. Dave is still there holding my hand, telling me once again that I'm going to be OK, calmly helping me breathe more slowly. The nurse tells us she's going to find a doctor to prescribe me some more pain relief. I lie there and Dave helps me focus on breathing.

'That's right,' he says. 'In and out, in and out – you're doing really well, hon, you're doing really well.' The doctor eventually arrives, does some checks and asks me where my pain is on a scale of one to ten. That's a hard question, because I'm British. I go for a seven, so as not to make it sound like I'm making a big deal, but also to communicate I'm experiencing the worst pain my body has ever known. He nods, says something to the nurse, then leaves. The nurse then lifts the mask off my mouth and releases liquid through a syringe into my mouth. Apparently it's morphine, and it's amazing. I am calm. Dave continues to stroke my hand, talking calmly, still focused, unmoved, strong, present. I feel sleepy. I enjoy breathing, the long, slow breaths calming me, slowing down my heartbeat which no longer feels like it's trying to escape from my chest. I want to lie here and never be moved. The threat of waiting for the doctor to return, of them taking action, investigating, making a decision means once again that a life has been lost. If I stay here, my body calm, numbed by morphine, I won't need to think or feel ever again.

Drifting in and out of consciousness I float between peace and trauma. Red blood. Nurses covering it, cleaning it, pads soaking it up. Still, quiet, Dave calmly telling me I'm doing well, to stay calm, to relax, to breathe. My experience of what happens next is beautifully clouded by the morphine. There was a nurse, a doctor, a torch, a speculum, forceps, an amazing hug and two cups of tea in polystyrene cups. Praise the Lord for morphine, is all I can say.

After being monitored for another hour or so, I'm eventually allowed to go home. I didn't really want to leave; it was nice being looked after and going home meant we had to pick up that familiar script, reciting lines we wished we'd never have to repeat again. The doctor told us they would run some tests on the baby and that we'd now be referred to a Recurrent Miscarriage Clinic for investigations. Sat in my wheelchair, I wait in the hospital foyer for Dave to bring the car round with a single phrase running through my thoughts. It was one that shocked me because it jarred so much with what had just happened. It shocked me because it's just not a phrase I've used for a long time; it's not a phrase I've wanted to use for a long time. I see Dave pull up, running back towards me to wheel me over to the car.

Once settled in the seat and the chair given back to reception, we begin to drive away, that phrase still repeating itself over and over again in my mind: 'God is good, God is good.'

The morphine eventually wears off, forcing me to feel. Dave fulfils his manly duty of ringing parents and texting friends. Messages come back, the word 'sorry' filling our mailbox. I sleep. Joy and Becky come over after work. Joy washes up and makes us a cup of tea and Becky unpacks a bag of treats from M&S for us to enjoy over the weekend. I manage to stand and chat to Becky and Joy, but when they leave I take myself back upstairs to the bathroom. A miscarriage doesn't suddenly end, the pain doesn't stop quickly. It's really good at dragging itself out for a long time, and so I go up to the bathroom and I wait for it to end.

I've been upstairs for about half an hour now, sat on the toilet, my body doubled forward, elbows digging into the bare skin of my legs. Although nowhere near as bad as earlier, the pain is still clinging on and sitting bent forward is about the only position that's helping me feel a bit better. But sitting alone upstairs in the bathroom means I start to remember, over and over again, the images of today, the pain, the blood, the loss. '*Dave!*' I call out. '*Dave!*'

'Yeah!' he responds from downstairs.

'*Can you come up here?*' I can hear his footsteps running up the wooden staircase, walking along the painted wooden floor-boards on the landing towards the bathroom.

'Can I come in?'

'Yes,' I reply. He pushes the door open, and sits down on the grey-tiled step leading into the bathroom.

'Are you OK, honey?'

I lift my head up and turn it to the right to look at him. 'No, of course I'm not alright.'

'I'm sorry,' he responds gently, and I start crying.

'Why did this happen again? What's wrong with me? Why can't I keep a baby inside me?' The tears and snot are free-flowing now.

'I'm sorry, hon. I don't know why it's happened, but it's not your fault.'

'But I don't understand!' I cry out between the sniffing and the weird hiccupy, burpy thing that I need to find a better name for. 'It's not fair! It's just not fair! Loads of other women have babies, why can't I?'

'I'm sorry, hon.'

'Why do you keep saying sorry?' I stare at him, my desperate sadness rising into anger. 'Why are you saying sorry? It was your baby too! All you do is apologize like I'm the only one who's going through it! What about you? Look at you! You're just sat there like nothing's happened!'

'I'm sorry, I . . .'

'*Stop* saying sorry! Why am I the one that's always crying but I've never seen you cry? Why won't you cry? Do you not care what just happened today? We lost a *baby*! We lost *our* baby! And it was our third baby! We've lost three children and you can't even cry! Just *&*%! cry, will you!' I watch Dave stand up and walk towards me to sit on the edge of the bath next to me. I sit upright. He takes my right hand.

'I can't cry in front of you.'

'But why? I cry in front of you all the time. What's different?'

'When you miscarry, you're so upset and you're in so much pain I just want to be strong for you, to help you feel better. You're the most important person in that moment.'

I grab some toilet roll to wipe my nose; why had I not thought of this earlier rather than wiping an increasingly slippery hand across my face?

'You're amazing at looking after me, but when you stay strong it makes me feel more alone in what I'm going through. When I cry and you don't, it makes me feel weak because I can't cope like you can.'

'When you had the last miscarriage, I cried when I spoke to Andrew.'

'Why didn't you tell me?'

'I wanted to be there for you. I wanted to be strong.'

'But the miscarriage affects both of us.' I lean over towards Dave, still sitting on the edge of the bath, put my right arm around his shoulders and pull him closer. His shoulders start to shake, I feel the salt water from his eyes on my neck, his tears helping mine flow more freely.

8

Walking on Eggshells

I wish there was something I could wear; maybe a badge that told people to be gentle with me. I'm stuck in that middle bit with nothing to show for the pain I feel – no plaster or limp. I keep Googling 'How long does it take to get over a miscarriage?' but nothing comes up. It's just women talking about getting pregnant again; the story of the in-between has no voice on the internet.

My friend Clare, from uni, lost her husband this year. She's only 31. She's now writing a blog about life as a young widow and in her most recent post she wrote about how she thought we need twenty-first-century mourning clothes.[1] If we lived in Victorian times, she would have been fine; she could have dressed in black and everyone would know.

I've not lost someone who lived on this earth, someone who had a job and got married, but I agree with her. No one can see the wounds inside me. When I walk through Chester whilst everyone else is at work, I keep my distance from the other pedestrians. I'm worried that if they get too close and brush past me, I'll break.

I only leave the house at times when I won't see anyone I know. I've been off work for four weeks; the doctor signed the sick note and I didn't argue. I haven't replied to messages from colleagues or agreed to meet up with anyone apart from the Weigh and Pray girls because I don't look ill. I don't look any different. The damage is on the inside; the wounds run deep but no one can see them.

I wonder what twenty-first-century mourning clothes would look like. Would they still be black? I'm not even sure whether I'd be allowed to wear them. My friend Clare would; she's earned them. But I don't know where my mourning fits. Even if I was allowed to dress in black, when would I stop? When would it be time to change back into my normal clothes? After the death of her husband, Queen Victoria wore black for the rest of her life, but Clare says she doesn't want to do that. I guess she believes she won't always be sad.

I return to work quietly. I leave the house earlier than normal to make sure I'm the first to arrive. I make a coffee then head back to my desk and turn on my computer, worrying about the number of emails waiting for my reply. As I move my hand towards my mouse, I notice a folded piece of paper half-tucked under my keyboard with my name on it. Inside is a beautiful letter from one of my colleagues. In it she has written her story of failed IVF, miscarriage and childlessness. Her description of pain perfectly describes how I'm feeling. She wrote about the struggle and the sadness that still rises within her, but promises there is still life to be found and a future to be lived.

I hadn't realized how much I needed to hear from someone else who knew what I was going through until I read that letter. It didn't stop me from crying in front of a male colleague later that day, or from freaking out about the number of emails waiting for my reply, but it changed how I felt about my story because now I knew I wasn't alone.

When I arrive home after my first day back at work, there is a letter waiting for me with the date of our recurrent miscarriage appointment.

I never imagined we'd have three miscarriages. I remember the first time the doctor told us about recurrent miscarriage tests and how they only investigate you after three miscarriages, but I didn't even really listen to him because I didn't believe it would happen to us; but it did. And so, one week after my return to work, now we're back again, sat in another hospital waiting room. So far today I've had an internal scan, a hysteroscopy, a dye test and now we're waiting for blood tests. I know it takes two people to make a baby, but the only thing Dave has had to do so far today is hold my hand and tell me to relax. Nothing about today has been relaxing. Every time I lie down for another investigation, I relive that morning in A&E. I try to relax as much as I can, but it hurts. Every part of me hurts.

'I'm a bit nervous about the blood test. I don't like needles,' Dave tells me as he fidgets around in his chair, checks his watch and starts tapping his foot on the floor. I look up from my magazine and glare at him.

'Elizabeth Lowrie?' I put the magazine back on the coffee table and head towards the nurse. 'Would you like to join her as a bit of moral support?' the nurse asks Dave.

'I'm not very good with needles,' he tells her.

'It's OK,' she reassures him. 'Just don't look at it.' I hand her the sheet of paper given to me by the doctor with a list of what he wants to test me for. 'Well, I hope you had breakfast because you've got a lot of tubes to fill!' She sits me down in the big armchair and lines up the test tubes. Dave looks at them, then back at me; he already looks like he's going to faint. 'Sharp scratch!'

Dave stares at the ceiling whilst I talk to the nurse about her plans for the weekend as she fills tube after tube with my blood. 'This is the last one, I promise,' she smiles.

'Finally! It's his turn next!' I tell the nurse, pointing at Dave as he inspects the fluorescent light above his head. She sits Dave down in the chair next to me and checks the sheet of paper with his name on. I watch Dave taking deep breaths in and out to prepare himself as I apply pressure to my arm with the piece of cotton wool the nurse gave me.

'Right, I think I'm ready,' Dave shakes his head and takes two more deep breaths.

'Sharp scratch . . . Aaaaaaaand you're done!' says the nurse.

'Is that it?' I ask her.

'Yes, they only needed one sample.'

'Phew! Well, I'm glad that's over,' says Dave. The nurse and I both glare at him. I wish I could have taken the whole day off work, but after my return-to-work meeting with Human Resources, I don't really have a choice. According to my HR rep, I need to make sure I don't rush back to work too soon, but at the same time, if I do take one more sick day I won't get paid. So, really, I don't have a choice. I need to be here this afternoon, anyway, because I'm meeting one of our moderators, and I've still got more essays to collate before she gets here.

Esther is one of my favourite moderators. She replies to emails promptly and is funny. I've not met her yet, but I feel like I know her really well from the months of emails and phone calls we've exchanged. Esther arrives promptly with time to spare before her meeting so I suggest we make a drink. 'I'm sorry I've not been in touch much over the past few weeks. I've been off sick,' I tell her, as we sit drinking our coffees.

'Are you feeling better now?' Esther asks. I don't know what to say because I don't actually feel any better and I'm getting really tired of pretending.

'Actually, no. I still don't feel that good.' I hesitate. 'I had a miscarriage . . . it was my third, actually.'

'Oh Lizzie, I'm so sorry. That's terrible. You poor thing.' She puts down her coffee. 'Life can be really s*** sometimes, can't it?' I love this woman! She's a Methodist minister's wife and she swears – amazing! 'A few years ago I lost a baby and I wrote a book about it; I can send you a copy, if you'd like? It's not about how to survive a miscarriage or neonatal death; but much more about expectations and how we might deal with them. You might find it helpful, you might not, but I'm happy to send you a copy.'

'Yes, I'd love that. Thank you so much.'

'Right, ladies! Dinner is ready!' Jo proudly announces, as all the Weigh and Pray ladies carry dishes filled with food and place them on the table. Tonight we're at Jo's house, or 'coordinated Jo', as Steph likes to call her. Becky and I met Jo and her husband, Tim, at church after they moved here from London, so we invited her to join Weigh and Pray. We've also got two more new members: Chantal who is tiny and married to the tallest guy I know; then there's Fran, who's American, hilarious and probably the most Christian out of all of us, which is good, because I think we all need a bit more God in our lives. All three of our new members are thin, so we've decided to ditch the scales and focus on the food.

I go to grab the ceramic dish holding steamed broccoli and Jo stops me. 'No, Lizzie, you don't need to do anything tonight. Just go and sit down.' Chantal takes my hand and leads me into the dining room.

The chicken tastes amazing; the potatoes crunchy and fluffy all at the same time; the gravy, glossy, deep with flavour; the broccoli, courgettes and carrots soft, but still with that bit of crunch. Even Gommie ate some of the vegetables, so they must have been good. Roast chicken is now my favourite comfort food, reminding me of what it feels like to be hungry again, the flavours waking me up, healing found in each mouthful. We talk, I listen. We all have seconds – of course – and then it's time for the great debate of the evening. Do we have custard or ice cream with the apple crumble? Joy will want custard, I know it. Gommie's pretty traditional in her taste, so I reckon she'll go for custard too. Chantal's probably thinking about how custard is more work for Jo than ice cream; Becky's rooting for ice cream tonight; and Fran's American, so she's probably wondering why we're deciding between one or the other. 'What would Lizzie like with her crumble?' Jo asks. They all turn to look at me.

'Um, I think I'd like custard.'

'Well, if Lizzie wants custard, then we're having custard,' Jo says, getting up from the table. Becky and Chantal start collecting plates and cutlery, I go to grab some serving dishes and Fran tells me to stay put and relax. Joy counts the raised hands showing who wants a cup of tea with their pudding. I know it's only custard and mugs of tea, but right in this moment I could not feel more loved, which makes me feel like I need to cry even more. Jo's apple crumble and custard is as good as I imagined; custard was definitely the right choice. After a few minutes of quiet with the occasional 'mmmmm' and a couple of loud 'yummo's from Joy, Gommie suggests we start to fill out our notebooks with what people would like prayer for this week. We all agree, grabbing our individual notebooks and pens from bags and coat pockets, ready to share.

'Lizzie, how are you?' asks Fran.

I look up from my bowl and the tears are already falling, the mix of salty and sweet on my lips, tears falling into my custard, creating little pools of clear liquid on top of my delicious pudding.

'Oh, honey.' Fran walks round the table towards me and puts her arm around me. Sitting next to me, Chantal takes my hand again. Slowly, one by one, Becky, Jo, Joy and Gommie move from their places and their pudding and gather round me, a holy huddle of brokenness, perfectly illuminated by candlelight.

Esther's book, *The Gingerbread House*,[2] arrived at the office today. I started reading it in my lunch break and am now sat up in bed rushing through the pages; her words articulate a story and a struggle I see so much of myself in. Scattered throughout the pages of the book are poems written by a friend who'd lost her husband. The poems speak of the journey of grief, something that I don't really know much about. The poems are beautiful and painful to read, but they're teaching me so much. I grab my journal from my bedside table and copy one of the poems onto the first page.

Walking on Eggshells
I'm walking on eggshells,
Into the future,
Taking each day at a time,
And not looking back,
And not looking forward,
For behind is loss,
And ahead is the unknown
Sometimes I can grasp
The gift of the day,

And hold it as such
With my being,
But at other times
The tide rises
And the misery surfaces
Once again.[3]

This is what the middle feels like, fragile and confusing and always changing like the sea, and now I know this is what it's supposed to look like, I guess I need to settle into it for a bit.

I don't want to always feel this way, but middles must end at some point. I don't know when, I don't even know what the end of this would even look like. But if my friend Clare believes she won't always wear black, then I have to believe I won't always feel this sad. Right now, I'm in the middle of something, but I'm not the only one, and the stories I've been trusted with have taught me that the middle isn't something to be afraid of.

9

No Perfect People Allowed

All I've ever wanted to do is fit in. I think it's because for the majority of my life I've been almost a foot taller than my peers. I spent my childhood feeling like a giant and most of my school years towering over the rest of my class and waiting for all the boys to catch up with me, but sadly most of them never did. All the adults in my life kept telling me how lucky I was to be tall, but I didn't agree. Instead, I grew up searching for tall friends and fleeing the Petite section in Next for fear of setting off an alarm that would declare to the whole world I didn't belong.

Thankfully I've married a guy who's slightly taller than me, and most high street shops now have a 'tall' section, so I no longer have to buy men's jeans and ugly shoes. I thought I'd grown out of this awkward pain of feeling deeply out of place along with my Doc Martens and my tape recordings of the Top 40, but I was wrong. I appear to have reached that stage in life when everyone around me is obviously having sex because they're all pregnant. I'm currently receiving pregnancy announcements on an almost weekly basis and each announcement drives home the painful conclusion that my life doesn't measure up. I don't know where this feeling came from; it's new and I don't want to feel this way. These feelings are dark.

I keep trying to push them down and ignore them, but they keep creeping back, telling me I don't belong.

Weigh and Pray feels like a little haven; there are no pregnancy announcements and no comparison. The other safe place in my life is church. Life has made me cynical about the faith I used to have. I don't trust slick churches and shiny Christians. But Christ Church isn't like that. Hidden between rows of terraced houses, it may be small and messy and it never starts on time, but I feel like I've stumbled across something beautiful.

This morning I meet Becky at the back of church, where we both grab some fresh coffee served up in the mugs we donated from the café. 'Where's Dave?' Becky asks as she passes me a croissant.

'He's got man flu.'

'Oh dear.'

'Yeah, he's really grumpy when he's ill, so I'm glad to get out the house.'

'Poor Dave!' Becky sympathizes as we walk across the church with our coffee and croissants to claim our usual pew at the back. No one else sits there, apart from Jo and Tim. It's tucked into the recesses of the ancient building, the light from outside dulled by its journey through the small stained-glass window above. The back pew doesn't judge you when you cry; it also gives you an escape route before or at the end of the service if you don't want to talk to someone. I used to sit at the front of church, but that was before.

'I've got to speak to Andrew after the service,' says Becky, as she watches me shake off the mountain of flaky pastry that's stuck to my jumper after eating my croissant way too quickly. 'I've been looking through the church accounts for Andrew and, well, there's no money.'

'What?'

'The church has no money.'

'Do you think he's got any idea it's this bad?'

'No, not a clue.'

'Well, that's going to be a fun conversation.' She smiles at me, just as Andrew steps into the middle of the church to start the service, his dog collar poking out between his thick blue woollen jumper and his bushy beard that looks like he's preparing to be Santa at the Christmas party.

Andrew's recently moved the pews so they're in a semicircle around the edge of the building, leaving a big space in the middle where he's put an old wooden lectern. Behind him to the right is the gilded pulpit, raised high above the congregation. Directly behind him are the carpeted steps leading up to the ornate gold fancy bit. I don't know what it's called; we never use it – maybe it's a sacristy or chancel or altar bit, I don't know – it's just really fancy. In most other churches moving the pews would be the most dangerous thing a vicar could do, but none of us at Christ Church are that precious about how things *should* be.

'Who's that?' Becky asks, pointing at the guy who's slipped into the pew in front of us.

'I don't know, I've not seen him before.' I nudge Becky and she smiles – he's young and good-looking.

We stand and sing. There's a bit of feedback from the ancient sound system at the beginning of the first song. Everything at the front of church is run out of one socket with a multitude of extension cables – Dave reckons it's all going to blow one day.

A new guy, Dan, is leading worship. He moved here when he split up with his wife. He's an amazing musician; his voice is strong, but there's a fragility to it that makes it even more beautiful as it rises up into the vast space of the echoey church.

Andrew starts preaching from the front and thirty minutes later he's standing right in the middle of the church, having pushed the lectern forward across the dusty parquet floor. His passion for the message he's preaching is always matched by the force with which he pushes the lectern forward. This is why I love going to church; sometimes I don't know why I'm here, but then I hear Andrew talk about Jesus and I always feel better. He talks about Jesus like he loves him. He talks about Jesus like nothing else matters. He talks about Jesus in a way that helps me to believe everything will be OK.

I notice Becky glancing down at the folder of spreadsheets balanced on the wooden ledge of the pew in front, next to the Bibles, as she waits for Andrew to finish praying at the end of the service.

'Right, I'm off to find Andrew. Do you want to come with me?' she asks.

'It's OK. I'll let you break the news,' I smile.

'Thanks!' She jokingly rolls her eyes then walks over to Andrew, who's hugging people and listening to their stories. I notice the guy who arrived late is still sitting on his own and I know I should talk to him.

'Hi!' I lean forward to the pew in front to get his attention.

'Oh, hi.' He turns to face me.

'Hi, I'm Lizzie. What's your name?'

'I'm Neil, nice to meet you.' He extends his hand to shake mine.

'Is this your first time here?'

'Yes, I've just moved to Chester.'

'Oh right, where were you before?'

'A small town just outside Manchester.' He pauses. 'I was a vicar at the local church there.'

'I keep meeting lots of vicars at the moment! My friend Fran, her husband's going to train to be a vicar and Andrew, the vicar here, is encouraging my husband and I to think about training too. So, have you got a new vicar job?'

'No.' He looks down for a moment, 'I've just got a job at an accountancy firm in the city centre. The vicar thing didn't really go to plan.' He looks away.

'Well, you're in the right place,' I smile. 'Pretty much everyone here is recovering from something that didn't really go to plan.'

'Thanks.' We both look at each other awkwardly. 'I should go,' he says. 'It was nice to meet you.'

'You too.'

Tonight Dave's driving us to another meeting with Richard. Richard is basically the guy who helps you discern whether becoming ordained is the right thing and if it is, then he sends you to a national panel. I've learned a bit about the whole process because Fran's husband has gone through it and they're about to move to Cambridge for him to train. This is our third visit to Richard. Before each meeting we have to read books and write an essay on one aspect of the selection criteria. Andrew thinks both Dave and I should think about becoming vicars which sounds ridiculous – me being a vicar – but I promised Andrew I'd go with Dave so that's why I'm here.

'Lizzie and Dave, it's so lovely to see you!' says Richard as he welcomes us into the oversized vicarage, which is sat next to a row of houses half its size. He makes us cups of tea and directs us to a room where the walls are covered in books towering over the four wing-back armchairs. 'So, we're going to chat about your essays and about your previous experience of leadership.' He pauses to take a sip of his tea; he speaks very slowly, leaving long pauses which seem to be a sign of a deeper spirituality I am yet to experience. 'Let's start with Dave.' He picks up the printout of Dave's essay and his notepad, filled with comments and questions. 'So, Dave, it appears that people have recognized your call to leadership from a young age?'

'Yeah,' Dave replies. 'It's not something I recognized in myself straight away, but over the years, even when I was at primary school, people in my church believed God had told them I would be a leader one day.'

'Ex-ce-ll-ent,' Richard says, drawing out each syllable of the word for an unnecessary length of time. 'How do *you* feel about this calling to leadership?'

'Well, I guess I'm just taking the next step to see what might be possible. I think both Lizzie and I,' he looks over to me, 'we both believe we will go back into some form of Christian work, and we think pioneering in the Church of England might be a good fit.'

'Ah, yes,' says Richard. 'Pioneering. It does seem like this very much lends itself to your experience, trying something new.'

'Exactly, yes,' says Dave. 'A lot of people have encouraged me to explore becoming a pioneer in the Church of England so that's why I'm here.'

'Yes,' says Richard, 'obedience. That is why you're here; obedience to the calling and to those who've recognized it in you – a very brave and wise decision, Dave, very brave and very wise.' Richard places his clasped hands over his knees and leans forward. 'What about you, Lizzie? It appears your journey into leadership hasn't been quite so smooth, am I right?'

'Um, yes, I suppose.'

'Reading your description of your time in Wales after university makes me think there are some aspects of your past that you are yet to deal with.'

'Perhaps,' I respond. 'It was a really difficult year, working for someone, a Christian leader, who told me he thought I wasn't good enough for the role.'

'Well, yes, of course it would be; it appears the fact you are a woman didn't help with this, either?'

'No, no it didn't; I think that was part of the problem. I hadn't come across people who didn't believe women could have an equal leadership role to men and I guess, well, it knocked my confidence a lot.'

'Well, yes, of course it would,' says Richard, tipping his head to one side in a pastoral manner. 'You know my wife is a vicar too, and I believe it's very important to encourage women to step into leadership, but it has to be from a healthy place, and I wonder if you need more time before progressing any further on this journey?'

Relief and regret sweep over me. 'I think you may be right,' I confess. 'In fact, we've also been having a tough time at the moment.' I glance over to Dave, then the floor, then back to Richard. 'I don't really feel like I have anything to offer; I do believe I might go on to work for the church in some way in the future, but I don't feel I have what it takes to be a vicar.'

'I think you're getting confused about what Christian leadership is.' He pauses again, takes a sip of tea and leans further forward. 'You see, leadership isn't about whether we feel adequate, it's a matter of whether we feel called. Christ is the one who equips us. The question you need to ask, Lizzie, is one of calling, not adequacy, because in Christ you are more than enough. And yes, I wonder whether right now, you may need to take a break and work through some of the more painful parts of your life that you're still carrying.' He picks up my essay. 'You may indeed still be called, but perhaps now isn't the right time.'

After our meeting with Richard, Dave has a date for his meeting with the national panel and I am left to focus on my other calling, the role every woman is expected to carry out – motherhood. Three miscarriages mean I get to find out what's wrong. The investigations began with blood tests, and lots of internal scans before an appointment with a geneticist to check we're not related.

Our investigations have been shared between three consultants – there's Mr Johnson who's scary but efficient; he's also Becky, Joy and Jo's gynaecologist, which I try not to think about. Then there's Ms Reid who seems lovely and keeps telling me my best option is to pray. If a vicar told me this I would be encouraged, but when a highly qualified consultant tells me to pray, I start to worry. Finally, there's Mr Miller, who's very excitable and looks like Michael Ball.

The multiple blood tests and the number of cameras, probes and hands that have gone up me, not to forget the Pixar lamp used to illuminate parts of my body I've never looked at myself, were not nice in any way. But at least we were finally doing something; we were searching for answers and it helped me feel a bit more positive about the future, until today.

'I'm sorry, we can't find anything.'

'Sorry?' Dave leans forward to make sure he's hearing this right.

'Everything looks fine.'

'But what about the miscarriages?' I add, 'Isn't there anything we can do to stop this from happening again?'

'No.' I really wish Mr Johnson was more of a talker. 'There's nothing you can do for now, just call this number the next time you get pregnant.' He hands me a slip of paper with the number for the Recurrent Miscarriage Clinic and shows us out his office.

This is not the life I want; it's not even one I want to talk about because it just seems to illustrate how incredibly flawed I am. Somewhere there's a list, I don't know where it came from or who wrote it, but there's a list of criteria that declares what a good life looks like and right now my life doesn't come anywhere close.

This Sunday we arrive late to church again. I blame Dave, it's in his genes. We're just in time to hear Andrew's booming voice across the PA to get everyone to sit down. The service is already ten minutes late starting but no one's bothered, we just keep talking as we slowly move towards the pews. 'I've got something very exciting to share with you today,' he says. He's already pushed the lectern forward about a metre so it must be good. Jo and Tim sneak to the back and we all move down the pew to make space. Becky and I popped round to their house last night with lots of M&S foodie treats. They'd just found out their fifth round of IVF had failed. This was their last chance – five was the limit for them.

'Hi,' Neil whispers as he slides in next to us. We're running out of space on the back row.

'I've been reading this incredible book,' says Andrew, 'and I believe God has spoken to me about what kind of church we need to be.' He pauses, his hands holding on to the wooden lectern. 'Christ Church is not a place for perfect people.' His deep voice booms over the microphone and the lectern slides forward. 'No perfect people allowed,' he repeats, looking around the church, trying to catch people's eyes. 'That's right,' he continues, 'no perfect people are allowed in this church, not one. If you're not perfect then this is the place for you.

If your soul is worn out, worn thin, this is the place for you.

If you're depressed, anxious, tired and fed up, then this is place for you.

If you've had enough of the way things are, this is the place for you.

If you're sad today, this is the place for you.

If you're mourning, bereaved or grieving, this is the place for you.

If you're at the bottom of the pile, this is the place for you.

If you're lonely, this is the place for you.

If you're struggling with addiction, this is the place for you.

If you're divorced or single or widowed, this is the place for you.

If your life doesn't measure up to what you think it should look like, then this is where you belong.'[1]

The lectern is now in the middle of the church and Andrew's still pushing it forward.

'If you feel like an outsider, you're in the right place because this is a church full of outsiders!'

Andrew's voice bellows through the microphone, the lectern is almost at the other side of church and some people have to turn their heads to look behind them to see him. Some people call church 'therapy' and I'm OK with that; we, the ones who turn up every Sunday, need it.

'You're not trash, you never were. You need to know that God not only loves you immensely, but he also *likes* you!' I glance over to Becky and Tim and Jo, absorbed in the words Andrew's booming voice is speaking over us. In the pews opposite are some of the guys from AA who used to come into the café and next to them is Dan, the worship leader. This building holds so many painful stories. I know people struggling with depression, with family breakdowns, unemployment, grief, singleness, divorce and childlessness. I've never been part of a community like this in my life; previously I wouldn't have thought a church full of people whose life doesn't look like it should would be a good thing, but it is and it's beautiful.

Andrew keeps talking and I look up once again to that statue of Jesus hanging on the cross, looking down on the congregation below. I imagine the people who sat at the foot of the cross when he died and the people who sat at his feet when he was teaching and eating – they were mostly outsiders: women, prostitutes, widows, tax collectors, the poor, those who were fully aware of what made them different. Their lives may not have fitted into what society defined as the good life, but they were the ones who first saw Jesus for who he really was. They called him the Saviour before the disciples,[2] they worshipped him before the rich and the educated and they were the first to witness his resurrected body. I think it's because they were the ones who knew they needed Jesus – they knew they needed a saviour.

10

Business Time

~

'I'd want Reese Witherspoon to play me,' says Steph. We're discussing who we'd like to play us, if someone did a film about our lives. I'm torn between Kate Winslet and Miranda Hart. Joy is struggling to cook and join in the conversation, so she's standing in the doorway to the living room wielding a large knife, whilst the rest of us flinch as she unknowingly waves it around when she speaks. She's making this bacon, cheese and puff pastry thing from her new cookbook, which sounds amazing.

'Dinner's ready!' Joy yells, completely unnecessarily, as we're only in the next room and can actually see her walking towards the table with the food.

Becky slides along the bench closer to me and further from Joy, who's still talking and waving the knife. I'm more focused on the smell of bacon and melted cheese and less worried about the knife. As she serves up, Joy begins to tell us about the doctor's appointment she and Rob had today.

'It went OK, the doctor was helpful. He's going to refer us for tests to see if there's a reason why I've not got pregnant after four years.' I want to hear about what happened, but I also really want to eat that pie sat in front of Joy. 'They're going to do blood tests for both us and Rob will have to do a sperm test.'

'How do you feel about it?' Steph asks, pushing the pile of empty dinner plates closer towards Joy.

'Alright, I suppose. I mean, we don't really know if there's anything wrong yet. I suppose it depends on the test results.' Gommie takes the knife off Joy and finishes cutting the pie and putting it onto plates. Becky passes a full plate to each of us and Joy continues, 'It was strange the way the doctor dealt with it, though – he just started talking about IVF and hormone treatment. Rob was surprised he didn't ask us about sex; you know, check we were doing it right.'

Steph's struggling to swallow her mouthful of pie quickly so that she can say something about sex, I can see it – she's desperate to make a comment but can't because she's got a mouthful. Becky gets there first. 'What? Like diagrams of the best positions or something?'

'Yeah,' Joy responds. 'I mean, you go to the doctor to talk about trying to get pregnant and they never talk to you about sex; they just go straight to the medical issues. What if we're doing it wrong? Or, what if there's an optimum position?'

Steph finally finishes her mouthful. 'Babes, do you need me to talk to Rob, you know, to give him a few tips?'

Becky and I are huddled next to each other on the bench, sniggering.

'Alright! Alright! I'm trying to eat here!' Gommie shouts.

But Steph has only just started, 'What about after sex? I mean, did he not talk about lying down and sticking your legs in the air or jiggling around a bit to help the little swimmers get there?'

'No! He did not talk about that! He just talked about medical intervention and diet, like cutting out caffeine and alcohol. To be honest, it would have been really awkward talking to him about sex; I mean, he was clinical about the whole thing.'

'Well, he doesn't sound like much fun,' Steph comments as she fills her fork with another mouthful of pie.

'Sooo, what did people get up to at the weekend?' asks Gommie, bluntly changing the subject.

Steph's not ready to move on, though: 'Well, we all know what Joy and Rob were probably doing.'

Becky and I are sniggering, Joy is focusing on eating her pie and Gommie pretends she's not listening.

The following day I'm home first from work, changing out of my work trousers and into my trackie and a baggy hoody from my pre-uni gap year. Sat on the sofa with the Prof and a cup of tea, I catch up with more episodes of *Friends* before Dave gets home. Half way through my third episode in a row, I hear the key in the door. The Professor hops off the sofa and Dave walks straight into the living room. I've paused Ross and Steph mid-argument on the telly; he only has to glance at the screen to realize what I'm looking at.

'Looks like you've been watching something very intellectual whilst I've been slaving away at work!' He bends down to kiss me on the forehead and carries on through to the dining room. 'I've just remembered I've got a meeting at church tonight; it starts at half-seven.'

'So, when are we going to do it, then?' I jump off the sofa and follow Dave into the dining room.

'Does it have to be today?'

'Um . . . yes! When I peed on the ovulation stick this morning, there was a smiley face.'

I'm really enjoying using the ovulation sticks at the moment. Seeing the smiley face can feel almost as good as seeing the two lines on a pregnancy test. My body has done something right; I've peed on a stick and it smiled back at me – it was this smile that currently controlled our sex life.

'We could do it when I get back from the meeting.'

Dave's got a meeting about becoming a vicar. He's got a three-day super-intense interview next week so it's not long until we'll find out if he is destined for vicardom. We've already decided on a college in Cambridge if he gets through. Our decision to go to Cambridge may have been more to do with the fact it reminded Dave of Hogwarts rather than any deep spiritual reasons; he did also like the sound of the course, and Fran and her husband, Jon, are already there after leaving Chester a few months ago for Jon to train, so at least we'll have two friends.

'I suppose,' I say. 'It just depends what time you finish your meeting. I don't want to go to sleep too late – I've got work in the morning.'

'It's 6 o'clock, we could do it now.'

'What about dinner? I was going to make chilli.'

'How long does that take?'

'About half an hour.'

'Well, we've got time then.'

'I suppose.'

'How about we do it now, but set an alarm for half an hour's time to make sure we leave time to have dinner before I go out? I know we need to have sex but I'm not going to let that spoil my dinner.'

'OK, let's do it quickly now, then.' We make our way to the bedroom. Dave sets a timer on his phone and we get down to business.

Half an hour later, I'm dressed, downstairs in the kitchen chopping an onion to make the chilli. I love chilli, it's a great comfort meal, the spicy mince and kidney beans in a thick tomato sauce – amazing! One of the things I love about chilli is all the things you can eat with it; it's just so versatile. It goes great with nachos – which I love – or if you want to be healthy, you can have it with rice. Then there's the toppings: sour cream, guacamole, maybe a handful of grated cheese sprinkled, or a couple of squares of dark chocolate melted in at the last minute. I start to fry the onion in the hot oil as Dave comes down the stairs. He walks through the dining room and into our little galley kitchen. He briefly stops and kisses me on the cheek; his hand gently curls around my waist. His lips quickly leave my skin and he carries on walking past me to the bin where he removes the lid and lifts the overstretched bin liner out, ties the top closed and carries it outside. 'It's bin day tomorrow,' he comments on his way into the yard.

The onions are soft and translucent and they squidge as I push my wooden spoon against them in the pan. Now the fun bit. I tip in the garlic, chilli powder, cumin, coriander, smoked paprika and cinnamon and fry them off in the oil with the soft onion. The smell rises as I quickly stir the spices, coating the onion until it changes colour to a rich, burned red. The draft from the open back door is quickly shut out when Dave comes back into the kitchen, locking the door behind him, allowing the kitchen to fill with the smell released by the warm spices. He tears off a new bin liner from the roll under the sink and slowly rubs the edges of the liner between his fingers until the bag finally opens, and he places it in the bin, firmly closing the lid. I tip the soft, aromatic terracotta onion into a bowl and start to brown the mince.

'So, if today was the first day with a smiley face on the ovulation stick, we need to do it tomorrow as well.' I break up the wiggly worm-like pieces of meat with my wooden spoon as they slowly change colour and texture. Dave's leaning against the doorframe between the kitchen and the dining room.

'I suppose so,' he responds. 'But I'm thinking it might be best to go with what the doctor said and just do it every two to three days; I looked it up online as well – it's to do with sperm quality.'

'Oh. Are you sure? The box said to have sex every time you see a smiley face as well as a couple of days either side of it.' The kettle clicks off and I pour the boiling water onto a stock cube, stirring to dissolve it in its plastic jug. I pass Dave a tin of tomatoes and a can opener. 'Honestly,' he adds, 'I think it could be better to do it this way rather than with the sticks. It gives time for me to restock the good stuff. Do you want the tomatoes in here?' I nod and he tips the contents of the tin into the pan with the cooked mince, stirring to mix them together. I add the stock and the onion spice mix to the pan, turning the heat down for it to simmer.

'So,' I say, 'if we do it your way that means we need to do it again on Thursday, and then maybe Saturday?'

'Yep,' Dave replies as he throws the rinsed tomato tin into the recycling bin.

'But my parents are coming at the weekend.' I stir a tin of kidney beans into the gently bubbling mixture, the dark red nuggets popping out of the rich tomato sauce coating the meat.

'Oh, I forgot about that. We could be really quiet?' I look at him. 'What? What's the problem? It'll be fine.'

'I don't know. I mean, I know we can be quiet but they'll only be next door. Plus, they get up really early now, so they'll be awake way before us – they're bound to hear something. I don't think I could do it with them in the house.'

'OK, well, how about we do it Friday morning before work and then Sunday evening once they've left?'

'Yeah, OK, that sounds alright. But will you be able to do it early in the morning? You're not exactly good with early starts.' I scoop a spoon of chilli out of the pan, blow on it and take a mouthful to taste.

'Yeah, I'll be fine. This is different. I'll be waking up to have sex – I think I can manage.'

I dish up the rich, dark red chilli into a bowl, grating a couple of squares of dark chocolate, leftover from a baking experiment, on top.

It's Friday morning. The alarm goes off at seven, it's business time. Dave puts his arm around me and we both lie there for a bit. He kisses me, but I still feel so sleepy I barely kiss him back. We lie still for a bit longer, me resting in Dave's arms, head on his shoulder. I check my phone. 'It's half-seven! How did that happen? We must have fallen back to sleep! Oh no! Dave, wake up!' Dave's eyes open slowly to see my phone right in front of his face showing him the time.

'What! What's going on?'

'We slept in! We need to get up!'

'What about having sex?'

'I don't think we've got time now!'

'Yes, we do, it's fine, we can be quick.'

'Are you sure?'

'Yeah, of course. I mean it's that or having sex tonight with your parents next door, and now your dad's got his new hearing aid he's pretty sharp.'

'OK, let's do it now, but it's got to be quick.' Dave starts kissing me – lips, neck – his fingers move through my hair. It feels nice, then I remember the car tax needs renewing. 'Have you sent off the car tax form?'

'What?'

'The car tax needs renewing; we had to send that form off.'

'Yes, it's fine, I did it yesterday.' His hand slides round my waist, we start kissing again, I pull his body closer to mine.

'When you get home tonight, will you help me with the cleaning? The bathroom really needs doing before Mum and Dad arrive and we need to put the hoover round.'

'Yep, that's fine,' Dave says whilst lifting my hair and kissing my neck. 'You know these conversations aren't sexy, don't you?'

'Sorry, I keep getting distracted. Let's get down to business, then.'

11

More Tea, Vicar?

~

It's 7 o'clock, the alarm is beeping right next to Dave's head and he's not doing anything about it. 'Dave? Dave?' I roll over and poke his arm. It's his alarm; he's the one who's got to go to morning prayer. 'Dave?'

'Mmmm,' he responds.

'Your alarm's going off. It's time to wake up.'

'Oh, oh yeah.' He rolls over, turns it off and goes back to sleep. I close my eyes and try to relax; this is not my responsibility.

'Argh! Dave, it's 8 o'clock!' I grab his arm and start shaking him. 'You've got to be at college in fifteen minutes!'

'What?'

'Quickly! Get up!' He sits up in bed rubbing his eyes, then turns to me.

'Can you drive me in? I've still not worked out the cycle route and I'm really late.'

'Fine.'

Cambridge is not built for cars. At 8:30 we arrive outside the red-brick college draped in purple blooms of wisteria. 'Thanks, hon, bye, see you later.' Dave kisses me, grabs his bag, slams the car door shut and I watch him run through the archway, across the empty quad and into the chapel, wondering if this is what every morning will be like for the next three years.

On my way home I somehow end up on a dual carriageway and turn what should be a fifteen-minute journey into a forty-minute one. When I eventually arrive home, I slam the door shut and instantly wonder why I was so stressed about getting home quickly because I have absolutely nothing to do today. I turn on the radio in an attempt to drown out the silence of a house that's far too big for two people, and I eat my breakfast in the dining room across the hall from the kitchen. I try to pray about my day to what feels more like a brick wall than the Almighty God of the universe.

I make a coffee and head down the dark, cupboard-lined hallway with my journal in one hand and my coffee in another. I'm going to make a prayer journal. I write a list of the days of the week and then begin to put names of friends and family next to them. I stop at Thursday; I've overfilled the first few days, and I'm not that great at praying anyway, so I decide to give myself a long weekend off.

I turn the page and write a list of tasks that include finishing off the unpacking, posting a birthday card, applying for jobs, making a doctor's appointment and learning how to pipe frosting on a cupcake. A half-finished prayer journal and the desire to improve my cake-decorating skills can only mean one thing: yes, that's right, my husband is now training to be a vicar.

'So, how was it, then?'

'Yeah, it was really good,' He replies, gulping down a pint of squash. 'It took ages to walk back. I have to cycle in tomorrow.'

'Did you meet some nice people? You know, normal people?' I ask, leaning against the kitchen worktop, trying to act super-chilled.

'Yeah.' He fills up his pint glass again.

'And . . .?'

'And what?' Dave looks at me blankly.

'Any other information? Like names of people, where they're from, do they have wives?' I say, glaring at him.

'Oh. I met this guy Andy, he's a pioneer as well and, ummm, he likes Tim Keller.'

'Well, maybe you could start a Tim Keller fan club and talk about all his Christian books and critique his sermons together.'

'Maybe we will,' Dave says, filling another pint glass with squash. 'Oh, and he's married.' Finally, something helpful.

'Did he say anything about his wife? Like her name or whether they've got kids?'

'Not really . . . I think she's called Rach . . . oh, and she's really tiny.'

'Seriously? Is that all? Did you meet anyone else who's married?' I can sense the desperation in my voice, but I'm pretty certain it's lost on Dave.

'Oh yeah, there were loads,' he reassures me. 'So how about you – how was your day?' He walks up and puts his arms around me.

'OK, I suppose.' He hugs me.

'I'm sorry, honey, it will get better. You've got Spice tonight; it'll be really good to meet some of the other spouses. I'm sure lots of them feel the same as you.'

The spouses' group is called Spice. There's also a spin-off group called Crafty Spice run by the cool, arty spouses. Tonight is my first Spice meeting.

I walk through the stone archway entrance to the college and across the quad towards a building where I head up the wide carpeted staircase. I find myself in a large kitchen filled with teapots and female voices. Scanning the room, I notice a long wooden table at the end of the kitchen filled with immaculately decorated cupcakes, biscuits and sponge cakes, and one guy standing next to it, doing his best to blend in.

Unsure about what to do first, I head towards the cake, admiring/coveting the piping skills on a batch of cupcakes before shoving one in my mouth, then head over to talk to the one guy in the room. 'Hi, I'm Lizzie.'

'Hi, Lizzie, I'm Ian.'

'Hi, Ian. This is weird, isn't it? It's almost like it's our first day of school again.'

'Yeah, I suppose, although I didn't go to an all-girls' school.'

I grab another cupcake. The volume of high-pitched voices lowers as we're ushered into the principal's lounge. I'm handed a sticky label with my name on and step into a beautiful high-ceilinged room with lead-framed windows and draped ceiling-height curtains, furnished with a kind of old people's home eclectic style of sofas and wing-backs. With far more people than chairs, we all remain standing before being told to mingle again and find out more about each other. I start with the woman stood next to me who tells me she's in her final year.

'The college is amazing!' she gushes. 'The friends I've made here will be friends for life!'

'So do you feel ready to become a proper vicar's wife?' I ask.

'Well, my husband's definitely ready to move. He's more of a leader than me, plus we've got three kids so I'm not sure how much I'll be able to get involved in. Do you guys have kids?' she asks.

'No.'

'Well, make sure you make the most of all the spare time you have while it lasts!'

'Yeah, good idea!' I fake a laugh whilst scanning the room, and notice a group of ladies in the corner, giggling. One of them has bits of orange in her hair and a really cool chunky orange necklace. I wish I was hanging out with them.

'Would you like another cupcake?' A large tray of pastel frosted cupcakes appears in-between us, held by a very tall, smiley woman with long, shiny brown hair and a pastel pink blouse. 'Hello, I'm Rosie.'

'Rosie and her husband arrived the same year as us. She's an amazing baker as you can tell.' My new friend points at the exquisite display of cakes in front of us. 'She's also a very talented musician; she plays the harp.'

'And our youngest sons were born in the same week!' adds Rosie. 'They're practically inseparable!'

I smile at them both, unsure what to do with all this information.

'So, do you have kids?' asks Rosie.

'No.'

'I'm sure it won't be long until you join the club!' She nudges my arm with the giant tray of cupcakes and winks at me. I offer a half-hearted smile and look over longingly to the group of cool, laughing ladies in the corner. The volume of women's voices rises all around me; even Ian seems to be having a good time.

'Right, ladies, keep mingling!' says one of the Spice reps. I say goodbye to Rosie the harpist and her friend and move onto another group of two women, one with four kids, another with three and we talk about our husbands and housing and baking for a few minutes before dispersing. Why does everyone have kids? And why are they all so content and gracious about supporting their husbands? I feel so inadequate. There has to be at least one person here who I have something in common with. I begin scanning the room for someone a bit younger, who maybe hasn't had time to get pregnant yet, but then I remember I'm surrounded by Christians, most of whom probably got married as soon as they turned 20 and began having biblically named children not long after.

I spot a woman standing by herself in the corner of the room by the window and walk over to her. Maybe *she* is the one. She's very thin and pretty but we could still be friends. I introduce myself, asking questions about where she's moved from and what her plans are, trying to hide my excitement when I hear she has no job *and* no children. 'We should meet up; maybe we could go for coffee this week?' I suggest. She looks at me, pausing before responding to my desperate invitation to hang out.

'No.'

The voices from huddles of women bonding and laughing rise up around me, dragging me back to that horrible teenage paranoia when you believe everyone has a best friend but you. There are the women who work, the stay-at-home mums and then me and this other woman who, for some reason, has decided she doesn't want to be my friend. The evening is almost over and I still haven't found my tribe. I glance over to the corner where I saw the lady with the cool hair and her friends laughing, and they're still there! They totally ignored the mingling rules! I turn to leave my *non-friend* and head straight towards them. I don't care if I look desperate; these women are rebels and I want them to be my friends.

'Hi, I'm Lizzie,' I announce, as I step into their huddle. Rach, Julie, Cath and another Rach, who's tiny – maybe she's the wife of that guy Dave was talking about? They introduce themselves to me one by one. I'm instantly drawn to Cath, not just because I love her South African accent, but because she's the same height as me, which provides a rare opportunity not to feel like a giant, especially as I'm currently standing between tiny Rach and Julie who are about half my size in every way.

We rush through all the classic small talk questions; jobs, homes and kids. Cath tells me they're all first-years, and all their husbands apart from Julie's are training to be pioneers like Dave, which explains why they didn't obey the mingling rule.

'I think our husbands have already met,' I tell tiny Rach, as we all grab another one of Rosie's cupcakes from the tray as it passes by.

'That's it, ladies, make sure you all take one!' says Rosie. 'I can't take any home, otherwise my husband, Stephen, will eat them and after three years here, he needs to cut down on his cake consumption!' I'd already heard talk about the weight people have put on whilst at the college.

'Soooo, are you ladies ready to become vicar's wives?' says Rach as she eats the frosting off the top of her cupcake.

'Do you think we'll get training?' Julie laughs, slowly peeling the cake case away from the soft vanilla sponge.

'What? Like vicar's wife training?' says Rach, and we all look at each other and start giggling. 'Maybe we'll get trained in flower arranging and baking!'

'Well, I'm going to fail because I can't bake,' whispers Julie, covering her mouth with her hand to make sure no one else hears.

'Me neither!' adds tiny Rach, leaning into our huddle.

'I'm afraid I like to bake,' confesses Cath, 'but that doesn't mean I want to stay at home baking all day! Joel and I have always done ministry together so it would be weird if I just left him to it. Obviously life's going to change for us very soon,' she says whilst pointing at her bump, 'but I don't want that to stop me from making the most of being here.' Slowly I begin to feel more hopeful. Cath may be pregnant but she still wants to lead alongside her husband. I thought I was the only one.

'I'm going to try to go to some of the lectures,' I announce.

'Oh, I wish I could do that, but I'm commuting to London for my job,' says tiny Rach as she carefully breaks off pieces of sponge and frosting to eat. 'This cupcake is amazing!'

'The sponge is so light!' adds Cath.

'Like a tiny cloud,' says Julie. 'That must mean there's no calories, right?'

'Do any of you ladies watch *Bake Off*?' I ask, and we spend the rest of the evening talking about soggy bottoms and Paul Hollywood's blue eyes until we're thrown out of the Principal's Lodge and left standing in the car park swapping numbers before heading back to our vicar-to-be husbands.

'Well? How was it?'

'Mostly awful, but it got better at the end,' I tell Dave, standing in front of the TV to make sure I have his full attention.

'Why was it so bad?'

'Everyone has a kid or a job apart from me.' He reaches for the remote to switch off the TV now he's realized this conversation will not be a quick one.

'But you can't be the only one.'

'Everyone has a job or a baby or both, apart from me and this other girl who doesn't want to be my friend.' I can't believe how immature I sound right now.

'But it got better, right?'

'*Eventually.*' His positivity is so annoying. 'I met this group of ladies at the end of the night. They've still all got kids or jobs, but we had a laugh talking about *Bake Off*. Most of them are married to pioneers as well.'

'Well, Thursday is community day, so that's another opportunity to meet people. There's a Spice meeting in the morning and spouses can join us for lunch, then there's afternoon tea and the chapel service and dinner altogether. That should be good.'

It turns out community day is not good. I had obviously not received the memo that Thursday mornings were essentially a mums' and toddlers' group. Sitting in the middle of a group I have been avoiding for the past three years just made me want to cry. After the Bible study I find myself trapped in a conversation about the need for more biblical toys at the college, oh, and these theologically sound toys should really be made out of wood, not plastic; it's better for the children, apparently.

'Shall we grab a coffee?' Rach and Julie appear just in time to save me just as the conversation moves on to breastfeeding. We leave the clusters of women chatting away in the quad, enjoying the early autumn sunshine. We cross the lawn, carefully navigating a path between the two toddlers aggressively throwing tiny stones at passers-by and a competitive croquet match and head up the wide, stone steps to the common room. The common room has everything a trainee vicar could need: old threadbare sofas, oil paintings of famous vicars, coffee, a tuck shop and table football. We grab a coffee and a seat in the corner of the room under a huge, leaded-glass window. 'Where are the kids?' I ask.

'We gave them to the men,' Rach replies.

'It's good for them,' adds Julie. Rach actually has four kids and Julie has three, but their youngest kids aren't old enough for school yet.

'So, how are you ladies doing?' asks Rach.

'I really miss my job,' says Julie. 'Of course, I know this is the right place for us and I get more time to spend with my little man before he heads to preschool, but I miss working at my old school.'

'Oh, mate, I'm sorry. It's only two years; hopefully we can both survive it!' says Rach.

'How come you guys are only here for two years? Dave and I are here for three.'

'Because our husbands are old,' says Julie.

'It's hard because two years isn't long at all! There's no point putting roots down, but at the same time I want to do something. I can't just stay at home!' says Rach, brushing the dashes of bright pink flecked through her hair out of her face.

'How about you, Lizzie, how are you feeling about being here?' asks Julie.

'Well, I am applying for jobs at the universities; that's what I used to do. Then I've signed up for some lectures. Other than that, I don't know.' My voice trails off and I look at the floor. I can't even convince myself I'm excited about being here: I don't really care about work, I don't want to work in university admin all my life, I'm not even that good at it, but I need something to do, some kind of purpose. What I really want is to be a mum, but I can't tell *them* that.

It's Monday again, but today I have two things in my diary: a doctor's appointment and Spice. I know, life is getting pretty hectic right now.

I arrive at the surgery with a handbag filled with hospital letters. I need to get referred to the Recurrent Miscarriage Clinic and the fertility clinic; it's been eighteen months since I was last pregnant and I need to find out why. Eventually I'm called into a room that looks like it has never been tidied. There are papers everywhere, stacked on the floor and piled around the computer. Sat at the desk is a doctor who looks like he's been here as long as the dusty files surrounding him. I'm pretty certain he's not brushed his hair or changed his shirt and beige tank top in that time either.

I sit down and immediately launch into my backstory whilst clutching on to the wad of hospital letters in my hand.

'Hang on a minute,' he says. 'I just need to get some of this down.' He swivels his chair to face the computer and I watch him type up our conversation using just two fingers. It is painful to watch. I witness each spelling mistake and then the pause to find backspace and start again. I start rocking to distract myself from grabbing the keyboard and typing up my medical history for him. Eventually he stops typing and turns his chair to look at me. 'So, what can I do for you?'

'Well, I need to get referred to the Recurrent Miscarriage Clinic in case I get pregnant again, and I also want to get referred for fertility tests because we've not been able to get pregnant for a while now.'

'Hang on, young lady! Let's slow down; so you say you want to get referred to the Recurrent Miscarriage Clinic?'

'Yes.'

'Right,' he turns to face the computer again. 'I'm not sure how to do that. I think if I click on this here . . .' It's impressive how slowly he is able to move the mouse and hover over the icon before clicking on it. He then writes and rewrites the word 'recurrent' four times before spelling it correctly. He clicks enter, then spins his chair back round to face me. 'OK, that's done. Now what were you saying about the fertility clinic?'

'Well, I've not got pregnant in eighteen months and I wondered if you could refer me for tests?'

'How old are you?'

'Thirty-three.'

'I'm afraid you need to be trying for two years before you're referred, so you'll have to wait a bit. There are other things you can do that might help your fertility, though.'

'OK.'

'Losing weight is one of them,' he says. 'I mean, you don't need to lose loads of weight but a bit won't hurt.'

'Sure, I know I need to lose weight. I can do that.'

'How are you feeling at the moment?' he asks.

'Um, not great.' I can feel the tears swelling up. Why did this computer-illiterate man start being nice to me? It's making me cry.

'Well, you've not had an easy time.' He passes me a tissue.

'No, I suppose I haven't. We've just moved here as well, and I don't have a job.'

'Can I just ask: how often do you feel sad?'

'All the time.'

'How long has this gone on for?'

'A few months, but it's got worse.'

'Have there been moments when you've felt happy recently?'

'No.'

'My dear, I think you might be depressed.'

'Oh,' I pause. I've been depressed before, but I hadn't thought about it since we moved, and now I can see what he means.

'I think it might help if I prescribe you something, just a low dose of antidepressants to help give you a bit of a boost. Is that OK?'

'Yes, um, yes, I think that might help.'

'Right, well, you know whilst you're taking these you can't try to get pregnant?'

'What?'

'It's not safe to take these whilst you're trying to conceive.'

'So if I take them I can't get pregnant?'

'That's correct.'

'Then no, I don't want them.'

'Are you sure?'

'Yes, definitely.'

'OK, well, we can leave it for now, but I want you to book in another appointment in two weeks so we can reassess this.'

'OK.' I grab my hospital letters and head back to our empty house.

At 4, the front door clicks open. I hear Dave throw his rucksack on the floor, slam the door shut, then walk into the kitchen. The tap is running, he fills a glass with water, starts drinking it and I wait. 'Helloooo?' he calls out.

'Hi.'

'Where are you?' I don't answer, I'll let him work it out. 'Oh, there you are!' He comes into the lounge and joins me on the sofa.

'Man, that was a full-on day, we had our first Greek lesson and it was so good. I know I've never been any good at languages, but I think that was partly because we hadn't been taught any grammar. Anyway, the Greek lecturer is so good, he's a great teacher but he's also so passionate about Jesus, he goes from Greek to preaching about Jesus in one sentence. And then we had a New Testament lecture, you should definitely audit that one, the lecturer is amaz . . .'

'I saw the doctor today,' I cut into his conversation.

'Oh, was that today?'

'Yes. I had told you.' I fold my arms and stare at him.

'So, how did it go?'

'Nothing happened. He's going to refer me to the Recurrent Miscarriage Clinic and we can't have IVF because we've not waited long enough.'

'But we haven't even talked about IVF yet.'

'You want to have a baby, don't you? If we could have IVF then we'd get a baby.'

'But,' Dave pauses. I know I've thrown him; he likes to take time to think things through. 'But doing IVF doesn't mean you'll get pregnant; it's only about 30 per cent successful any-way,[1] then there's the risk of miscarriage, plus we haven't talked about the ethics of it.'

'Just because you're training to be a vicar, you want to discuss ethics! I don't care what Jesus thinks about IVF, I want to get pregnant and IVF could help us.' I get up off the sofa and turn to walk away from Dave, down the corridor towards the kitchen. 'We're not eligible anyway, I'm too fat!' I shout.

Tonight is our first vicar's wife evening at Spice – our chance to meet and listen to the wisdom of a real-life vicar's wife. I feel sorry for Ian; he stopped coming a couple of weeks ago; it's not like our sessions are really geared towards him.

'Everyone loves to see a family in the vicarage.' Margaret is exactly what you'd imagine a vicar's wife to be – a small, smartly dressed lady with cloud-like hair and a gentle voice. She's sitting in the large green wing-back by the fireplace with a room full of women hanging on her every word; some are even making notes. So far, Margaret hasn't said anything I want to write down and, if that last comment is anything to go by, I won't be making any notes tonight.

'A lot of people talk about how stressful the job is. Do you have any advice on how to cope with this?' asks this cool, tall girl who apparently has no kids and no job, but I've still not managed to talk to her yet because she keeps disappearing before I get the chance.

'When your husband returns home, don't bother him with your day. Listen to him. Let him offload. Be calm and attentive to his needs.' I look over to Rach, who's sat next to me and looks as shocked as I am.

'What about unexpected visitors popping round the vicarage?' asks another lady, who's sitting by the door to the kitchen.

'Well, it can be quite busy at times,' Margaret says gently, as though she was so Christian she never got annoyed with anyone. 'You need to decide what to do when unexpected visitors arrive, but I find it's always helpful to have spare food in the house and, if in doubt, just bake a cake.' Judging by the culinary display covering the kitchen table this evening, I think all the women in this room will be amazing at this.

'Do you have any advice about how to choose a curacy?' asks a really smiley girl sat in the corner.

'Well, dear. There are all sorts of different curacies. Some are large churches, some in villages, some will be very rural. We were in a small village in the Cotswolds.' Margaret pauses, catches her breath, her eyes focus, her face falls, her tone changes to a quieter, more tentative voice. 'Some of you will have to go up north. Is there anyone here going up north?'

A third-year called Jane raises her hand slowly, looking around for support, but no one joins her.

'Oh. Just one of you. Where are you going, dear?'

'Bradford.'

'Bless you.' One of the Spice reps thanks Margaret, who looks angelic, the soft lighting resting on her gentle features. A card and flowers are presented and a generous applause is offered, accompanied by nods of agreement and admiring glances towards this woman who's spent the majority of her life managing children, a vicarage and a vicar.

Margaret interrupts the clapping to add one final piece of advice. 'One more thing before I go.'

The room is hushed. A couple of the women in the far corner reach back in their bags for their notepads, clicking their pens into action. Others stop reaching for their coats, poised, hoping for some kind of easy solution to making the most of life in a vicarage.

Margaret rests her delicate hands on her lap. She straightens her back; her gentle smile settles into a more serious expression as she composes herself to offer her final words to the young women gathered around her.

'A lot of vicar's wives have found that it can be really helpful if they have sex with their husband before they are scheduled to preach.'

The room is silent. Amy's admiration falls from her face. Nervous laughter rattles from huddles around the room and it suddenly feels very stuffy. I notice that none of the women with their hovering pens consider this piece of advice noteworthy. Bodies start to move, those on the floor standing and stretching; the high-pitched chatter slowly picks up pace as more people find their voices after the shock of Margaret's closing piece of advice.

'Yep, not sure about that last comment.' Julie comes over. 'I don't think I'm going to tell Rich about that last bit. I'll never hear the end of it.'

'Me neither. If Martin finds out, he'll be telling me he's got five sermons a week!' adds Rach.

As I drive home, back to Dave and our massive, silent house I try to focus on the funny parts of this evening. I mean, seriously, how is sex before a sermon going to help? It just makes guys really sleepy! I'm trying to stay positive, but I can't shake this darkness that keeps rising up within me. It's a weird mix of dread and sadness. I just can't move past those words 'everyone loves to see a family in the vicarage'. How could an offhand comment by a gentle Christian lady cause me so much pain? Rather than feeling affirmed and encouraged, I feel accused and judged and worthless. I thought I was entering into a world where I would feel at home, a safe place, but instead I've entered into a world clad with chinos, checked shirts, middle-class conversation, extravagantly fertile women and cake. I'm not saying this is necessarily a bad thing, but the Church of England definitely isn't going to win any diversity awards any time soon. I'm white and middle class and married; I've never been a minority. I fit the vicar's wife stereotype in so many ways, I even love baking! But there's this one role, this one identity I do not possess and I have never been more aware of it than I am right now.

12

Feasting and Fasting

'Well done! You've just completed your first Silver 7!' The lady at the weigh-in station grabs my card and sticks a silver number seven on it. 'Are you going to stay for the meeting?'

'Um, yeah, I thought I would.'

'That's great! Take a seat and we'll get started soon; we'll make sure you get a shout out for your first Silver 7 as well!'

'Thanks,' I reply, quickly grabbing my coat, shoes and Weight Watchers file and clumsily carrying them over to the rows of blue plastic chairs facing the giant before-and-after photos of our group leader. I look along the rows and head towards an empty one before realizing this is my one chance to meet people who aren't Christians, and choose to sit next to a lady on the third row. 'Hi there,' I cautiously greet her.

'Hi.'

'How did you do this week?' I ask, hiding my shiny number 7 in case she had a bad week.

'Alright actually, I lost two pounds.'

'Me too,' I respond. 'So, how long have you been coming here?'

'This is just my second week – how about you?'

'Um, I've been coming about a month.'

'I've just given birth so I'm trying to lose a bit of baby weight.' My new friend pauses. 'I actually gave birth but my baby died, so I thought I'd come along here to try to get healthy again and, um, you know, give me something to focus on.'

'Oh, I'm so sorry.' I pause; do I tell her I've lost babies too? No, it's not the same. I mean, she met her baby, she actually looked pregnant; I should just keep quiet. 'That must be really hard for you.'

'Yeah, it's been really difficult,' she replies before our leader jumps up to the front to start the meeting.

'Right, ladies! How are you all this evening? Well, so many of you have done well today, hands up if you've got a Silver 7.' I reluctantly put my hand in the air. 'Let's give them all a round of applause, shall we? Excellent! Well, first I need to tell you about an exciting new Weight Watchers product available now. It's powdered mashed potato!' I look at my new friend and raise my eyebrows before we're all given a demonstration of how to make mashed potato from a sachet. 'It's great! It's so easy and it's only two points.'

'One and half points!' yells out one of the helpers at the back.

'Oh yes, thanks!'

The lady at the back nods and goes back to counting out the Weight Watchers toffee crisp bars. I imagine she knows the points value of everything. She's one of those ladies who's been helping at Weight Watchers for years; she knows all about the diet plan but also doesn't seem to have lost any weight. After the mashed potato demonstration we talk about our 'danger zones', sharing the times we're at our weakest and find it hard to stay on track, setting a new goal for the week ahead before the meeting ends. I turn to say goodbye to the woman sat next to me. I want to talk to her more, to tell her I've lost babies too, but compared to her I don't think my babies count, so I wish her well and we go our separate ways.

'We were talking about "danger zones" at Weight Watchers tonight and I think we need to restrict the use of the waffle iron,' I tell Dave, my face still flushed from cycling home.

'What! But you gave me the waffle iron for my birthday. You can't give a present and then make rules up about when to use it – that's a crime against humanity!' I watch his reaction, half-joking, half-genuinely disappointed, but I don't care. I want him to know what it feels like to be deprived.

'It's OK, we can still have waffles,' I tell him. 'But I think we should only have them when we have people round. That way we won't eat as much.'

'That still doesn't sound fair.'

'It's just that it's hard to make waffle batter for two. I'm doing so well at Weight Watchers right now and it would really help if there was less temptation in the house,' I explain.

'Do I have any say in this?'

'No.'

Something's not right between me and Dave at the moment. I realized it the other night when we were having dinner with a couple from Dave's college and we totally overstayed our welcome. I watched our hosts yawning but I didn't want to go home. Not because I wanted to linger further in the moment but because I didn't want to go home with Dave and be in the house, just the two of us. I don't know if he felt the same way, but that night we arrived home around midnight and went straight to bed without saying a word, lying there on opposite sides of the bed, keeping a quiet, polite, yet painful distance.

In my mind Dave has everything; he has purpose and ambition, he's getting good marks at college and he's enjoying his course. I've managed to get a part-time job at Anglia Ruskin, the *other* university in Cambridge. But whilst I'm assessing whether students at a business studies college in Trinidad and Tobago are allowed extensions on their essays, Dave is pursuing his calling. We've always been equals, but somehow, in my mind, I've turned this into a competition, and right now I'm losing.

The struggle we're inhabiting doesn't mean we're not 'trying' or 'ttc' as all Fertility Friends[1] put it. We're living the most boring, sensible and organized life in order to get what we want. I'm ready for pregnancy, I've even researched the maternity leave policy at work, and I can't wait to finally claim it.

Every Thursday night I meet Dave in the car park so we can walk into college together for the chapel service, followed by dinner with everyone at the college. Before we arrived, I imagined this would be the highlight of the week, but in reality it's a gauntlet of pain. The chaos of 2.4 children and one on the way overshadows everything and leaves me wondering whether there's even any space left for my story. I know it's purely a statistic thing, but when you're one of the few who don't fit, it's horrible. Of course, I don't want the story I'm living in right now; no one would. It's certainly not a story that belongs here in the fertile, middle-class Christian world of trainee vicars, which is why I'm so focused on leaving it behind.

When Dave and I step into the chapel this evening, we turn left and climb up the narrow spiral staircase to the balcony; a tiny space crammed with old wooden benches that's home to those who turn up late and don't want to be seen. I quickly shove my bag and coat under the bench, slide in next to the other latecomers and watch the service played out from a distance. Once the service is finished, we wait for everyone to file out from the seats below us before clambering down the ancient staircase and heading towards the dining hall. The college dining hall reminds me of Hogwarts, but without the enchanted ceiling. The tall echoey space is filled with rows of long wooden tables and benches looked down on by carved stone busts of old white guys.

After finishing off a plate of shepherd's pie that tasted more like a plate of mashed potato with a sprinkling of mince, I'm now reluctantly eating a fruit salad that's really just tinned peaches and a few grapes. I watch Dave eating his crumble and custard whilst we're both subjected to the excited storytelling of a 20-something trainee vicar in a cravat sharing how God has *blessed* him and his wife since they moved to Cambridge. 'I mean, it's just amazing how God was really *in* our move to Cambridge: my wife was offered the first job she applied for two days after we arrived and she loves it, we've settled in so quickly to life here and made so many great friends and then we've just found out my wife's pregnant! God is so good! It just goes to show if you trust in him, he will bless you.'

Dave and I both nod reluctantly.

'Yeah,' Dave replies.

'I know!' Our excited friend pushes the long wooden bench back to stand up. 'Well, guys, it was great to talk. I hope you both have a good weekend. See you soon!'

'Bye,' we both reply, waiting to make sure he's left before sliding down the wooden bench with our trays, stacking our dirty crockery and cycling home.

'What do you think he meant by saying God was *in* his move?' I ask Dave, who's cycling beside me across Parker's Piece, one of the many green spaces in the centre of the city.

'Well, I suppose he and his wife have had a lot of answers to prayer since they moved here and so he's just acknowledging God's part in it,' he responds, weaving his bike from side to side on the path to slow himself down so that I can keep up with him.

'What does that mean for us, then?' We stop at the traffic lights, unlike most other cyclists in Cambridge.

'What do you mean?' Dave looks at me.

'Well, if God was in their move because of all these good things that happened to them since they've arrived, what about us? Does that mean God's not with us? Does it mean we're in the wrong place?' I feel my throat tightening, a lump rising up. I swallow, flick my right pedal up and begin cycling again to cross the road.

'I don't think it means God's not with us just because things are difficult at the moment,' Dave shouts across to me, indicating left to cycle over the railway bridge. My mind is filled with questions but I'm cycling up one of the few inclines in Cambridge so there's no chance of me actually being able to articulate what I'm thinking until we're coasting down the other side. What's shocked me about what happened this evening is that I know I used to be like our young cravat-wearing friend and I'm pretty certain I've said the same thing and sounded just as annoying as him in front of those who were struggling. I get my breath back and the breeze from our downhill cruise cools my face.

'I just . . . oh, it just makes me angry. Why is everything so hard for us? It doesn't need to be. Also, what about Cath and Joel? I mean, they've just arrived in Cambridge the same time as us for Joel to train, and now Cath has breast cancer and a two-month-old baby! What about them? We've all got the same God; we've all sacrificed stuff to be here. What's God playing at?' We pull up onto the pavement and stop outside our blue garage door, our faces flushed from the cycle home. Dave drags the garage door open, we place our bikes inside, he then drags it closed and we walk round to the house in silence.

It's like there's two sides to this faith I proclaim; one is rosy and joyful and filled with guys in cravats celebrating, and the other one is dark and filled with cancer and dead babies and questions. I used to be so articulate about God and now I have nothing to say, no wisdom to offer; I'm only versed in the side where everything works out. I'm lost. God and faith have become unintelligible. But maybe one day I'll be like that guy we sat with at dinner; one day it will be my turn and I'll arrive at the other side of whatever this season is and everything will make sense, even God.

It's Monday night, which means its Spice. This week we're having a prayer and worship night. I don't want to pray and I don't want to worship. I've not prayed for a while – it doesn't seem to make much difference – but I decide to go because I know my new lady friends will be there, and I know a third-year called Lucy is bringing cake and she is the most amazing baker – she can even make macarons. After tea and the lightest genoise sponge cake I've ever tasted, we sing a few songs and then we're left to pray. Some of the spouses had divided areas around the large living room, kitchen and landing with Bible passages, quotes and activities to prompt our prayers and our thoughts about God, and we're encouraged to wander through the rooms and spend time at each station.

I walk through the living room slowly, scanning the texts laid out around the room and head to the huge, carpeted landing because no one else is there. There's a prayer station in the corner, by the door to the kitchen, and I kneel down in front of some sheets of paper with psalms printed on them. I pick up one of the sheets and read the first line. The words are angry and I love it. I read it again slowly:

How long, LORD? Will you forget me for ever?
How long will you hide your face from me?
How long must I wrestle with my thoughts and day after day
have sorrow in my heart? . . .
Answer me quickly, LORD; my spirit fails.[2]

I write the verses down then I pick up the Bible lying next to
the printed sheets of verses and flick through its thin pages
until I reach the Psalms. I scan each psalm for words of desperation, anger or frustration at God and copy them into my journal. I sit there for the next forty minutes searching for angry
words and copying them down, filling the pages of my journal
with words describing how I feel.

'My God, my God, why have you forsaken me?'

'My soul is in deep anguish. How long, LORD, how long?'

'I am worn out from my groaning. All night long I flood my
bed with weeping and drench my couch with tears.'

'Save me O God, for the waters have come up to my neck.
I sink in the miry depths, where there is no foothold. I have
come into the deep waters; the floods engulf me. I am worn
out calling for help; my throat is parched. My eyes fail, looking
for my God.'

'Why, LORD, do you reject me and hide your face from
me?'[3]

I bet I look really holy, but I'm not. The rebel in me rejoices
in the thought that amongst all these incredibly faith-filled
women I had spent the whole evening getting angry at God.

This anger I feel towards God at the moment is fuelled by
every part of my life. Nothing is right, nothing is working as
it should be. I also really hate the word 'spouse'; I've only ever
seen the word 'spouse' on a form before and now it's my title. I
am now identified by who I am married to. Dave and I made

this decision to come to Cambridge together, we made this commitment to serve the church together, but apparently the next three years are about Dave.

Instead of feeling encouraged and inspired, I just feel incredibly de-skilled. We are still married, but we are no longer equal. Right now the only part of my life that's going well is Weight Watchers. I even get shiny little stickers as evidence. I never thought weight loss would be something I'd be good at as I don't like the discomfort of feeling hungry, but my target weight is in sight.

I got another Silver 7 sticker this evening and I'm now celebrating with a low-fat cookie baked by our Weight Watchers leader. The cookie is sucking all the moisture out of my mouth and Karen is waiting expectantly for feedback on her first adventure into healthy baking. Still unable to speak, I kind of nod encouragingly at her, unable to break the news that this is probably one of the worst things I've ever eaten; I'm not even sure if it should count as food.

'They're only half a point!' she tells us, passing the tray of leftovers to one of her helpers sat at the back who stops counting fruity chews to put four in her mouth at once.

I look to my right towards my new friend, who's just pulled a bottle of water out of her handbag and is now frantically opening the lid to get the liquid down her as quickly as possible to wash away the remains of the cookie.

Once the meeting has ended, we stay seated to catch up with each other; last week I found out my weight loss buddy is a Christian. I was kind of hoping she wasn't because I feel like I've got enough Christians in my life right now but, after reluctantly telling her we're in Cambridge for my husband to train to be a vicar, she told me she attends a local Baptist church.

'How are you doing?' I ask her.

'OK. I still haven't gone back to church,' she replies.

'Oh, don't worry about that,' I respond, perhaps slightly too quickly.

'It's just really hard to go back there. I don't know what to say to people because they all prayed for us and for the baby, but then he died.' She's looking at me expectantly; I think she's waiting for me to say something to help her, but I feel just as lost as her right now.

'It's OK to find it hard; there's no rush to go back to church. You need to look after yourself,' I respond.

'Yeah, I suppose so. It's just that I really believed God would answer our prayers and he didn't.'

I desperately wish I had some great answer to share that would make her feel better and explain every detail of what God's up to in this, but I have nothing. I think she's expecting me to know what to say because I'm going to be a vicar's wife, but I'm totally out of my depth here. 'It's not fair,' I respond. She nods in agreement.

'When I was pregnant, I used to talk about how great God was and how amazing it was that he'd given us a child, but now I don't know what to say. I don't know how to talk about God from this place; I don't know how to talk about faith from this place; I've never been here before.' She shifts in her chair. 'I'm sorry. I must sound crazy.'

'It's fine,' I reassure her. 'To be honest I feel the same way right now and I think God's OK with that. Maybe you should check out the Psalms. I've found them so helpful.'

'Oh, I don't know. I've not read the Bible for ages.'

'It's OK, the Psalms are different. Loads of them are angry. In fact, I think more than half of them are angry. Lots of them show people complaining to God, demanding to know why he's not showing up. I've never really heard anyone pray like that before, but if it's in the Bible then it must be OK.'

'Oh, well, maybe I will have a look at them, then,' she smiles, and I give her a hug before we go our separate ways.

The next day I'm not in work, which is great because I still have no idea how to do my job. To celebrate, I've decided to clean the house; it's not a glamorous celebration, but I know I'll feel better once it's done. Also, if I hoover really fast, maybe I'll burn some Weight Watchers points. I drag the vacuum cleaner out from the cupboard under the stairs and quickly slam the door shut before everything falls out of it, and then my phone rings.

'Can I come over?' asks Rach. She's calling from her 'office', which is basically her massive people carrier. With four kids she's constantly driving around Cambridge dropping kids off and picking them up, and when she's not doing that, she's driving to the supermarket to buy me crisps and/or chocolate.

'Yeah, come over; I'm meant to be cleaning the house so any distraction is always welcome.'

'Awesome! I've just got to stop off at the shops first; see you in about ten minutes.'

Rach arrives with a bar of white chocolate with dried raspberries in it. I make some coffee, and we carry both through to the lounge. 'So, how's work?' Rach asks.

'It's OK, but I still don't really have any idea what I'm doing.'

'That's normal, isn't it?'

'Yeah, I suppose, although it's been over a month since I started and I still can't work the photocopier.'

'It'll work out, mate. What about the other stuff? You know, with the doctor; have you got an appointment for the Recurrent Miscarriage Clinic yet?' Rach is the first person here I've told about the miscarriages. It took a while to build up to it, but I was so relieved once I'd told her; even though we've only known each other a few months, it already feels like we're established friends. As soon as I told her, I felt relieved and a little bit less alone. Rach keeps telling me it's OK to feel sad, and hopefully one day I'll believe her. Rach begins to open the chocolate and offers it to me. This is another one of my danger zones – talking about hospital referrals with chocolate present. I break off a couple of squares; this is medicinal.

'We've got a date, it's next month.'

'That's good, you've got a date. I mean, it took almost a year, but you've got a date, yay!' She does a mini Mexican wave. 'How are you feeling at the moment though, you know, about the baby stuff?'

'It's OK, some days are good and some days I still feel sad.' I break off another couple of squares of chocolate.

'I feel like a rubbish friend because I don't know what to say.'

'I'm just glad I've got someone to hang out with who doesn't talk about their kids all the time.'

'Do you think you could tell me what it feels like? You know, what it feels like for you now having lived through three miscarriages?'

'No one's ever asked me that before.' I pause, unsure how much to share. 'Well, it hurts, like it's actually physically painful. It hurts here,' I point to my heart. 'It hurts when I remember what we've lost; I mean, I don't think about it all the time, but it's always there just under the surface. It's so frustrating because it's been nearly two years since the last miscarriage, and I should have got over it by now, but it won't stop hurting.'

'But of course it's going to hurt, it's part of your story,' Rach reassures me.

'So, you don't think it's bad that it still hurts?' I ask.

'No, of course not.'

'I just wish I didn't always feel this sad; it's so lonely.' I break off two more squares of chocolate, dappled with specks of vanilla pod and dried raspberries. 'To be honest, the most painful bit for me at the moment is when I'm at the college; before we arrived, I was worried it might be difficult because of our story, but it's worse than I thought – there are just so many families!'

'Tell me about it!' Rach adds, 'I mean, I like kids, obviously, but I don't want to be surrounded by them all the time; so if I find it hard, then I can't imagine what you must feel like.'

'It's just, well, oh, I don't know, I just want to fit in and it feels like not having children is stopping me from doing that.' I watch for Rach's reaction, worried I've shared too much or that I sound like a 13-year-old, but she just nods, her expression filled with compassion. 'It just makes the sadness worse,' I manage to get the words out before the tears start to run down my face.

'Oh, mate, I'm so sorry.' Rach hugs me. 'I wish I could make it better; I wish it wasn't this way.'

'Me too,' I reply. 'Me too.'

We finish the chocolate and a second cup of tea before Rach has to pick up her daughter from nursery and I have no choice but to reluctantly embrace my wifely duties and actually clean the house and cook the dinner.

'What are you cooking?' Dave asks, walking into the kitchen with a sweaty sheen from cycling home, and lifts the wooden spoon sat resting in the big pan on the hob to taste the contents. 'Mmmmm,' he nods approvingly. 'Chilli?'

'Weight Watchers chilli,' I correct him.

'Oooo.'

'I've made a big batch because I need to drop some round to the Turners'; they've just had a baby.'

'Oh, is it your turn on the meal rota again?'

'Yep.' At the beginning of term the Spice meal rota sounded like a good idea, but I had totally underestimated how many babies could be born during one academic year at a vicar-training college. This is about the fifth meal this term and I'm wondering whether there should be some kind of reward system – when you've cooked a certain number of dinners you get a new saucepan or exemption from the next rota. 'One day I'm going to be on the Spice meal rota,' I tell Dave. 'One day people are going to make food for me,' I repeat under my breath as I tip the chilli into some Tupperware. Every meal I make is another reminder I've not yet earned the right to be part of this community.

'I've been thinking, hon,' Dave tells me whilst filling up another spoonful of chilli to 'taste test'. 'I think you should tell the lady you met at Weight Watchers about the miscarriages.'

'Who? The lady whose baby died?'

'Yeah, I know you say it's different, but I think it might help her. I reckon you'll find you're both going through the same things.'

'I don't know.' I take the spoon from Dave, worried there won't be any chilli left for us. 'I don't know if it would sound insensitive; I mean, she gave birth to her baby – a miscarriage is nothing compared to that.'

'You can't compare suffering like that.' I can hear the exasperation in his voice. 'Look, I just think you might feel less alone if you told her; you might find someone to talk to who understands.'

'What, so it's not just you having to listen to me?' I ask, then turn my back on him to start washing up.

'No, you know I don't mean that . . . I just . . . oh!' Frustration rises in his voice. 'I think you'll find you have more in common than you think.' He walks over to the sink, puts his hand on my waist and turns me towards him.

'I suppose she's the only person I've met here who's lost a child,' I tell him.

'Yeah, that's what I mean. I think you should talk to her.'

'OK, well, maybe I will. Maybe I'll try to chat to her after the next Weight Watchers meeting.'

'Sounds like a good idea.' He pulls me towards him and wraps his arms around me.

'Dave?'

'Yes.'

'Can you drop the meal off to the Turners' later? I don't think I can face it.'

'Of course.'

The next week, as I'm queueing up to be weighed, I look over to the rows of blue plastic chairs searching for my friend, but I can't see her. I take off my shoes and coat and cardigan and step on the scales. 'Well done! You've lost another four pounds. You're only two pounds away from your target weight.' One of the helpers looks up from the Weight Watchers magazine display with a thumbs-up for me.

'Thank you!' I reply, proudly handing over my weight loss book to be filled in.

'I'm going on holiday to Italy soon, so I'm looking forward to sunbathing by the pool and not feeling self-conscious,' I tell her.

'Oh yes! Maybe you should pop out and buy some new clothes for your new figure? A new dress or some strappy tops?'

'Maybe I will,' I tell her. 'I mean, I've earned it, haven't I?'

'Definitely,' she agrees with me. I grab all the clothes I stripped off before getting weighed and find a seat with an empty chair next to it for my friend. I can't see her in the weigh-in queue, but sometimes she's a bit late. I put my Weight Watchers' folder on the chair to save it for her.

This week the talk is about visualizing our goals. As I sit there, I think about the swimming pool in Italy and wearing a vest top without worrying about showing off the tops of my arms. I imagine Dave being distracted by my thin figure and forgetting about all the ways I frustrate him and how my sadness has dragged him down for so long. Then I think about an appointment with the recurrent miscarriage consultant and how impressed he'll be when he weighs me and sees how much I've lost. I briefly think about getting pregnant and how my new svelte body will look with a pregnant belly, but I stop myself before I get carried away.

The meeting ends with one of the helpers reading out a quote she found online by the Dalai Lama about being yourself, before everyone rushes off to have dinner. I stay seated and scan the room carefully, but I can't see my friend anywhere. My sadness surprises me; I wanted her to know she wasn't alone, but she's not here. I grab my coat from the back of the chair and stuff my Weight Watchers' folder into my handbag and head home, visualizing the new clothes I'm going to buy and, more importantly, the Italian food I'm going to eat on holiday.

Siena is a city I fell in love with during my six months of studying in Italy, and I can't wait to show it off to Dave. Thankfully, he falls in love with it too, and we spend days wandering the narrow, cobbled streets of the city, exploring churches and galleries, drinking wine under the shade of restaurant umbrellas in piazzas and sampling platters of cured meat, local cheeses, pizzas, fresh pasta coated in rich ragú sauces and cooling off in the shade of the ancient city walls with the most stunning pistachio ice cream.

We watch the preparation for the Palio with the medieval banners hanging from the buildings of each district; the parades and drums, and the ceremony of matching horses with their riders in the Piazza del Campo. We spend days by the pool, reading and sunbathing and we travel through Tuscany, past fields of sunflowers and ancient walled towns before ending our holiday in Florence, overwhelmed by art and sculptures and more beautiful Italian food. We return to Cambridge with sunburned legs (just me) and bottles of Chianti to a positive pregnancy test.

When I saw the two lines on that stick, I thanked God.

13

The End

~

I'm sat on a soft brown leather sofa, my puffy red eyes staring out the window of a third floor flat and across the tops of Chester city centre's historic black and white buildings. I was really looking forward to a few days back up north, visiting friends and escaping the flat Cambridge landscape, but our trip hasn't really gone to plan. Dave is sitting next to me holding my hand and talking to the three vicars sat across from us, each one of them leaning forward, concern furrowing their brows, compassion in their voices.

'We need to work out what's best for Lizzie,' Dave tells them, each one nodding thoughtfully in response. I think this is a great question but I don't have a clue what the answer is. Ralph, a vicar friend from our church in Chester, begins to talk and my broken body sinks further into the sofa, resting in the relief that my husband and the three other guys sat in Ralph's flat this Sunday afternoon are going to help me.

I look over to the fresh pot of coffee sat brewing on the old wooden chest Ralph uses as a classy coffee table, but the rich aroma does nothing to drag me from the haze of despair surrounding me. I don't even care about the posh Waitrose biscuits laid out on a plate next to the coffee, that's how bad things are. Dave squeezes my hand and turns to look at me every now and then to check I'm OK, his gaze longing to make everything better. I trust him, but right now I'm so lost I can't even imagine how I will ever recover from this.

Two months before ending up on Ralph's sofa we arrived home from our holiday in Italy, tanned and excited for the future. I can remember taking the pregnancy test, telling myself over and over that I'm probably not pregnant and it's all in my head until I saw the two lines appear and everything changed. Dave and I shared the news with friends and family, cautious not to broadcast it but wanting to invite those close to us into our current reality and potential future.

I remember laughing on the phone, chatting to Rach, who's now training to be a doula, telling her I could be her first client – she could practise on me for free! I recall Cath's reaction, exhausted from chemo but still celebrating this answer to the prayers she'd faithfully offered up for us. We had four weeks of reserved joy, reminding people we'd been here before and that nothing was certain, when inside it felt like we were living out the most wonderful story of loss turned to hope. Then I saw blood.

I locked myself in the toilet cubicle at work, bile rose up in my throat as I silently and repeatedly spat the word 'no' into the floor. I heard other women enter and leave the cubicles either side of me; toilets flushing, doors locked then unlocked, taps, hand-dryers and conversation, the soundtrack to my nightmare. Eventually I managed to stand. I splashed cold water on my face and patted it dry to soothe my blotchy red cheeks and walked across the large open-plan office towards my desk, my body cast in stone; numb and deadly cold. Impervious to the ringing phones, tapping keyboards and conversations, I turned off my computer and picked up my bag and coat from the back of my chair.

'I'm not well, I have to go home,' I told my desk buddy. She looked up from her computer just as I turned to leave. I wasn't going to wait for her reply; there was nothing she could say that could help me now.

I phone Dave. 'I'm bleeding.'

'Where are you?'

'Just outside work; can you come and get me?'

'I'll come now. Do you think . . . Do you think it's happening again?'

'I don't know.'

Fear consumed every part of me: fear of loss, fear of pain, fear I'd never recover from this. I rang the Early Pregnancy Unit from the car after Dave had picked me up. I told them what was happening, I told them how bad my previous miscarriages had been, I told them I was scared. They told me to wait.

For two days I stayed in bed, in and out of consciousness, the heat of the summer breezing through the open windows. Dave stayed with me, his long legs stretched out on the bed next to me, reading, playing on his phone and watching me sleep. I cried and yelled and anesthetized my soul with trashy novels and TV. Every few hours I'd ring the Early Pregnancy Unit, begging them to let me come in. I wanted to know what was happening. I wanted a scan. I wanted to know if I was carrying a corpse or a heartbeat. I wanted help. They told me to wait. I cried. They told me to come in.

We drove past the swanky new maternity unit with its contemporary exterior, covered in huge double-glazed windows with its fancy glass-fronted atrium and parked up outside the old 1960s tower block that houses the Early Pregnancy Unit.

We took our usual spot in the waiting room underneath one of the few windows that open. We sat down on one of the mismatched chairs underneath a curtain rail and next to a bedside table screwed into the wall from when this used to be a hospital ward. As we flicked through tattered magazines, we spotted a photo of our friend on the poster for the chaplaincy team that she hasn't been in for five years.

'Elizabeth Lowrie?'

I followed the sonographer to her room, carrying with me a tiny shred of hope. In an attempt to feign control, I anticipated the worst, but somewhere deep inside I was still holding onto this shy, excited fragment of expectation that maybe mine would be one of those stories where everything works out OK. Maybe mine would be the miracle story.

'There's no heartbeat.' The sonographer pointed at the hazy black and white image on the screen next to my head. 'If you look here,' she zoomed in, 'you'll see there was never a baby, just an empty sac.'

Does this news make my loss better or worse? Apparently, it's quite common, but the frequency of this diagnosis offered me no comfort as I was quickly moved to another ward where they gave me a drug to start contractions and some painkillers before leaving me in a ward filled with other women waiting to miscarry.

Eventually the baby or non-baby came; I felt it, my contractions increasing, running deeper. I wanted it to hurt more. I wanted the pain of my loss to manifest itself physically to prove it was far greater than an empty sac. I knew when it was over. It's the same every time. You can feel it leaving your body because of the emptiness it leaves behind.

The nurse silently cleared everything away before returning with her clipboard and a cup of tea. 'We can't let you go until you've drunk this.' I took cautious sips of this truly British tonic and watched her write 'missed miscarriage' on my notes.

Does that mean it's a miscarriage that never existed? She caught me reading her sheet: 'It's also called a silent miscarriage.'

'That's a terrible name for it.'

'This is your . . .' she flicked through my notes, 'fourth miscarriage. You should probably get some counselling. We used to have a counsellor in this clinic but they cut the funding so she's not here any more. There is a waiting list I could put you on, but to be honest it's so long you'd probably have to wait more than a year to get seen.' She stopped writing and closed the pale brown folder. 'I think that's everything for now.' She picked up the empty plastic cup next to me. 'You've finished your tea, so I'll call your husband in and you can go home.' She got up from the chair next to my bed ready to leave. 'Oh, and don't forget to take a pregnancy test in a week and phone us with the results.'

'Yep,' I nodded, familiar in the post-miscarriage ritual of *paying for another* pregnancy test just to make sure you're 100 per cent certain you've not wasted anyone's time.

We left the clinic in silence and stepped back into the familiar ritual of sharing our unwanted news with those we'd celebrated with and set up camp on the sofa with a plate of cheese on toast.

The long-awaited summer holiday from Dave's training slowly turned into a long summer of hell. The term-time residents of Cambridge left us in a city filled with tourists and English language students wandering the cobbled streets with matching rucksacks. Most of the friends we'd made over the past year had also left for the summer to placements and holidays and to no doubt have the time of their lives. Our long days were filled silently watching the 2012 Olympic coverage, nursing a mood so low, no amount of British Gold medals could lift it. I occasionally left the house to go to the doctor's to extend my sick leave, but other than that we remained on the sofa, watching races and matches and staying up until the late hours of the evening to see the highlights of what we'd already seen. Occasionally Dave would venture into the garden to do some weeding or mow the lawn, which was weird because he hates gardening. I could hear him through the open double-glazed doors from our lounge leading into the garden, swearing under his breath. When the lawnmower stopped working, I heard him kick it; I also think I heard him throw some of the tools back into the shed, metal clattering against metal, causing a small shelf to fall on top of them, and the shed door being slammed shut.

The day after the Olympic closing ceremony we packed up our car and headed to Chester for a wedding. Whilst we weren't really in the mood for celebrating, the opportunity to re-treat back into the comfort of old friendships was just what we needed, and after a ridiculously long journey on the M6, we arrived at Becky's doorstep, exhausted, grieving and longing to be looked after.

On the day of the wedding, Becky and I headed straight to our familiar back-row seat at Christ Church, the church Dave and I were married in four years before. As we quietly waited for the bride to arrive, I looked up once more at the statue of Jesus hanging on the cross, red blood running down his face from the crown of thorns placed on his head. It's not the best illustration of 'God won't give you more than you can handle', but then maybe that was the point.

We watched a young couple make promises before God and their family and friends. Dave preached, the congregation wor-shipped, the vicar prayed and I managed to get through most of the service without crying. I didn't know why I was crying. I'd given up trying to work it out; the grief within me was far bigger than a miscarriage. It was bigger than four miscarriages. It was bigger than me.

Once I'd sorted out my face in the back of the car with Becky's emergency breakdown kit, we drove to the reception. Becky and Dave guided me in and out of conversations, towards the Prosecco and the trays of finger food and eventually towards a quiet corner of the walled garden of the reception venue. I didn't speak; I couldn't. I just wanted to escape all these people and this noise. There were so many people I knew here, people I hadn't seen for a year, but I didn't want to talk to them. Normally I would have loved the opportunity to catch up with old friends, but that was when I had stories to share.

The speeches started after our dinner of hog roast and chocolate brownies. I listened to embarrassing stories and declarations of love and gratitude but I didn't feel part of the celebration. I was surrounded by people and laughter but I felt like I was an observer; I wasn't living in their world any more and I didn't believe I ever would again. The best man stood up and started talking and then it happened; I recognized what was happening straight away. The fear, the sickness rising and then suddenly I had no idea where I was. I could hear people around me laughing, relaxed back in their chairs, enjoying the best man's stories about the groom, but I had no idea what was being said. I felt the pain grow across my forehead making me feel sick and even more disorientated.

I turned to Dave. 'Why are they laughing?'

He looked at me, confused. 'Hon, it's funny, he's . . . Wait, are you OK?'

'I don't know where I am.'

Quickly and gently Dave helped me up from my chair and took me outside to one of the rattan sofas laid out for wedding guests to lounge on with glasses of Prosecco, and I started to cry. I wept and wept and wept; I had no control, no awareness of what was going on around me. I've no doubt people heard me wailing and saw me crumpled up on that sofa but I didn't care; there was nothing left of me to care. Becky and Dave sat next to me, their arms around me, whispering words of comfort and staring down anyone who tried to approach us. I kept waiting for the crying to stop like it normally does, but it didn't; it was endless. All my energy was channelled into crying; it flowed out of every part of me, but it still wasn't enough. I was so frustrated because no matter how hard I cried I knew my tears wouldn't even come close to expressing how much I hurt. My whole body rose and fell with such force it felt like my soul was trying to turn me inside out because it could no longer withstand the ferocity of my grief; it had destroyed me.

Eventually I was gently taken to the car, arms around me, holding me up as I stumbled along the gravel car park to the soundtrack of the first dance playing in the distance.

I woke up late the next morning alone in our bed and lay there listening to Becky pottering around downstairs. I waited for that feeling of relief to come after a night of crying – you know, when you wake up and realize life's not as bad as you thought – but it never came. So I plodded downstairs in my pyjamas to Becky and a big mug of tea. 'Where's Dave?' I ask her.

'Oh, he's gone to Ralph's.'

And so here we are now back at Ralph's, the day after the wedding and about six hours after Dave met with Ralph this morning, talking about what to do with me. After meeting with Dave this morning, Ralph contacted the new vicar of our church in Chester, Graham, and another vicar friend of theirs also happened to be in Chester this weekend.

'The most important thing is that you guys are looked after. Training comes second; you need to be in a place where you can get the support you need. If you want to leave Cambridge, we can make it work; you just need to decide where the best place is for you guys.' I look at Dave, recalling all the reasons why we chose Cambridge, his excitement about the course, the world-renowned theologians, the resources, his enthusiasm for the pioneer teaching sessions, reasons that went far deeper than the fact it looked like Hogwarts. How could I do this to him? Cambridge was where he wanted to train.

'I think it would be best for Lizzie if we left Cambridge,' Dave replies, looking back at me, his face flooded with concern. I feel his hand squeeze me; the sensation of it reminds me I'm in the room and not just observing from behind a thick wall of glass. I sink further into the sofa, relaxing into the relief that these guys want to help me.

'We can sort out a placement with Christ Church.' Graham adds, 'There wouldn't be a problem with that; in fact, it would be great to have you guys there.' Squeezing my hand again, Dave turns to look at me, his eyes desperate for me to find peace. I long to run away, to escape, to hide, to be looked after, to seek refuge back in this place that feels like home. The depth of concern and genuine desire to help us in our sorry situation offered by the men in this room is seductive, an offer to just hand our lives over to them and let them sort it out.

They keep talking details and I lean back into the sofa trying to ignore this one tiny, single, lonely thought whispering to my soul, telling me that if I run away, I might never deal with my pain. This decision to stay or run away is the last freedom left to me and the opportunity is irresistible. Sat there on the soft brown leather sofa in Ralph's apartment we prepare to leave Cambridge. Ralph pours more coffee, passes round the plate of biscuits and we begin to plan.

My story, however, was obviously not meant to be an easy one; it did not move neatly and smoothly back to familiarity and rest. A few days later our request for Dave to transfer colleges is declined. Instead we are offered a choice – either Dave pulls out of vicar training and we move back to Chester, or we return to Cambridge. United in the belief that Dave should continue his training to be a vicar, I am left with no choice but to return to Cambridge and look this fight in the eye.

14

The Beginning

'So how's your summer been?' I'm walking through Terminal 5 at Heathrow, chatting to a trainee vicar from Dave's college on our way to security. I look ahead to Dave and the rest of our small group of travellers from the college, chatting away.

'Not great,' I reply, conflicted by how much truth I should share with her, especially as we're about to spend the next ten days together. I don't want her to think I'm too messed up.

'I'm sorry,' she replies with a kind smile.

'It's OK.' It's not really, but I'm British so this is what you're supposed to say. 'I wasn't very well,' I reply, briefly distracted by the pastry display in the window of a café we're walking past. 'I started to have these migraines when I lose my memory. I've had them before, but the hospital's worried it might be epilepsy, so I've got to go for tests when we get back from Denver.' We both grab a plastic tray and place it on the conveyor belt in front of us and pile our tiny transparent bags of liquids, bags, phones, passports, coats and watches into our trays before they reach the scanner. 'Well, hopefully this trip will be a really good break for you and a chance to relax.'

'Yeah, hopefully,' I respond, before stepping through the scanner, collecting my luggage on the other side and heading towards the rest of the group.

There's six of us from the college in total: a tutor called Dan and three trainee vicars, Dave and me. I can't quite believe I'm here, to be honest; I doubted I'd even be able to survive to the end of August, let alone be able to get on a plane and visit a church in Denver. I'm not exactly on a spiritual high right now. I don't know if I even like God any more. But thankfully we're not visiting a shiny mega-church filled with fake smiles; instead we're hanging out with a church founded by a ska-punk band and a Greek-American pastor, called Scum of the Earth. Dave's really excited because he used to be a massive fan of the band who co-founded the church. For the past couple of weeks he's been reminiscing about his youth, digging out old CDs and telling me stories of when he used to go skateboarding in Liverpool back in the nineties. I spent the nineties listening to Take That and dreaming of marrying Mark Owen, until I realized he was too short for me, but a church that describes themselves as being for the left-out and the right-brained is pretty much the only church I could see myself in right now.

After a ten-hour flight, free alcohol and a couple of good films, we're greeted by Mike, the pastor of Scum and his wife, Mary. Dressed in baggy cargo shorts, white trainers and a Hawaiian shirt, Mike looks nothing like you'd imagine the leader of a church for punks, goths and homeless guys would look like. Oblivious to our British reservedness, Mike and Mary welcome us like old friends.

'Oh, you guys are just adorable!' Mary cries out as she grabs my cheeks then hugs me like I was one of her own kids. 'Lizzie? You wanna ride with me?'

'Mary? Can you remember how to get there?'

'Oh, Michael, don't you worry.'

'But on the way here you turned the wrong way onto the freeway and drove away from the airport.'

'Michael, I'll be fine! We'll get there, won't we, Lizzie?' I nod, unsure if riding with Mary is a good idea, but even if we don't ever find the house, I know the journey will be entertaining. 'Oooo! I know! Let's have a girls' car and a boys' car! Wouldn't that be fun?' Mary starts jumping up and down and clapping as we load our cases into the car.

Mary was right; she knew where she was going. She was even able to drive us to the house without getting lost whilst talking nonstop for the entire journey. We're all staying in the same house; some friends of Mike and Mary are away for a couple of weeks and have offered their home for us to use and it feels like we've just stepped into a glossy magazine. The house has a hot tub, fire pit, pool room, air-con and many bathrooms, and each room displays its own colour scheme complete with matching accessories; we're going to be spending the next ten days in luxury. Mary shows us where she's stored the groceries she bought for us, including ten tubs of Ben and Jerry's. 'I couldn't decide which flavour to get you guys so I bought 'em all!' she tells us excitedly.

The following morning Mike arrives carrying a tray of doughnuts in one hand and in the other, a tray of takeaway coffees from a local roaster and coffee shop his daughter works at – thank you, America! Drawn by the smell of sugar and caffeine we gather round the table.

'OK,' says Mike. 'I've got a few things planned for our time here.' He pauses to watch us politely wait for someone else to pick the first doughnut. 'You British take so long to make a decision!' He leans over, picks up a doughnut. One by one we follow Mike's lead, leaving a moment of reverent silence as we all bite into the soft clouds of sugary dough.

'This tastes incredible!' says Ruth, pointing at her double chocolate doughnut. Ruth used to be a chef before she started

training to be a vicar, so she should know. Next to Ruth is
Dan, quietly enjoying his New York cheesecake doughnut.
Dan's the reason we're all here; he'd met Mike a few years ago
whilst on sabbatical and ever since then he's taken a group of
students to visit the church each year. To the right of Dan is
Kate, who was the first one up this morning, fighting jet lag
to prepare breakfast for all of us, which included learning how
to use the coffee maker, for which I will be eternally grateful.
Naomi is the other trainee vicar in our group; she is beautiful
and is currently managing to eat her glazed doughnut without
covering herself in sugar. Naomi is tall and slim and clothes
just hang off her perfectly. She wore a white linen suit to travel
in yesterday and when she stepped off the plane after a ten-
hour flight she still looked immaculate; there was not a single
crease in her suit.

'Right!' Mike wakes us out of the euphoria of fresh doughnuts and coffee 'I've set up a few meetings with different pastors in Denver; it's the most popular place in the US for people
to come and start up a new church. Incredibly God seems to
have called all these people to this place with great scenery,
amazing summers and even better winter sports, so there are
plenty of people to learn from. But first I think we should have
some fun. I thought we could go check out this food festival
and then go to a ball game. We'll head to the Rockies later on
in the week.

'As long as there's time to hang out in the hot tub with beer,'
adds Dan.

'Yeah, sure, there'll be time.'

I already love Mike; it's almost like he knew my aims for
this trip are comfort eating and relaxing. He's someone who
makes you feel better just by being around him. He's fun and
easy to talk to, but when it comes to Jesus, he's very serious, not

in a judgemental preacher-y way, it's simply because he's way more interested in the state of your soul than anything else. When we're talking, I wonder if he already knows; I wonder whether God's given him some kind of supernatural insight to see what's happened. Or maybe he's heard a voice: 'You see that girl there, the tall one with curly hair? She's broken and I want you to help put her back together.' I kind of wish God would do that, then Mike could tell me what to do. He could tell me everything is going to be OK. I'd like that.

We spend the afternoon on a culinary tour of America; I try funnel cake – deep-fried batter in sugar, a giant ice-cold pickle on a stick that looks as dodgy as you might imagine, and a lot of slow-cooked meat. At the ball game, we watch home runs whilst eating foot-long hot dogs and eventually head back to the house for a cold beer in the hot tub.

'So, how's your summer been?' asks Dan. The rest of the group have flaked out one by one, heading upstairs to catch up on sleep, leaving Dan, Dave and I to finish off beers as we watch the sun set. I take another swig from my beer and glance at Dave to indicate it's his turn to take this one; besides, I don't know how honest we should be. When you hold so many secrets, you're constantly trying to work out how much of the truth you should filter out, partly to protect yourself and partly to protect the other person who has no idea what they're getting themselves into.

'Well, we tried to leave college this summer,' Dave replies.

'Oh . . .' I knew we'd made him feel awkward. 'Can I ask why?'

'Well,' Dave looks over to me and I nod. 'Lizzie had a fourth miscarriage and it's just been really hard; there are a lot of great people in Cambridge but it's not the same as having those long-term friendships like the ones we have in Chester, so we thought it would be better to move back there, and I could do my training by distance learning.' Dave pauses and takes a sip of beer. 'We couldn't leave, though. We had to stay in Cambridge and I had to continue my studies at the college, or I'd have to stop training.'

'Oh, I'm so sorry. But I'm also glad you're staying.' I was waiting for him to challenge our cowardly response, or offer one of those stock Christian phrases about God having a purpose or us needing more faith. 'You know, you can always talk to Helen and I if that helps?'

'Actually, that would be great,' Dave looks over to me again, briefly, with a faint smile. 'It might be good to chat to you both about marriage stuff too, if it's OK? It's not been easy.'

'Yeah, of course we can do that. We'll sort out a date before we leave and you can come round for dinner.' Dan takes another swig of his beer. 'You know, I believe you guys are going to do some amazing things in the future; it might not feel like it at the moment, but God is going to use you both to make a real difference.'

'Thanks,' Dave replies. I nod in agreement, unable to speak, barely able to believe the words spoken over us but longing them to be true.

'I started Scum because I knew if I didn't, no one else would,' Mike tells us the next morning as we sit around the dining table with mugs full of fresh coffee and a tray of cinnamon buns.

'You also started it because you got fired from your old job!' adds the pastor of a local Presbyterian church who has joined us for the morning.

'Well, yeah, there was that as well,' Mike laughs as he takes a cinnamon bun from the middle of the table. 'I'd been meeting up with the lead singer of this ska-punk band to talk about Jesus and read the Bible together, and I suppose I kind of became their pastor . . . As the band's popularity grew and they also began inviting fans at their gigs to a Bible study, the group kept growing, and after a while the fans started turning up to the church where I was the young adults and singles' pastor at the time, but it wasn't working. I mean, it looked like what church should be like – this unholy mix of seniors dressed in their Sunday best and a couple of rows of young adults with body piercings, tattoos and crazy hair. But they were in such a different place to the rest of the congregation both culturally and spiritually. It was really hard for them to get up and attend church early on a Sunday morning after being out until the wee hours.

'After a few months I believed God was prompting me to start a church for these guys; a lot of them lived really chaotic lives and they needed a pastor, they needed a church where they didn't feel like the odd ones out. The decision to start Scum wasn't an easy one; it was around this time that I was asked to leave my post at the church I'd been working at. I knew if I was going to start this church I needed a salary, and I knew the guys who come to Scum would never be able to support me financially; they could barely support themselves – plus we had four young kids, and I just didn't know if I could put Mary and the kids through this. I told God this, I told him if he wanted me to start a church for those who felt like they didn't fit, then he had to provide the finances for it. At the time I was offered a very well-paid job at a big church in Denver, but I knew if I didn't start Scum, no one else would. There were plenty of other pastors out there who could do the job I'd been offered at this big church, but no one was going to start a church for the left-out; these guys needed Jesus just as much as a church full of respectable Christians. I chatted and prayed with some friends about it and a few weeks later the money for half a salary came through. God had answered my prayers, so I turned down the other job and started Scum.'

'Where does the name Scum of the Earth come from?'

'It's from Corinthians, though the guy who came up with it wasn't even sure where it was in the Bible.' Mike pulls out a business card from his wallet. 'It's a slightly different translation to the one we're used to, but the word "scum" is closer to the original Greek.' He lays the card out in front of him.

> To this very hour we go hungry and thirsty, we are in rags, we are brutally treated, we are homeless. We work hard with our own hands. When we are cursed, we bless; when we are persecuted, we endure it; when we are slandered, we answer kindly. Up to this moment we have become the scum of the earth, the refuse of the world.' (1 Cor. 4:11–13 NIV 1984)

'I didn't like the name at first. I thought it was a really bad idea; I had to raise money from good, respectable people and I'd be asking them to write a cheque out to "Scum", but I'm glad we went with it now. A lot of those who come to Scum identify with the name because they've been treated that way. But the name "scum" also implies that being people of faith doesn't mean we're better than anyone else. We're not about judgement, we're just aware of our need for God. The message most of these guys need to hear is that God never sees us as scum.' Mike pauses. I swear he's looking at me.

It's Sunday and Mary's driving us to church. 'I've never really been an upfront person – I let Mike do that. I'm just here to make sure these guys all know they're loved. I've just gotta keep lovin' them, no matter what happens or how they mess up, I just keep lovin' them till they believe it,' Mary tells me.

I love Mary, I think she's awesome, but I wish she'd stop looking at me when she's driving. I can hear Dave describing the 'BLAT' in the back of the car. Ever since he had it for lunch the other day he won't stop going on about it. The 'BLAT' is a burger bun filled with bacon, lettuce, avocado and tomato and I'm pretty sure Dave wants to marry it. I focus on the road in front of me. The nausea from the migraine/fit I had yesterday is still lingering at the back of my throat and my head feels bruised by whatever keeps attacking my mind. Staring at the road ahead seems to help, plus it means at least one of us is looking where we're going.

'Hey, man, good to see you!' We're greeted at the door by a guy with neon dyed hair and a lot of piercings all over his face. I am embarrassed by how middle class I feel right now. The other day Mike told us how the church council had decided the smokers should be the welcome team as they're already standing around outside before the service starts, which is genius. They've also learned from experience to keep drunken hecklers away from the preaching inside, so some of the welcomers stay outside with them until they sober up.

Even though Scum's church building was built years before the church was started, it looks like it has been made specifically for them. The ornate entrance decorated in broken pieces of ceramic and coloured glass and the paint-splattered floor have been left as a tribute to its previous occupant who was a mosaic artist. The interior is an eclectic mix of murals, fairy lights and works of art hanging from the walls and the ceilings. Similar to how the stained-glass windows of ancient European churches and cathedrals were used as an artistic representation of God's story, Scum's entire building is a vibrant, creative, contemporary expression of what faith looks like for the left-out and the right-brained (and it even extends to the finest toilets in Christendom). One of the most powerful examples of this is the large crucifix hanging on the wall in the main worship space; made up of significant items donated by members of the church, including the last thing someone stole before they met Jesus and a troll doll salvaged from a car wreck that someone miraculously survived.

'This is the first church I've been to where no one's told me I have to cut my hair and take out my piercings if I want to keep coming,' says the girl sitting next to me. 'It's basically one of the few places where I actually feel like I belong.' I don't know many people who are able to say that about church.'

'Really?'

'Yeah, this place is pretty special.'

'It sure is.' We both smile in agreement and then turn to look at the front as the service begins. I didn't know what to expect, maybe a mosh pit at the front of church during the worship, but that's not what happened. We sang and prayed, just like you would in any other church. The service was creative; there was poetry and the musicians made the worship songs their own, but it wasn't church trying to be cool, it was just church. It was a genuine, honest and humble expression of church where Jesus was the focus and homeless guys wandered in and out at the back.

After about half an hour of singing, we head down to the basement for food. The guys who started Scum wanted the meal time to be sacred and so it became part of the service; they wanted the time of sharing lives over food to be more significant than small talk over a cup of coffee and a biscuit at the end of church. We all grab paper plates and queue up for helpings of pulled pork, burger buns and salad. 'You see that guy serving up the meat?' Dave leans forward to whisper into my ear.

'The one with the bum bag?'

'Yeah. He's a world-renowned theologian.'

'Really?'

'Yeah, I've used some of his books in my essays. Mike told me he and his wife have been serving at Scum for years. They wanted to be part of a church where they knew they could make a difference.'

'That's awesome,' I reply, watching this respected scholar as he served up pulled pork to a long line of hungry misfits. The first time I came to Scum was fight night,' says the guy sitting next to me; he's got those earrings that make your ear lobes bigger. I'm trying not to stare but I can't stop looking at them.

'Oh man, fight night was awesome!' says his friend, who starts laughing.

'What happened?' asks Dave.

'Well, we were all eating down here and then these two guys who obviously knew each other from somewhere else started shouting and then punching each other. The fight was broken up pretty quickly, but right then I knew this was the church for me. It's a church that knows it hasn't got it all together, it's not polished, it's just a bunch of people who are hurting and trying to love God and each other.'

'Man, I heard about fight night before I even started comin' to Scum!' says another guy at the table, who introduced himself as a goth poet – I've never met a goth poet before.

'How did you end up at Scum?' asks Dave as he pours more Scum of the Earth hot sauce onto his plate.

'Well, I'd grown up going to church, my parents were super-religious, but then my dad left us when I was a teenager and that was it; I stopped going. I just thought all Christians were hypocrites. A friend started coming here and kept inviting me so I eventually gave in. I'd planned to show my face then leave part way through the service, but I didn't, I stayed. Scum has become like family to me; my own family is super messed-up, but now I've found somewhere that feels like home.'

We carry on talking and eating until we're shepherded back upstairs for the rest of the service. We listen to a sermon, share communion, sing a few more songs and pray together.

'Right!' Mike comes over to us at the end of the service. 'You guys ready to go to the best Greek restaurant in Denver?' We all nod our heads. I've only been here five days, but I'm pretty sure I've stretched my stomach because I'm already feeling a bit hungry again. As we head out the church, Mike invites everyone we walk past to join us, including a homeless guy who rides with us to the restaurant.

When we arrive at Greek Town, there's a huge, long table running through the middle of the restaurant reserved for Scum that quickly fills up with the unlikeliest bunch of people I've ever seen in one place. Dave and I sit down the end of the table opposite this guy with a massive long beard who had spent most of his life in prison, but now he wants to be a pastor and start a church like Scum somewhere else. He keeps talking about how God's forgiveness has changed his life; he knows he doesn't deserve it, but as soon as he accepted it, he became a new man – that's grace.

His isn't the only story of transformation we hear that night; the evening is filled with the tales of misfits and how the grace of God is changing their lives; we also have conversations with people who simply came because they'd been invited.

As I eat my bodyweight in feta cheese, I can't think of anywhere else I'd rather be right now. I know the struggle I carry with me is nothing near what some of these guys have gone through, but there's no comparison amongst this group who define themselves as being 'on the outposts of society'. There's something about sitting around a table and eating together that draws you closer; obviously it helps when the food is good, but there's more to it than that. I think it depends on how you approach it: whether you come battle-ready to defend, or longing for connection.

As I share food and stories with a group of people my mum once told me to never hang out with, I feel happy, or content, or something like that; it feels good, whatever it is, and I've not felt like this for a long while.

On our last day in Denver we're eating Mary's apple crisp with half and half, which is basically apple crumble with cream, *for breakfast.* I love this, but I don't think it would be good for me to live here. The coffee is brewed and we're waiting for our final guest, a guy called Ryan. Before he arrives, Mike briefs us.

'Now, Ryan's a really humble guy, so he probably won't really talk about how he pastors some very famous people and he's also provided counsel to some important politicians, but the only reason he does that and stays humble is because God beat the snot out of him.'

A few extra people from Scum have come to join us so we gather in the large sitting room, sinking into the oversized sofas ready to listen to Ryan's story about his move to Denver. He didn't want to move here, but through a number of miraculous events, God made it clear that he was meant to move to a town outside Denver to plant a church. Although Ryan's church is much bigger and sounds more mainstream that Scum, they are also changing their community. We hear amazing stories of crime rates dropping, of people becoming less religious and more like Jesus as they actually get to know people in their neighbourhood. Then we get to the famous and important people, the bit I'm a little ashamed to admit I've been most looking forward to. Of course, he doesn't name anyone, but he does give us a glimpse into the human condition of the soul. 'These famous, influential and talented people, they're as messed up, depressed, broken and insecure as the rest of us.'

I watch Dave, sat on the sofa opposite me, soaking up and loving these stories. He's needed this time away. He needed to be reminded of what church can be like.

'I think I've talked enough now,' Ryan concludes. 'Shall we pray?' The rest of the room nods in agreement. I sink deeper into my super-soft armchair, the red fabric arms rising up, surrounding me with comfort. I close my eyes along with the others around me who all have their hands stretched out, palms up, ready to receive.

The smell of fresh coffee still lingers in the air. 'Just ask God to speak to you.' Ryan's words hover over the expectant silence. I open my eyes and glance around the room; everyone looks like they're relaxing in the presence of an old friend. I close my eyes again. At first the silence feels oppressive as I struggle to rescue my thoughts from dark places. I feel like a fraud. I haven't prayed since it happened. Since I last saw blood. I cried out to God then; I begged him to protect the life inside me; I asked for a miracle, for him to intervene. But all I got was silence. I begin to focus on my breathing, clearing out memories of the past couple of months, allowing the silence of the room to fill my mind. I sit there for a while, breathing in the peace and intimacy of this moment.

Then it happens.

A thought? A voice? I don't know, but I definitely hear something in my soul and it doesn't come from me. The words that are now filling my mind are clear and precise, the same sentence repeated over and over, rising from the deep, springing up from the darkness and shaking my soul awake with a shock. Is this God? My throat is tight, my jaw clenches in defiance. The room is silent but deep in my soul I'm fighting back against the words I heard: 'No! I can't do that! It's too hard, I'm not ready!' I sit still, swallowing back tears, continuing to battle against those words and the terrifying challenge they carry with them.

Ryan begins to talk slowly, gently, bringing us back into the room. I open my eyes and everyone is crying, tears streaking their faces. But the atmosphere in the room isn't one of despair or sadness, it's peaceful. These aren't tears of lament; they come from a more sacred place, one of acceptance and pure, perfect, healing love. 'Did anyone hear anything? Did God say anything to you?' Ryan asks. Slowly people begin to share specific words of hope for people in the room, people they never met until today, words that speak to the parts of their lives they keep secret. I believe God is here; this is the only explanation I can give for what I'm witnessing. Words and tears pour from people's hearts as their souls hear exactly what they need to hear. I wait, hoping someone has something for me, something nice and encouraging, but they don't. I've already had my message from God, but I don't want it. I can't share it either because I know if I tell someone what I heard, I will have to act on it, and I'm not ready yet.

Ryan ends with a prayer and we stand, working our way round the room, hugging each other. Across the room I see Dave, his tears matching mine. He walks towards me and I let him hold me, words superfluous to this moment, our embrace becoming increasingly tight the more we realize how deeply we need each other. My damp face rests on his chest, the sacred words I heard are turning over and over again in my mind, my discomfort with them lessening, but I'm still not ready to say them out loud.

Later on that evening, after another debrief in the hot tub, I go back to our room and pull my journal out from my suitcase. Turning to an empty page I write the words I heard earlier, ink on paper making the first step.

Your desire to have children cannot be your focus, you have to put it to one side. Put it to one side and start living again.

I turn the page of my journal again and write two words in big swirling letters: 'The Beginning'. It's time to change; it's time to push this crazy life-consuming obsession to be a mother to one side and start living.

15

Owning It

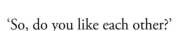

'So, do you like each other?'

'Yes.' We look at each other to check we agree; if you'd seen us in the car on the way over here, you wouldn't have believed us.

'Well, that's a great start!' Helen announces. We're sat on the leather sofa opposite Dan and Helen, waiting for them to fix us.

'OK, so we're going to start with communication; here's a sheet for you guys to fill out. You need to put a number from one to five, indicating how much these statements resonate with you. Five is the highest – just go with what your gut says.' She passes two sheets of paper to us. I search around in the depths of my bag for a couple of pens for what feels like an eternity until Helen gets up off the sofa and grabs two pens from the kitchen for us.

'Thanks,' I reply. The numbered statements are all about how we receive love. I scan down the list to find the ones that describe me best. I keep glancing over to Dave, but I can't see what he's writing; he's writing a lot, probably about how mis-understood he feels.

'Right, time's up!' Helen says five minutes later. 'So, Lizzie, tell me which statements you scored highest.' I tell her the numbers that most reflected me. 'OK, so for you what matters most is attention, words of affirmation and quality time. Does that sound right?'

'Yeah, that sounds like me.' I look over at Dave, hoping he realizes how he's not offering any of those to me right now.

'Great, so Dave, what about you?'

'I've just got two; number five and number seven.'

'Well, seven's not a surprise!' Dan pipes up.

'What's seven?' I ask.

'Affection,' replies Dan. Helen looks at me, rolling her eyes.

'Yeah, pretty much every guy has affection at the top of their list, including Dave.' She adds, 'It's mostly to do with sex.'

'What's number five?' I ask, trying to move the conversation on to something less awkward.

'Five is respect,' Helen responds. I look over to Dave, who's nodding. Respect has never crossed my mind.

'What does respect even look like?' I ask, half-joking, half-genuinely serious. Dave looks over to me, visibly hurt; maybe it's not just me who doesn't feel loved right now.

We drive home from Dan and Helen's in silence. I want Dave to say something, anything. I want him to tell me he loves me, I want him to be interested in how I'm feeling and tell me everything is going to be OK, but he doesn't speak. As we brush our teeth and get ready for bed, the anger inside me keeps rising. I don't want to speak first; why should I? I'm always the one who speaks first. If he loved me, then surely he would talk to me. If he loved me, he would want to help me, he would want to understand how much I'm hurting, how much I hate this life I'm living. I slide under the covers and my heart is raging. What is wrong with him? He turns the light off and I lie there stiff, wide awake and fuming.

'So, do you want to talk about tonight?' I ask, trying to stop my voice from cracking. I don't want him to know how much he's hurting me. He should know what to do, he should know how to support me, I shouldn't have to make him talk to me.

'I'm tired.'

'Oh, I'm sorry I didn't realize you were too tired to work on our relationship.'

'No, it's not . . .' He sighs, then rolls over on his side to look at me. 'What do you want to talk about?'

'I don't want to force you.'

'You're not forcing me, it's just . . . Oh I don't know, it's just that I don't know what to say.'

'Were you there tonight? Were you in the room when I talked about how I needed attention to feel loved? Well, silence isn't exactly the way to do that.' I turn over onto my left side to face the wall, with my back to Dave.

'Tell me what to say! Tell me what you want to hear!'

'It doesn't work that way.'

'Well, maybe I'm not the right person to help you.' I feel Dave turning over onto his other side and now we're both lying there with our backs to each other.

'Maybe you're not.'

The next morning, we start the day as if nothing had happened; I'm too tired to talk to someone who doesn't want to talk to me; besides I'm going to see a counsellor in the afternoon, so maybe she can tell me what to do with Dave. It was his tutor who suggested counselling. Ever since we tried to leave, she's been trying to find ways to support us more. I think she's really worried about us; but then I imagine there aren't many people who try to leave because their wife can't handle it. Louise, the counsellor, used to work at a hospital before the budget cuts, but now she's set up on her own so she can keep helping people. I feel like a bit of a fraud; surely her services are more for people who have lost actual babies, not empty sacs and barely formed foetuses.

'Lizzie?' Louise pops her head around the door.

I follow her into a sunlit room filled with scented candles, floral cushions and a delicately placed box of tissues. She looks at me gently; she's one of those people who you know is comfortable in her own skin – her beautiful, soft, glowing skin. 'So, Lizzie, can you tell me a bit about your story, about what brought you here to this moment?'

I open my mouth and everything just tumbles out. I'm not talking, I'm weeping and speaking at the same time – it's quite an achievement. The softness of her voice and her compassionate response invites me to keep talking. I want to be fixed and I believe she can fix me.

'Firstly,' she adds, 'it's no wonder you're struggling; you've been through so much loss and trauma, and you need to stop apologizing to me every time you explain how you're feeling. You have nothing to apologize for. You are allowed to feel this way. It's completely normal after what you've gone through.'

'Thank you,' I mumble as she passes me another tissue.

'Secondly, the experience of miscarriage and infertility can feel very lonely and I think the root of a lot of what you're feeling is isolation.' Her words wash over me like a balm as she offers me the words to describe what's happening; just naming what I'm feeling is healing.

'There's also something else I sense we need to talk about though. It seems to me that you've lost who you are in the midst of all this; does that make sense?'

'Yes,' I think back to what God said to me in Denver. 'Yes, it does.'

'Do you know what you want to do with your life?'

'No.' I look at the floor. 'I want to be a mum.'

'Wanting to be a mum isn't a bad thing, Lizzie, but you're putting all your energy and dreams into this one role. Having a child won't live up to all this expectation; imagine the pressure that child would feel!'

'I hadn't really thought about it that way.' I pause. 'I guess how I am wouldn't be a great place to bring a child into right now?'

'Yes, I think you could be right.' Louise takes a sip of water from one of the glasses placed on the coffee table between us. She must drink a lot of water to have skin that shiny. After allowing this revelation to hang in the air for a little while, she continues: 'This may sound strange, but I keep imagining you stepping into a house that's been empty for a really long time and you're throwing open the shutters. The house isn't ready for people to live in it yet, but there's definitely life there.'

I grab another tissue. I look down at my hands, cradling a collecting of soggy, scrunched-up tissues. I can feel the soft tissue against my skin, I can feel the tears slowly sliding down my face, my eyes stinging from the salt water that surrounds them. I am flesh and blood and bones on the outside, but inside I feel very empty, just like the house Louise talked about. I can picture it in my mind.

'It doesn't sound strange at all.' I think about Louise's encouragement that there's still life in the house and I imagine opening the shutters, then the windows; allowing the sunlight and fresh air from outside to pour into the empty space and bring it back to life.

'Lizzie, I think you need to find out who you are again, and I think coming to see me is the first step towards this. Does that sound like something you're open to exploring?'

'Yes,' I pause and look down at the bobbly biscuit-coloured carpet. 'It's just that I don't know how I let this happen. I used to have so much ambition and so many ideas.' I keep staring at the carpet, ashamed by how lost I feel in front of this capable and put-together woman. 'I don't want to be like this any more. I don't want to live like this. This isn't me!' I watch the tears fall onto the carpet, creating dark spots as the liquid soaks into the fabric.

'This is going to take time, and for now you need to be OK with just being; you don't need all the answers yet. Also, this is something you need to do for yourself; in future sessions we'll talk more about your relationship with Dave – it might even be helpful for him to join us for a couple of sessions. But right now, this is about you and rediscovering who you are again and you're the only one who can do this. I can help you, but you have to do the work yourself. Do you understand?'

'Yes,' I nod my head slowly. I'm so disappointed in myself, but I'm also so relieved.

'Do you have a notebook with you?'

'Yes.' I pull out my journal.

'It might be helpful to make a few notes of some of the stuff we're talking about.' I grab my pen; we keep talking, and I start writing:

It's OK for Dave to have his own thing. I need to allow him to own it and for it to fill his life.
It's not either/or. I need to rediscover who I am alongside working out how to grieve for a family. I don't need to be sorted before I move on to the next thing.
I don't need all the answers yet. I can just be content with knowing I want more and for my life to change without actually knowing all the answers.

Term starts with the traditional afternoon tea and bouncy castle. Dave and I reluctantly walk through the stone archway and into the chaos of a world we tried to run away from. I don't want to be here, but I don't want them to know that. I grab Dave's hand, the solidarity of our story drawing us closer together. I don't have the energy to approach people; instead, we just stand there, the two of us, lost. I watch children running and laughing, students and spouses embracing each other, sharing stories of their summers. Everywhere I look there are babies and pregnant bellies, reminding me of what I've lost and what I long for. It feels like there's this invisible wall that separates us from the crowd and we're just spectators, observing the lives of those who are moving forward whilst ours is stuck in this repetitive story of loss. When people approach us, we offer our pre-prepared answers about Denver and my migraines/epilepsy because it's just easier; people know what to do with it.

'Hey, lovely!' Rach hugs me. I notice she's added flecks of orange into her hair and she's rocking a new pink and orange necklace.

'I love the hair!'

'Thanks! Hey, how are you guys doing?' Rach is one of the few people who actually know what happened this summer, including when we tried to run away.

'OK.'

'I need to talk to you. I've got an idea!' Rach says excitedly.

'Ooo, tell me!'

'So, you know I was doing my doula training this summer? Well, it was great and all that, but something about it just didn't feel right. It was hard because I was learning how to help women give birth and how to support them, but I couldn't stop thinking about you and everything you've gone through and how hard it is for you right now. Obviously I think being a doula is a great thing and I've wanted to become one for ages, but what about women like you, who have miscarried?

Or people who are struggling to have kids? There's no support for them. So I chatted to my doula training lady about how I was feeling and if she had any ideas of what I could do and she told me about red tents. Now, they can be a bit of a weird American thing, but the idea behind them is great; they came from the Old Testament, when women had to leave the village when they had their periods because people thought they were unclean.' I think Dave heard the word 'period' because he's just pulled his phone out of his pocket and started scrolling through Facebook. 'The Red Tents became places where women would gather and share lots of significant life stages together; they didn't just go to the tent once a month when they were due on – there were also young girls who got their first period and women who were miscarrying as well as those who had just given birth. Basically, if you were bleeding, then you went to the tent.'

'Hence the "red",' I add.

'Exactly! So these Red Tents were the places where women shared what was going on in their lives, where they bonded over their pain. There's a book on it and I read it over the summer and I want to start a Red Tent. I want to start a Red Tent for women at the college who are struggling with miscarriage and infertility. I know at least one other person who's going through something similar and I reckon there's more.'

'Oh, Rach, that would be amazing! I know I'd find it so helpful and, like you say, there has to be more people, right?' I respond, stepping out the way of a double buggy.

'I'm so glad you're up for it. I just kept thinking about how hard it's been for you and how difficult it is being here surrounded by kids and pregnant women and how great it would be for you to have your own support. I've also spoken to Jane, the chaplain, and she thinks it's a great idea and she's going to help, because I have no idea what I'm doing! The only thing is,' she leans closer, 'I've got kids and Jane's got kids too; do you think that would be OK?'

'I know what you mean . . . but you're different, Rach; I feel safe with you . . . and you don't talk about your kids all the time!'

'I promise you, Red Tent will definitely be a kids-free zone!'

'Great.'

'OK, cool, I just wanted to check with you first. I'm going to announce it at the first Spice meeting tonight, you know, in case there are any first-years who are struggling with this as well.'

'Heyyy ladies!' Julie hugs me and Rach. 'Hi, Dave!' Dave nods back. 'Look, I really want to catch up but I'm doing my official Spice rep thing. I can't believe I volunteered for this,' she shakes her head. 'Anyway, I've been put in charge of the Spice buddies this year so I'm here to tell you who you've both been paired up with so you can introduce yourselves. Rach, you're buddied with a girl called Sarah, she's moved from Norfolk with her husband and three kids. I saw her a minute ago, she's just over at the bouncy castle chatting with some of the mums. Lizzie,' Julie turns to me, 'I've paired you up with Sheila, now let me see . . .' She scans the sheet of paper with a list of names. 'Oh, here we are!' She points at the line next to Sheila's name. 'Right, so Sheila and Elis moved from London.' She moves her finger along the list of information. 'Elis is here for three years, and – '

I scan the information on the sheet and look at the last column which says 'children'. I check to see what they've written: '2 cats'.

'I've just spoken to them and they seem lovely, they're over there.' She points to a girl with shoulder-length shiny, dark-brown hair, waving her hands in the air with excitement as she admires the cake table. Her husband is standing next to her wearing an ornate, flowery blue shirt with one hand in the pocket of his purple chinos and the other holding a paper plate as Sheila picks her favourite cakes and adds them to the plate. They're both short, but I've now just resigned myself to the fact that the Lord keeps bringing short friends into my life and I'm going to just have to get over it. Dave takes my hand and leads me towards the cake table.

'Hey, buddy!' Sheila opens her arms wide and pulls me in towards her.

'Hi,' I respond into her emerald green jumper. She holds me close to her for a bit longer before stepping back and grabbing Dave for an equally big hug. I offer an awkward half-wave to Elis and wait for Sheila to let go of Dave.

'Great hug, Dave! Don't worry, there are plenty more where that came from — so look out!' She jumps towards him with her hands out.

'Dave loves hugs!' I reply, laughing at how awkward he looks right now. 'So, as your official Spice buddy, it's my job to show you around and make sure you settle into life here,' I tell Sheila.

'Well, Dave already did a really good job showing us round when we came to visit earlier this year!' says Elis, slapping Dave on the back.

'Dave's the reason we came here!' says Sheila. 'Best tour guide ever!' she shouts out to everyone on the quad whilst pointing at Dave.

'What can I say? You guys were the only people I showed round, so I've got a 100 per cent success rate.'

'So, how was your summer?' I ask. They both look at each other. Elis runs his fingers through his mop of curly brown hair, making it stand up and adding at least two inches to his height.

'Not great,' Sheila replies. 'What about you guys?'

'Ours wasn't great either,' I add, looking at Dave. We all look at each other apologetically as Elis rocks back and forwards on his feet.

That night I watch as Rach nervously shares her announcement to a room filled with women, and two men – Ian now has a friend. Her cheeks flush as she stands and speaks. I feel like she's speaking on my behalf and on behalf of any other women in the room who feel like me. There have to be more; please don't let me be the only one. I scan faces and body language for any sign that there's someone, anyone, who feels the same. I spot Sheila over the other side of the room listening to Rach talk; she's smiling, but then she seems a pretty smiley person so that might not mean anything. Once the announcements are finished, Julie hands out name labels and we start mingling. Memories of last year and my struggle to find friends come rushing back, but whilst I'm not exactly in a great place, Rach's idea to start a Red Tent already makes me feel hopeful that this year might be better. I want to tell Sheila I'm going to Red Tent, just in case it's something that might help her, but instead we end up talking about Ryan Gosling. But we're going to meet for coffee tomorrow in my lunch break, so maybe I could try to mention it to her then.

I leave my desk at 1 o'clock on the dot. I can't wait to get out of here. I'd spent most of the morning building up the courage to ask the guy who sits next to me to help me retrieve the Business Studies exam marks that I somehow deleted from the student record system for the *entire* academic year. When I come out the office, Sheila's already waiting for me. 'Sooo, how's your morning been?'

'Not good! I *need* coffee!'

'Lead the way!'

When we arrive, the coffee shop is packed, but we manage to find a small table in the middle of the shop that's uncomfortably close to the couple sitting next to us, and order our coffees. Our drinks arrive quickly, accompanied by a little chocolate-covered coffee bean on the side.

We talk about Sheila's cats and coffee shops and our reluctance to be known as the vicar's wife. We talk about work and how Sheila left her job as a primary school teacher when they moved here for Elis to train.

'I'm not going to look for a job for now, I think I need to take some time for myself,' Sheila says.

'That sounds like a good idea. Moving house can be pretty stressful.'

'You're right.' She looks down at her cup of coffee. 'I think I need some time to recover too.'

'You mentioned you'd not had a great summer the other day.'

'Yeah.' The waiter bumps into Sheila's arm as he tries to clear the dirty crockery from the table next to us. 'It sounds like you guys didn't have a great summer either?'

I pick up the wrapper from the chocolate-covered coffee bean and start twisting it between my fingers. Sensing my reluctance, Sheila jumps back in to rescue us from the awkward silence. 'I'm hoping that coming here will be a fresh start for Elis . . . well, for both of us really. He's not been well.'

'I'm sorry.' The tables are so tightly packed in that it feels like we're sharing a coffee date with the couples on either side, so I lean in towards Sheila in an attempt to create some level of intimacy. 'I wasn't well either this summer.' The edge of the table is digging into my stomach as I lean further into our conversation.

'The thing is . . .' Sheila has her mouth open, but it takes a few seconds for the words to come out. 'What happened is

. . . well, Elis had a breakdown.' Sheila looks straight at me, anxiously waiting for me to speak, but I don't know what to say. The volume of conversations, the steam from the coffee machine and the clatter of crockery keeps getting louder, emphasizing the awkward silence. I may have chosen *the* worst place to have this kind of conversation.

'Oh . . . that sounds really bad.'

'Yeah, it was. He was signed off work for a couple of months. I should have seen it coming; we'd been having loads of fertility tests and then he was diagnosed with azoospermia, which basically means he has no sperm. Apart from some kind of a miracle, there is no way we will be able to have our own kids.'

'Oh my goodness, I'm so sorry, I didn't even know that was a thing. I didn't know it was possible to . . . you know . . . to have no sperm.' I swear the guy next to me stopped talking when I said 'sperm'.

'Neither did we. It was a complete shock to both of us. We'd just always presumed we'd be able to have our own kids and now we can't. Our only option is a sperm donor or adoption, but we've just moved so we're not eligible for either.'

'I'm so sorry for what's happened to you guys . . . and that must be such a tough decision to know what to do next.'

'It's probably a good thing that we have to wait for a bit before we can explore other options; it's all very fresh and I think we need some time together to work through stuff.'

'That sounds like a good idea.' I take a deep breath. 'Listen, I know this isn't anywhere near as bad as what you guys have gone through but, well, the reason our summer was bad was because I had my fourth miscarriage.'

'Lizzie,' Sheila puts her hand on my arm. 'Four miscarriages is not better than no sperm! That's ridiculous! We're both going through similar stuff and it sucks!' She's so much better at this than me.

'It does. It really sucks!'

'Listen, I'm not feeling very Christian right now; I've not been to church for months, but I wonder if God had a part to play in bringing us together as buddies?'

'Well, you know what? I'm not feeling very Christian right now either, but I think you could be right.' I smile.

'I was planning to go to the Red Tent meeting on Saturday. Are you going to go?'

'Yeah, shall we go together?'

'I'd love that.'

On Saturday morning Sheila and I meet under the stone archway entrance to the college. We climb a twisting staircase and step into a living room filled with mismatched sofas sunken with comfort and decorated with cushions that don't belong anywhere near the pastel shades of the floral sofa fabric. The small, leaded windows at the end of the room offer little light, so Rach has turned on all the lamps nestled between the sofas, creating a space of warmth and welcome. Jane, the chaplain, has also brought her candles – holy people always seem to have candles with them. Until we moved here, I'd never considered their significance, but every time Jane lights a candle, she does it with such reverence it's like she's inviting God into the space.

'Ooo, pastries!' Sheila claps excitedly at the selection laid out on the retro glass coffee table in the middle of the room.

'There's also coffee,' says Rach.

'Amazing,' I say. 'This feels like such a treat!'

'Well, that's what we wanted,' Rach replies. 'You've all been through so much and we want you to feel spoilt.'

'This is *way* better than what Elis will be having for breakfast this morning,' adds Sheila.

There's a little tap on the door and Esther, one of the second-year spouses, pokes her head into the room.

'Esther! Come in!' Rach says.

'Anna's just locking her bike, she'll be up in a minute,' Esther tells us. We cautiously all look at each other; we all know why we're here, but it remains unspoken. Anna arrives and we fill mugs with coffee, select a pastry and sink into the sofas. I feel nervous, which is strange because I know everyone in the room, but I've never done anything like this; I don't think any of us have. I cautiously peel my almond croissant apart as we chat about anything but why we're here.

Rach waits for us to finish the last crumbs of flaky pastry on our plates before telling us what she and Jane have planned.

'So, I know I've spoken to you all already about why I'm doing this, and Jane has kindly offered to help me. I've not done this sort of thing before and I'm not really sure how to, but that's why Jane is here; she's the professional! We've got a few ideas of what we could do when we're together, but it's really up to you guys; basically, we're here because we want to help.' We're all smiling and nodding in encouragement. Rach checks the sheet of paper she's holding in her hand. 'Firstly, I want you to know this is a safe space, you can say anything you want, there is no judgement and nothing you say will leave this room; also, I promise Jane and I won't get pregnant.' She looks over to Jane, who smiles. I've no idea how old Jane is, but I'm pretty sure she's past her childbearing years. 'Oh, and one other thing,' Rach adds, 'there will always be food.'

'Hallelujah!' shouts Sheila.

'Now, Jane's going to get things started with a prayer.' We bow our heads, close our eyes and Jane speaks words of grace and love over us, reminding us of how precious we are and how Jesus sees our pain and weeps with us.

'Oh man! You've set me off already!' says Sheila, grabbing the box of tissues on the coffee table.

'It's OK, Sheila, this is a place for tears,' says Jane. 'That's why we've got so many boxes of tissues.' She points to the boxes scattered around the room.

'You might regret saying that, Jane, because you've not seen how much I can cry!'

'You can use as many tissues as you need, Sheila,' Jane smiles. 'Now, when Rach and I were talking about this first Red Tent, we thought it would be a really good idea to start by simply sharing our stories, to help us get to know each other, but also so that Rach and I can better understand what you're going through. Is anyone feeling brave enough to go first?'

We all look around the room, willing someone else to volunteer.

'I'll start,' says Esther. Thank goodness, I did not want to be the first one to talk. I know Sheila, Rach and Jane all know some of my story, but they really don't have any idea how much of a mess I'm in. At least if the others talk first, I'll know what to hold back; I don't want them to think I'm a total nutcase. I relax into the sofa with the relief of not going first.

Esther leans forward, her hands clasped and her arms resting on the soft fabric of her patterned dress. 'Since we arrived here two years ago, I've had *a lot* of miscarriages . . .'

I listen as Esther shares a story I know so very well. Anna follows with her story of ectopic pregnancies and miscarriages and, once again, I can hear myself and my own pain reflected in the words she shares with us. Then it's Sheila's turn, and as I listen to her talk about fertility tests and the loneliness of the pain she carries, I am no longer scared of the story I carry within me because now I know I'm not the only one.

I'm not the only one who finds it painful when they're surrounded by mothers.

I'm not the only one who feels hurt and sad when they receive pregnancy news, and I'm not the only one who feels guilty and ashamed of feeling hurt and sad.

I'm not the only one who feels like they don't belong because they don't have a child.

I'm not the only one who struggles with social media and I'm not the only one who's blocked someone on Facebook because they're filling my feed with 'baby spam'.

I'm not the only one who finds the sight of a scan photo really, really upsetting.

I'm not the only one who feels like their husband doesn't understand them.

I'm not the only one who feels like their life is worth less because they're not a mother.

I'm not the only one who feels lonely.

I'm not the only one who can't stop crying.

I'm not the only one who's sick of being given advice and hearing stories of people who 'stopped trying then got pregnant'.

I'm not the only one who struggles with 'all age' church services – because, let's face it, they're really just for children.

I'm not the only one who's upset by the words 'church family' because it doesn't feel like a family when you're the odd one out.

I'm not the only one who wants to walk out when the preacher can't stop talking about how *as a parent* they understand God's love better.

I'm not the only one who hates Mothering Sunday.

I'm not the only one struggling to pray.

I'm not the only one who wants to punch the person telling me 'everything happens for a reason', or 'God won't give you more than you can handle'.

I'm not the only one.

Until this moment I thought there was something deeply wrong with me and so I kept all the mess inside. But today I'm here sharing every part of my struggle and the nods and smiles of these women reassure me I'm no more messed up than anyone else. All these tears and painful stories in one room should be depressing but somehow it's beautiful, and surprisingly joyful. This sacred space was crafted for us by two women who have no experience of what we are going through. Two women who chose to simply sit and listen to our stories; desperate to understand and even feel some of the pain we have been through. I have never had anyone cry on my behalf until today and it is beautiful and humbling.

As the morning goes on, we sink deeper into the worn-out sofas, exhausted by the emotion of sharing each other's pain. Our hands are filled with soggy tissues, but we're all smiling.

'Oh man, why am I such an ugly crier?' says Sheila, repeatedly wiping each eye with a wet tissue to remove the smudges of mascara. 'And where does all the snot come from?' she asks. The laughter and conversation that follow feels like freedom. I didn't know what I needed to help get through this, but I think I've found it.

16

Time to Prove

Dave and I are sat in another hospital waiting room, but this time we're at the epilepsy clinic, which is weird because I've not been diagnosed with epilepsy. I've not actually been diagnosed with anything. I've had MRI scans and tests with wires stuck on my head, but the consultant still hasn't come to any conclusions as to why I keep losing my memory.

'Elizabeth Lowrie? Hi, I'm your epilepsy nurse.' A short Afro-Caribbean lady offers her hand to shake both mine and Dave's before leading us into her office and indicating where to sit.

'Sorry?' I ask. 'Did you just say you're my epilepsy nurse?'

'Yes, that's right, I'm your epilepsy nurse.'

'But I don't have epilepsy.'

She looks down at my files in front of her and back up to me. 'Uh, yes, you do.'

'But no one told me I had epilepsy. I thought they still hadn't worked out what was wrong with me.'

'They have worked out what's wrong – you've got epilepsy.'

'Oh.' I look over to Dave, who shrugs apologetically.

'So, how do you feel about having epilepsy?' she asks, leaning forward in her chair.

'Well, I'd rather not have it,' I reply.

'Pah! Rather not have it!' she repeats, slapping her thigh and laughing way too loudly. 'That's a good one! Rather not have it,' she repeats, shaking her head, and making some notes on my file. 'Soooooooo, you can't drive until you've had a year without a fit, but it will be OK once we get you onto some medication. Now, with this medication you can't get pregnant, OK?'

'But I want to get pregnant. We're trying for a family. I mean, I've had four miscarriages, but we're still trying. Is there any medication that's safe to take when I'm pregnant?' I ask, desperately.

'No. If you want to get pregnant, you can't take anything. Also, you can't swim by yourself, cook or have a bath.'

'Oh.'

'Here's some leaflets for you.' She shoves a bundle of NHS leaflets about living with epilepsy into my hands and turns to her notes. 'So, Dave, you might need to be around to help Lizzie. What do you do for a living?'

'I'm training to be a vicar,' he replies. She stops writing, puts her pen down and stares at Dave.

'What? You? A vicar?' She slaps her thigh again, rocking back and forth, giggling. 'What do I call you? Bishop?'

I stare at her silently. Dave laughs. She grabs a tissue and dabs her eyes.

'No, just, well, you can just call me Dave,' he replies – still laughing. She continues making notes, muttering the word 'vicar' under her breath and smiling. Eventually she looks up from her notes to the two of us.

'Well, that's it, then. You'll see me every six months; keep a diary of your fits, and when you've had a baby, we'll sort out your pills.'

'OK,' I reply casually, because having a baby is that easy. I grab my handbag and we stand up to leave.

'Oh, and goodbye, your worship!' she says to Dave, giggling and kind of bowing at the same time until the door shuts behind us.

'Do you know Dr Hibbert from *The Simpsons*?' Dave asks.

'What?'

'He's a doctor who laughs inappropriately at sad things? Well, we just met the real-life version!'

'But it doesn't change the fact I've still got epilepsy, though.'

'Of course it doesn't; I'm sorry, hon.' Dave puts his arm around me as we head to the car. 'But she was funny, though.'

If feels like my body has decided to fully commit to the epilepsy diagnosis because ever since we saw my epilepsy nurse a few weeks ago, my fits have increased. My weeks are now punctuated by memory loss, followed by migraines and a lot of sleeping. This morning I woke up like every other morning over the past fortnight, confused, tired and unwilling to get out of bed. I have one final scroll through Facebook, then reluctantly trudge towards the bathroom to wash my face before spraying more dry shampoo into my hair, slowly pulling on the clothes I wore yesterday and trudging downstairs and into our cluttered kitchen. Dave's left the radio on, a trace of life left behind him after rushing out the house this morning for morning prayer.

I brush the crumbs off the kitchen worktop into my cupped hand and tip them in the bin. I then push my expanding collection of kitchen gadgets against the white tiles in an attempt to make as much space as possible. I bend down and grab my large mixing bowl and place it on the worktop ready to make a loaf of bread. There's very little I can do at the moment, but making bread has become like therapy to me. In an attempt to do something fun together that didn't involve babies or the Church of England, we've been attending a bread-making course. Our teacher is called Humphrey Montgomery; he has a wood-fired oven in his garden that he built himself and every week he turns up with shopping bags filled with ingredients from Waitrose – you know, just your typical Cambridge guy. Dave is Humphrey's favourite because his dough rises to about twice the height of mine. I think the guy next to me is jealous of Dave's skills because I keep noticing him watching Dave very carefully as he violently kneads his dough to get it to rise better.

I start humming along to the kitchen radio as I measure out each ingredient on the scales, tipping it into my mixing bowl without consulting a cookbook; a small achievement but one that I'm pretty proud of. I grab the olive oil sat next to the gas hob and drizzle some over the flour; the thick golden liquid sits on top of the ingredients in pools, waiting to be mixed in. I then pour in a glug of warm water, sink my right hand into the wet flour and begin to mix it with my fingers, enjoying the messiness of the process. I keep adding extra water until I've collected all the flour into a ball. I drizzle more oil onto the worktop and rub it onto the dark work surface, creating an ever-expanding circle with the warm greasy liquid whilst the rest of it soaks into my skin, anointing and softening my hands. After rubbing the roughly mixed ball of dough around the sides of the bowl to collect every last scrap, I tip it onto the counter and start kneading – stretching, folding, turning, stretching, folding, turning, stretching, folding, turning.

Ten minutes later – or, as I like to time it, four songs on the radio – I drizzle a bit more oil into the bowl, then tip the smooth ball of soft dough back into the bowl and cover it with clingfilm and a sense of satisfaction. The bubbling water of the kettle joins the voices on the radio for a short while. The radio will keep playing until Dave gets home. I even keep it on when I leave the house. I keep the radio on to stop the silence. I don't like silence; I'm scared of what it might tell me.

My phone beeps with a new message. I take it with me and leave the freshly made dough and the radio behind before slowly retreating back to the living room, through the dark, cupboard-lined corridor towards the lounge. I turn on the TV without thinking, so accustomed to my routine that it just happens. 'Routine' may be too strong a word; my day consists of very little, but it's habitual. Sometimes this pattern of life brings me comfort; on other days, like today, I feel trapped. My phone beeps from underneath the blanket with another message.

My body gradually sinks into the long, dark-red sofa, my head bolstered by the cushions at one end, my long legs just about contained within the arms of the sofa. I pull the soft, bobbly brown blanket over my body, kicking my legs to ensure it falls over the ends of my feet because I can't be bothered to sit up to sort it out – I'm too tired. My phone beeps again and I flick through the channels on the TV; people buying houses in the country, in the city, abroad and I settle on *Homes Under the Hammer*. I love seeing the finished product and finding out if they've made any money.

This isn't me right now. This isn't who I am.

I quit my job two weeks ago. It sounds pretty dramatic when I say it like that, but in reality, my career at Anglia Ruskin ended in an awkward mutual agreement with my line manager.

I realized I needed to quit my job on my birthday. I was refilling the A4 paper drawer of the photocopier at work, when I got my necklace stuck in it. I stood up and it snapped, scattering beads across the huge open-plan office and briefly attracting the attention of the sixty or so university staff working quietly at their desks. As I crawled around on my hands and knees chasing turquoise beads across the grey carpet-tiled floor, I realized I didn't belong here.

Quitting a job without having anything to go on to feels reckless and immature, but Dave keeps assuring me it was the right thing to do.

I didn't just leave because of the jewellery thing. If I'd left a job whenever I'd done something clumsy or embarrassing, I would have spent most of my life unemployed. I left because I wasn't coping. I wasn't coping with life and work and epilepsy. The necklace was merely the breaking point – hah!

The problem was that even on the days when my head was OK, I wasn't really getting any work done because I'd forgotten how to do my job. It was like my brain had stopped working. Most days I would sit silently at my desk waiting for an appropriate moment to ask the guy sat next to me another question about what I'm supposed to be doing. The rest of the time I would stare at my computer screen, petrified that I had somehow become unemployable.

I'm currently avoiding my mum's phone calls and I'm dreading seeing my counsellor, Louise, next week. Sheila's happy I've quit my job; she's been telling me to do it for ages. She wants an unemployed friend to hang out with who won't talk about babies all the time. I kind of admire Sheila; she's not working, but she seems fine about it. I, on the other hand, am not OK. No matter how I try to rationalize my decision to stop working, this heavy sense of failure continues to follow me around, hanging off me. I should be achieving things, not lying on the sofa watching daytime telly.

Telling people I have epilepsy, however, is way easier than telling someone I've had a miscarriage. It sounds really serious too, which kind of helps, but the reality is that the epilepsy diagnosis is like a very tiny cherry on a really dry vegan cake. No, actually, it's like that final kick in the guts when you're already dead on the floor. Lying here on the sofa, I try to rationalize what's happened, but the shame of failure consumes me; it's inside me, failure is part of me, it's who I am now.

The ending titles of my favourite daytime home improvement show roll up the screen. I glance at my watch and decide I should probably check on my dough. I shake the blanket off my legs and slowly trudge back down the dark corridor and into the kitchen, the radio battling against the sound of the TV in the distance. I slowly peel back the clingfilm wrapped over the mixing bowl and take a look at the dough: it's risen well and I can smell the yeast working away. I think about tipping it out on the counter and shaping it ready for its second prove but decide against it. I pull the clingfilm back over the bowl and walk out the kitchen, my slippers padding along the brown carpet and back into the lounge, knowing that leaving it will make a better loaf.

17

Salt Water and Honey

~

'Did you know? Anna's pregnant,' I tell Dave when he appears in the lounge, red-faced from his cycle home.

'Um, yeah, I heard today. It's good news, isn't it?'

'Yeah.'

'I mean, they've been through a lot.'

'Yeah.' I move my gaze back to the TV and he leaves the room.

'Rejoice with those who rejoice; mourn with those who mourn'[1] is the Bible verse we always talk about at Red Tent. I think it's a great verse because it tells us it's OK to feel sad, and it encourages us to be sad together rather than hide away; it's a verse that describes Red Tent. I'm only at the beginning of this journey of sharing my sadness, but I love that something in the Bible gives me permission to go there; it also makes me feel really Christian because I'm doing something the Bible says I should do. The only problem is, I don't know what to do with the rejoice bit.

When you're sad, it's incredibly hard to rejoice. I know the news Anna shared is good news; it's amazing, but when I saw her email, in my inbox I was scared to open it. I was scared because of the challenge it presented me with, the challenge to feel joy for another when I'm drowning in sadness. Her news makes my pain of longing even more acute.

When you're rejoicing, I think you can forget what it's like to mourn. I know I have. Someone else's sadness presents itself like a stain on your celebration, ruining your joy. Without me, the joy of the expectant parents would be complete. With me, I create a problem, a dark side to the good news of a pregnancy.

I guess I hadn't realized how costly that verse was. I hadn't realized the sacrifice required to put these verses into practice.

'Have you read the email?' Sheila asks, stepping through the door. She cycled over this morning to hang out with me; I had a couple of fits yesterday and still feel exhausted.

'Yeah.'

'It's good news, isn't it?' She pulls out a bag of Doritos and all four *High School Musical* DVDs.

'Yeah, it is.'

'It hurts, though.'

'I know.'

'I feel bad that I feel this sad.'

'Me too. Dave just made me feel worse; he acted like it didn't affect him at all.'

'It must have done. He probably just didn't know what to say.'

'Yeah, I suppose. That's one more thing to bring up at counselling, anyway! Do you want a coffee?'

'Always!' We move the Doritos, coffee and *High School Musical* DVDs into the living room, throw the soft blanket over the two of us and snuggle up on the sofa.

'Is it me, or is the whole world pregnant right now?' Sheila asks.

'Yep, about three months ago everyone had really successful sex and now they want the entire universe to know by posting photos of their womb on Facebook.'

'Ha! Exactly. I think all our friends had a diary party and coordinated their ovulation.'

'I know someone who planned her due date.'

'What!' Sheila grabs a handful of Doritos.

'Yeah, she's a teacher and she wanted to have the baby in September to make the most of her paid maternity leave. Apparently she flipped out because she ended up getting pregnant a month later, so the baby's due in October!'

'Oh, wow, that must have been *so* hard for her.'

'I know! Imagine having to wait a whole month!' I pick up the bag of Doritos and look inside. 'Oh, I think we've finished them.'

'What do you think is going to happen at Red Tent, you know, with Anna's news?'

'I don't know. I mean, in her email she said she wouldn't come any more, but that doesn't seem right.'

'I know, it's hard because it will feel awkward with her there, both for us and her, but we can't throw people out the group because they're pregnant.'

'Hopefully Jane will know what to do.'

'Jane will definitely know what to do.' I think Jane might be a saint; I swear you can see a faint heavenly glow around her soft blonde hair sometimes. 'Right!' says Sheila, picking up a *High School Musical* DVD, 'Do you fancy watching a bit of Zac Efron?'

'Of course.'

This evening Red Tent is at Jane's house. Whilst we're waiting for the lasagne to bubble, Sheila is telling Jane off for the amount of catnip she feeds her tabby; Jasper, Esther and I are laying the table; and Rach and a couple of female trainee vicars are sat in Jane's velvety green armchairs – our little group is growing. One of the trainee vicars who's joined us is Bee; we bonded quickly over coffee shops; she's a great dancer, and she's always in the library with Dave, working through the night to finish essays at the last minute. Bee's single at the moment and it's just as hard for her, if not harder, to feel part of a community with so many families. The oven beeps and Jane carries the lasagne to the table; it's almost bigger than her! We gather round the table to eat and continue the conversation about Jasper's catnip dependency between mouthfuls.

Our cheeks are blushed and shiny from the warmth of the food in our bellies, the wine, the laughter and the many candles – Jane sure does love her candles. The excitement of discovering this group of women and the privilege of sharing in their stories fizzes away inside me.

'Right!' says Bee, shouting over the top of our voices. '*Order!* Sheila, that means you!' she grins as she tells Sheila off.

'Yes, Miss, sorry Miss!' Sheila shouts back.

'Thank you,' says Bee. 'Right, to start with I've got postcards for each one of you.' She passes them around the table. They're all the same. On the front it says, 'Let's be awkward together'.

'These are awesome!' says Rach.

'OK, I want you to write your name on the postcard and then we're going to pass them round and write what we love about each other on the postcards.' Jane provides a pile of coloured pens and we all start writing, our words illuminated by candlelight. There is no awkwardness found in the silence that follows, just the comfort of companionship. The postcards are passed around, a patchwork of colour and encouragement written on them. As I write I realize my gratitude and love for each person will never fit on the back of a postcard; I don't even know if there are words to express what I feel about this group of women.

'When everyone's written on each postcard, just pass it back to the person it belongs to,' says Bee.

We begin to read the words gifted to us. I struggle with this bit; I find it easy to write lovely stuff for other people, but difficult to receive. I try to read the back of the card slowly to absorb what's been written to me.

'I love you guys!' Sheila says through tears. Jane puts the box of tissues on the table and we all start gushing about how much we love each other.

'I've put together a little liturgy for us to share tonight,' says Jane.

'Oh, Jane, you know how much I love your liturgies!' Sheila responds excitedly. Until Red Tent, I've never been much of a fan of liturgy. I've read through pre-written prayers hundreds of times in church and although the poetry is often beautiful, I find it hard to mean what I say when I'm using someone else's words. But now life is different; I'm different and I'm discovering how helpful liturgy can be when words fail you. The prayers Jane has put together are teaching us how to express what we're feeling and acknowledge our sadness, but they don't leave us there. The words we read together always move us forward; they always offer hope. Without them I'd be lost.

'I've created this liturgy to help us acknowledge how Anna's pregnancy news makes us feel. It's OK to struggle to rejoice over other people's news but we need to share this with God.'

I look down at the table.

'I want to be happy for them, I just hate how this makes me feel,' I share.

'There's no shame in grief,' says Jane. 'We need to acknowledge the reality of this situation and the battle between the grief and the joy that we feel.' She pushes her chair back away from the table, stands up and walks over to the kitchen counter, picks up two bowls and brings them back to the table. She then collects six tealights and a larger candle. 'Jesus never dismissed the pain he felt in certain moments of his life, and we shouldn't either. Tonight we are going to acknowledge how we feel about this news and bring it to God.'

Jane lifts the small ceramic bowls up one by one. 'This bowl contains salt water to acknowledge our tears, and this one is honey, to acknowledge joy, and we're going to use them as part of the liturgy.' She passes round the sheets with the printed liturgy on them, and we begin to read, joining Jane in the words written in bold.

A LITTLE LITURGY OF HOPE AND HEALING

Lord Jesus you wept over Jerusalem

Our tears were your tears[2]

We thank you Lord that you understand our pain and hear our cries.

You know we want to rejoice with those who are blessed with the gift of a baby,

But you know too how hard it is for us.

And so Lord Jesus we take a moment

To acknowledge our pain and the pain of all who long for the gift of a child.

A bowl of salty water is passed around.

We taste our tears:

– our envy

– our fear

– our anger and

– our longing

Father, forgive us

And set us free

We worship a God of grace

The word to us in Jesus Christ is

Our sin is forgiven

And so Lord, we come to you in hope.

We light a candle as we give thanks for your blessing on our friends

And we light candles for ourselves

As a symbol of the hope that is in us:

That you have made us

That you love us

And that you fulfil your purposes in our lives.

(We light six candles.)[3]

Walk forward from this moment in the peace and power of Jesus

May you receive all that you need for the journey,

May the joy of hope revive your heart,

And the Spirit bring restoration and healing to the broken pieces of your soul

Amen[4]

Jane takes the bowl of salt water and hands it to me; I dip my finger in, right down to the bottom of the bowl and then up to my tongue. I feel the liquid first, then the saltiness kicks in, overpowering and bitter to taste. Next Jane passes me the bowl of honey, its thick, golden contents shining in the candlelight. I dip my finger in, twisting it, careful not to lose a drop. The sweet nectar thaws my tongue, dispelling the traces of sourness. Honey. Made even sweeter and softer and more indulgent by the eye-watering saltiness preceding it. There is a reverence found in the silence as the bowl is passed around the table and the honey tasted by each one of us. I have a new respect for joy, for its value and the sacrifice it requires of me.

Eventually the silence is dispelled by hugs and chatter around the table, tissues are passed round, mascara smudges wiped clean, the kettle is boiled and those two bowls remain in the middle of the table. The salt water and the honey, both there together. Since when did it have to be one or the other?

18

Bread and Wine

⌒

'Hon? Are you OK?' I can hear Dave tapping on the toilet door.

'I just need a bit longer!' I splash more water on my face and check it in the mirror, but it's still red and blotchy. I'm just going to have to stay here until it calms down. I can feel a migraine beginning to creep over my head as well; last time this happened I lost my memory and had to spend two days in bed.

'You've been in there a really long time . . . I can't really come into the ladies' toilet so I'm going to find someone who can come check on you, OK?'

'OK.' I check my watch. Ohhh, I've been in here for half an hour already. The party's probably already well underway.

'Lizzie?' The door opens and tiny Rach appears. 'Are you alright?' I shake my head because I know if I talk I will just start crying again. 'It's OK.' Tiny Rach hugs me and we just stand there for I don't know how long, hugging in silence.

'I'm sorry, I feel so stupid. I thought I could do this, but Dave was right, we should have stayed at home. I . . . I just really wanted to come to his first birthday party. I wanted to celebrate with everyone! Cath's had such a tough year, the chemo made her so sick and now her son has turned 1, and I just wanted to be here to celebrate.'

'It's amazing you wanted to come,' she reassures me, 'but Dave's right, you don't have to be here if it's too difficult. Cath will understand.' Tiny Rach grabs more paper towels and hands them to me.

'I genuinely thought it would be OK, but as soon as we arrived I saw everyone there in the hall playing with their kids, and it made me so upset. Everyone here has kids apart from us. We don't belong here!' I wipe my nose with the rough paper towel tiny Rach handed me; they might be recycled and good for the environment, but they're really scratchy.

'Oh, Lizzie, you do belong – it's just that maybe right now you need to be kind to yourself. Just go home. Cath will understand.'

'I didn't even get to see the hungry caterpillar cake she made!'

'It's alright, I'll bring a slice home for you.'

'Thanks,' I smile. 'Right, I better go find Dave. I think he's a bit bored of standing outside the ladies' toilets!'

Tiny Rach puts her arm round me and guides me out towards Dave.

'So, do you think maybe we should just avoid kids' birthday parties for a bit?' Dave asks, as we walk to the car. 'I mean, obviously I love standing outside the ladies' loos for forty minutes, but there are probably more fun ways to spend an afternoon.'

'Yeah. I think you could be right.'

The following morning I'm lying in bed, repeatedly hitting snooze on my alarm. The memory of yesterday is still fresh in my mind as I think of excuses to get me out of helping my vicar friend Sue this morning. 'Beeeeeeeeeeeeeeep!' I check the time on my phone and turn off my alarm – with no suitable excuse, I have no choice but to get up.

I quickly butter two slices of toast and eat them standing in the kitchen before grabbing my handbag and gloves and heading towards the garage to collect my bike. Turning the key in the wooden garage door, scraping it across the concrete pavement to open, I grab my bike and helmet, kicking the door closed with great force to make sure it's locked shut. I throw my handbag into the metal basket hanging off the front of my bike, clip my helmet on and set off.

My eyes are watering from the force of the wind beating against my face as I turn a corner, but still the wind doesn't let up – why is it always against me? A big gust throws itself in my face, slowing me down. I glance down to my pedals to check I'm still moving forward. Thankfully, I am, and this epic workout is not in vain.

I arrive at my destination and manage to squeeze my bike in next to a Peppa Pig scooter, lock it and walk towards the school entrance. The lady on reception is friendly, but I feel like a fraud; I don't belong here. I tell her I'm not a mum, but I'm coming to Thirst, the mums' group run by Sue, the vicar. I sign the book, the door is unlocked and I'm shown to the room where Sue and a group of women are sat round a wooden table, drinking cups of tea. My throat tightens, my mind questioning why on earth I agreed to do this as I grab the only spare plastic seat left and sit next to a young woman with a baby.

Breathing in courage, I start talking to the woman on my right who introduces me to her 3-month-old daughter. She tells me about how Sue had baptized her daughter last week. Apparently, her partner isn't around any more; he left when she refused to have an abortion; she's got two other kids as well and now she's caring for them by herself. Sue introduces the rest of the women round the table, then introduces a time of sharing. Sue is incredible; she listens and absorbs every one of the stories shared as though they were her own. As each person speaks, I quickly realize this isn't just a coffee morning for primary school mums. I hear stories of struggle to provide for families as a single parent, of children with Asperger's and autism, social housing and food banks, illustrating a life far removed from the world of academia, privilege and great architecture that Cambridge is famous for.

My heart and my middle-class upbringing tell me I have nothing in common with these women. I've never experienced the struggle they inhabit. I don't know what it's like to be addicted to alcohol or abusive relationships. I may be struggling to find my place in this world, but these women are struggling to survive. I should feel out of place here, but instead I feel welcome. I'm surrounded by babies and conversations about school uniforms and benefits and battling a system that feels like it's always against you. I have nothing to contribute, no experience or advice, but I don't want to run away.

Fairy lights are sparkling through windows and I've filled our house with cinnamon-scented candles, offering comfort from the dark afternoons and evenings counting down to Christmas Day. Another Christmas without children. Another Christmas without answers, or even a promise of change. I'm running late again. I park my bike behind the college chapel, switch off my lights and unstrap my helmet, clipping it in my bike basket, and walk quickly round to the chapel door. The service has already started so I try to walk in quietly, cheeks burning red from the cycle ride through town and the contrast of a Cambridge winter evening with the warmth of bodies and radiators filling the college chapel.

I squeeze past the three parents stood up at the back, gently bouncing babies and kissing their soft skin, willing them to stay quiet so they can stay in for the service. I catch the eye of a dad standing by the door with his son strapped to his chest.

His eyes move from his peachy-skinned little boy and then awkwardly to me, my barrenness jarring with his newborn joy. I think the look he just gave me was pity, a kind of sad, apologetic glance, moving quickly back to his son and the world he knew. I then walk past another guy, gently rocking his daughter to sleep; I think his name is Steve; he's part of Dave's college fellowship group. Dressed in chinos and a checked shirt, Steve looks and sounds like he's posh, but he's actually from Luton – *or so he says.* Steve glances a silent hello as I brush past him. I find a seat in the corner of the chapel on a bench pushed up against the oak-panelled wall. I lean back into the hardwood panel behind me, longing to disappear into it.

I stand with everyone for songs and liturgy, I sit to pray and listen to the sermon, but I feel little unity with this body of people. I have found wonderful friends here who have shown me great love, but many just keep their distance. I'm pretty sure a lot of people know what's happened to us, but we don't talk about it. It's not their fault; I wouldn't know what to say either. The preacher stands and we sit, ready to listen. The passage is about Mary, the woman dressed in blue on Christmas cards, the woman who's celebrated for her fertility and admired for her mothering instincts.

'I've decided to go back to Thirst this week,' I tell Dave after the service.

'Really?'

'Yeah,' I reply. 'I know I didn't handle the birthday party well, but Thirst is different; I don't know why, but the fact they all have kids doesn't bother me as much.'

The next day I brave the icy winds of the Cambridge streets again and cycle to see Sue and the other mums for a second time.

'Hey, Lizzie!' As soon as I walk into the room, I'm welcomed by lots of hugs. My friend from last week comes over to chat to me with her daughter tucked under her arm, but her phone starts ringing, she checks the caller ID, then asks, 'Do you mind holding her?'

I awkwardly put my arms out to take her daughter from her. No one else in the room is watching. To them this is totally normal, but for me this is a big deal. As I hold her, my arms slowly start to thaw and bend to the shape of her body. I look at her face, the softness of her skin, her long eyelashes resting on her cheeks as she sleeps and I think about the miracle that she's still alive. I think I actually like holding her; she's beautiful, maybe even more beautiful because of the story she's living, because her mum chose life for her.

We gather around the small table in the school coffee room, our fingers warming themselves around mugs of tea, and stories of difficult children and invisible fathers and grief fill the space. 'How are you?' Sue asks the lady sat next to me with a toddler on her lap.

'Not great.' She looks over to me. 'My dad died on Monday.'

'I'm sorry,' I reply.

'I worry about my mum because she's far away, and because of the kids and life in general I can't see her as much as I should. I'm just exhausted.'

'Grief is exhausting.' Everyone looks at me.

'You're so right, Lizzie,' one of the girls agrees. 'I just feel so tired all the time!' Her little boy stretches forward to grab her mug of tea and she quickly hands him another bread stick. 'Have you lost someone close to you, too, Lizzie?'

'I've lost grandparents, but they had already had long lives so it was different . . . I have had a few miscarriages, though.'

'How many?'

'Four.'

My new friend holds my hand and tells me she's had two miscarriages, then two more of the women around the table share their stories of miscarriage as well. It feels like the table's just got smaller. I may not be a mother, but now I realize why I feel like I belong here – we're sisters who struggle, we're a community of sufferers. Our stories may be different but our struggles unite us. After more cups of tea, Sue starts the Bible study, and today we're reading about Mary *again* – it's Christmas, so of course it's Mary.

I've always found Mary hard to connect with; I mean, to start with the most famous thing she's known for – being a mother – is the one thing I'm not. But also, I've always struggled to relate to someone whose first response to the news of God turning her life upside down is one of praise, not fear or frustration. But reading her story now, with my new friends, I think Mary's actually pretty hardcore. She had nothing; she was a young woman who featured very low on the social scale, but she didn't let her status in the world determine her value, and yet her story shows God is interested in us, no matter how insignificant we may feel. I think that's why she was able to rejoice at the news of her pregnancy rather than freak out about what people were going to think of her and whether Joseph would still want to marry her. She may have been poor and weak and insignificant in her community, but she believed she was valued in God's world, and that's what mattered most to her. Just like our little group sat round the table this morning, none of us have much to offer, but that doesn't mean we don't matter to God.

It's another Thursday evening and once again the warmth of the tiny, ancient college chapel welcomes me into a community I still struggle to feel part of. I feel like I have more in common with the plaques on the chapel's historic walls than the people inside. There are memorials to remember missionaries who sacrificed their lives to tell the nations they are loved by God and others to remember the short lives of children who died during their parents' time here. The building retells the bittersweet story of life both outside and inside its walls. I watch the shadows of bare branches dance around in front of the ancient stained-glass windows depicting saints and sacrifice as I fail to find comfort from the words of the sermon preached from the front. I know there is truth and hope and beauty in this faith I share with those crammed into this chapel tonight, but if I'm honest, I'm struggling to find it.

Tonight we share communion, simple bread and wine, remembering what we have in common. Remembering our faith in Jesus and what his death and resurrection means for our lives on earth. We stand to make peace with each other; hugs and words of love and encouragement ripple through the chapel. I know the hugs are genuine offers of love and I receive them gladly, with the biggest hugs reserved for Rach, Sheila, Esther and Jane. We remain standing to sing and then repeat the words I've spoken countless times before, remembering the story of Jesus' death and sacrifice and the new life and hope that follows. The tutor at the front invites us to share in the bread and wine, and row by row, people walk up the aisle, kneel down before the cross and receive bread and wine.

I watch from the back as men, women, single, married, divorced, childless and parents walk towards the front, kneeling with their hands stretched out ready to receive. I watch the backs of their heads and I think about their stories, realizing I know more about the people in this room than I thought. There are three women diagnosed with breast cancer this year, divorcees, those struggling with singleness, others who were once at the top of their career who now struggle to cover the cost of raising a family on a trainee vicar stipend, and those who walk with depression and anxiety every day of their lives. I watch as they carry their stories with them as they walk to the front of the chapel, kneel down and put their hands out ready to receive, and I decide to join them.

At the end of the service the band continues to play, the chapel slowly empties as parents head out to collect children from their groups, and hungry students file out towards the dining hall, but I can't move yet. The music fills the small chapel warmed by bodies and an ancient heating system. I look across the aisle and see Esther, Ben, Sheila, Elis and Rach. Esther is crying; her husband, Ben, has his arm around her. Sheila, Elis and Rach have moved over to sit with them, reaching out to offer comfort. I walk over to join them, catching Dave's eye and inviting him to follow.

We fill the pew; Jane and Steve, the guy from Dave's fellowship group, are at the front of the chapel praying for those who weren't ready to leave the foot of the cross. Their hands are stretched out, resting on the shoulders of the students kneeling in front of them at the communion rail. The music continues to float over us. I reach out my arm to hold Esther's hand and look up to see Sheila crying too, and then my tears begin to fall down, soaking into my jeans. I can feel Dave's arm around my shoulder, the warmth of his body drawing me closer into him; I rest my head on his chest and look towards the communion rail and see Jane looking back at us all, inviting us to join her. We move as one, the six of us slowly shuffling forward to the front where we kneel, heads bowed, hands open, longing to receive something.

Jane steps forward inviting Steve to join her in praying for us, whispering to him that we're all part of Red Tent. He kind of looks at her a bit confused; she explains a bit more about what that means, and he steps forward to pray for us. As he stands next to Jane, he looks out of his depth but also desperate to help; the courage of his empathy keeping him in the room. Behind us stands Rach, her arms stretched up and out, reaching out to heaven on our behalf.

Tears are flowing, gushing, running down my face, and I don't care. I glance over to Dave, his head bowed, salt water running down his cheeks. I then turn to my right and see Sheila, Elis, Ben and Esther weeping. I look up to Jane and Steve, the two of them calling out to God on our behalf, their faces wet with tears. Music floats over us, tending to our souls as a couple of guys from the music group stay behind, piano and guitar ministering to our hearts as much as the words of the prayers spoken over us.

'Lord Jesus, I thank you that you are here with us now,' Jane prays. 'You know our hearts, you have counted every hair on our heads and every tear from our eyes,

You see Sheila's tears,
You see Elis' tears,
You see Esther's tears,
You see Ben's tears,
You see Dave's tears,
You see Lizzie's tears.
You see our tears on their behalf.
And you weep with us as we lift our broken hearts to you.'

Kneeling in front of the cross we cry with all our being, with muscle and sinew and flesh, with heart and soul and mind, with hopes and dreams and memory; there is nothing and nobody left in that room who is not weeping. It is a messy, unrefined and holy moment. A moment that takes us all by surprise, especially Steve, who soon found himself weeping with the rest of us. The only explanation for his tears I can think of is that they came from the heart of God.

19

Dare to Dream

~

Today is one of those perfect winter days when the air is crisp and the sun shines brightly. Ben drops me and Esther off at Rach's house, and we're greeted with fresh coffee and pastries. Rach has sent Martin and the kids to her mum's for the weekend, so we've got the house to ourselves. Sheila and Jane arrive, and we start the day with food and laughter.

After breakfast we head outside ready to explore the untouched white canvas of snow laid out in front of us. Invigorated by the sharpness of the air, our cheeks are flushed and our hearts full. We mess around, taking photos, climbing over branches and piles of chopped-down trees and create snow sculptures of varying quality, including snow boobs! Further along our travels through the snow-covered woods we discover a tractor that's just asking to be climbed on, and we persuade Jane to pose in the driver's seat for a photo before running towards the frozen river and bravely poking the ice that seals it with a giant stick. Walking through the woods, we continue to climb branches, play with snow and pose for silly photos. My heart feels free as I embrace this precious opportunity to mess around with my friends.

After a couple of hours of frolicking, a word I rarely use but one I believe is justified on this occasion, the cold begins to penetrate the layers of thick jumpers, winter coats and woolly hats, and we head back to Rach's. We bang our boots against the doorstep and celebrate the welcome offered to us by the radiator in the hallway. Home-made soup and bread appear on the table, steaming and aromatic. Lunch is followed by cups of tea and bodies stretched out on the huge red sofas in Rach's living room. I sink deep into the soft sofa cushions, my body relaxed from the laughter and craziness of the morning.

'You know, Jane and I are praying that one day we won't need a Red Tent,' Rach announces to the room. 'I mean, it's not that I don't like hanging out with you all, it's just that our dream is one day you'll all have families. That's why we wanted us to have this day together – we want to help you guys to dare to dream again. Jane and I can't just dream for you, you need to dream too.' We look around at each other, wondering who's going to speak first.

'Dreaming is scary,' Esther says.

'I know,' Jane responds gently, 'but you can't let disappointment stop you from dreaming of what could be.' My fists are clenched underneath the soft, red blanket laid over me.

'But what if it doesn't happen?' asks Esther. I'm so glad she's talking because I have no idea what to say.

'I don't know,' replies Rach. 'You're right, it might not happen, but also it could happen, you could be a mother, and if that's what your heart really desires, then you need to let God know.'

Sheila shifts around in the giant armchair and tucks her feet up underneath another one of Rach's red blankets.

'It might feel like you're protecting yourself by not thinking about the future and dreaming of what could be, but that's not how God designed us to live,' Jane adds. 'Firstly, you need to know that longing for a child isn't a bad thing, but your dreams shouldn't stop there. Our heart is for you to dream well and

dream bigger, to dream into your identity and your calling.'
I think back to the café and how big my dreams used to be. I
miss that. 'Your hearts have been broken, but we want to pray
for God to help you dream again,' Jane tells us.

I stare at the carpet, Sheila focuses on drinking her tea, and
Esther seems to be studying her nail varnish.

'We thought it would be a good idea to have this day at
the beginning of the year, to give you the opportunity to start
dreaming about what could happen, to open your hearts up to
what could be,' Rach tells us. 'Look at this verse.' She passes
round sheets with little liturgies on them and at the top is a
Bible verse.

Forget the former things . . . See, I am doing a new thing![1]

I scan the verse again and again. I know it's telling me to let go
of my disappointments and move forward into new life, but I
don't know if I'm strong enough to do this. Maybe God could
do a new thing in another part of my life, a small bit that won't
hurt if it doesn't work out. I look over to Esther and Sheila who
are both staring at the sheets of paper in front of them. Red
Tent is never this quiet.

'I love this verse,' Sheila breaks the silence.

'*The Message* translation of it is really good too,' Rach adds.
'Listen to this.' She picks up one of the Bibles on the coffee table.

Forget about what's happened; don't keep going over old
history. Be alert, be present. I'm about to do something
brand-new.[2]

'"Don't keep going over old history",' I repeat. 'That's what's
stopping the dreaming.'

'I love how the bit about something new happening is reliant on God – he's about to do something, it's not all on us,' Esther adds.

Our hearts begin to thaw and we start to talk, settling back into the familiarity of heart-sharing as we recover from the shock of this new challenge. The colours from inside glow through the windows into the waning light of a winter's afternoon. Jane is lying across the sofa opposite me, eyes closed, listening; Rach is reclining in her new IKEA chair; Sheila is sitting in the big armchair, her face sticking out over the top of the blanket covering her body, and Esther is curled up on the sofa next to me. Talk of newness, of moving forward and allowing ourselves to expect and anticipate new things fills the room. As we continue to talk, it feels like bits of God are beginning to drip into our dreams like drops of gold, refining and expanding our hope, letting the pain of the past slip from our fingers. I'm nowhere near healed, but I know deep down there is a wildness in my heart that craves adventure and newness and hope. As the sun sets and the glow of the candles on the coffee table and around the fireplace burn brighter, we read together from the little liturgy Jane put together for us.

THE AFFIRMATION
Let us affirm our faith
We believe that every moment of our life is important to God
Every struggle is honoured,
Every pain is felt,
Every courage is celebrated
And every small victory
Is marked with delight.
We believe

That every moment of our life
Is held precious,
Walked in by Jesus Christ
As though our experience
Is worth knowing
And our choices
Are worth making.
We believe
That every moment of our life
Could possibly hold
The dancing Spirit of God
As though we are a part
Of a great adventure,
The loved ones of the passion
Whose every moment
Could be a moment of grace.
In the name of Christ,
Who has walked every journey before you
And sees deeply into your heart in understanding,
We announce a new day.
Receive the grace of God
And the peace of the Holy Spirit,
In the name of Christ, **Amen**[3]

The 'dare to dream' day ends with dinner and wine. Anna joins us; I can tell she feels awkward, but she doesn't need to. We welcome her back into our world, our hearts softened and comforted by a day of laughter and soul-sharing. After dinner, Anna, Esther and Jane go home and leave Rach, Sheila and I watching *Dirty Dancing* in our pyjamas. At the end of the film and the bag of Doritos, Sheila and I lay out sofa cushions and sleeping bags on the lounge floor and talk about dreaming whilst lying there in the dark. I wait for her to fall asleep and slowly unzip my sleeping bag, trying not to wake her.

I tiptoe across the room, grab my handbag and head to the bathroom. I try to climb the stairs quietly, but they're so creaky; I pause half way, worried I heard someone, but the dark silence of the house reassures me I'm alone. Once I'm in the bathroom, I close the door slowly until I hear it click shut and then slide the lock across and turn on the light. I carefully remove the carrier bag filled with medication from my handbag. I do the injection first. Pinching the skin from my tummy together I push the needle in and feel the liquid burn into my flesh. Next the pessary – the less said about that the better. Once I'm done, I pack everything back into my handbag, gently unlock the door, creep back downstairs, zip myself back into my sleeping bag and wait for sleep.

The following morning our husbands arrive to take us home. Tired and full of pastries, coffee and laughter, I hold the conversations about dreaming in my heart, not ready to do anything with them, but knowing I can't ignore them. On the drive home, Dave turns the radio down and asks me a question I didn't want to answer.

'So, did you tell them you were pregnant?'

20

An Authorized Life

~

To Authorize: to give authority/power to someone; to give permission, to validate, to empower[1]

The curtain rattles round the rail, hiding me from the world. I can hear the guy next to me vomit. I watch pairs of feet hurry past the gap between the blue curtain and the floor. The two paracetamols given to me when I arrived have done nothing to help; I told the nurse it wouldn't, but I know she was just doing her job. I can't lie still; the pain from each contraction pushes my body around the bed with a force I can't control. This must be what writhing looks like. I can feel blood leaving me, turning the dry, crisp, white sheets crimson and damp. More feet pass by. The guy next to me is calling for a nurse, but on this busy Friday night I can hear the doubt in his voice. Another contraction, and I push my body further into the bed, glad to be finally lying down after two hours of waiting on a red plastic chair. Dave is sat next to me, the blue curtain a backdrop to his posture of despair. He's bent forward, holding my hand, his gaze moving from me to the closed curtain and the feet passing us by, and back to me again.

At 11:15 this morning I went to the toilet and saw blood. I sat there in a grey cubicle, bent forward, elbows pressing into my bare legs just staring at my underwear, bile rising in my throat, the word 'no' repeatedly screaming from my body. I sat there, listening to my friends' voices chatting in the small faculty kitchen at the college, just across the corridor from the ladies' toilets, my mind battling the shock pulsing through me, squashing it down in order to make a plan of how to go from sitting in a toilet cubicle with my trousers around my ankles to finding Dave and getting out of there.

Eventually I stood up. I walked out of the ladies' toilets, my body leading me forward into a future I dreaded.

'Can you help me find my husband?' My voice sounded cold, abrupt, business-like, cutting through the light-hearted conversations of the kitchen. A woman walked over to me; we stood on the landing between the kitchen and the toilets, and I told her. She put her arm around me and led me to the faculty office.

I sat on the sofa in the office, bent forward, repeating the word 'no' over and over, and let the woman I had spoken to in the hallway go off to find Dave. Once Dave had been called out of his lecture, I was helped down the stairs to meet him under the stone archway at the college entrance; I gave Dave my bag and we drove away, back into a story we had hoped we had left behind.

I watch as two feet stop in front of my curtain and the soft pale blue walls are pulled back to reveal the chaos of a Friday night in A&E behind it. The nurse steps towards me. She checks my blood pressure and tells me it's very high. I ask her for more pain relief. I tell her morphine has always worked well for me in the past, but she can't give me anything more until I see a doctor; apparently the gynae doctor has been notified but it could be a while. I show her the halo of blood surrounding my body and she promises to return with some pads. I tell her I've been here before and that I know what's happening; I tell her how bad the pain is; I ask again for more painkillers, telling her this is my fifth time and that I know what I need to help me. I tell her about the epilepsy, hoping that will help me get seen sooner, but it doesn't make any difference. She responds with sympathy, repeating the words she's already told me: I must wait until the doctor sees me. She brings me a glass of water, some pads and a cardboard sick bowl and closes the curtain behind her.

I knew this would happen. I rang the Early Pregnancy Unit as soon as we got home this morning to tell them I was bleeding. I told them how bad my miscarriages are and they said the same thing they always say: that I can't see them until the pain is unbearable or I lose too much blood. I tried to follow Anna's advice and cried down the phone but it didn't work. I told them it's likely I'd end up in A&E, but they just repeated their instructions.

I sip my water; Dave passes me the sick bowl. I tuck it under my chin and we go back to watching the feet hurry past the closed curtain. I listen to the guy next to me tell the doctor he's drunk two bottles of vodka today and listen as the two pairs of feet meet in front of my curtain to discuss the woman a few beds down who is twenty-three weeks pregnant and also waiting for a doctor. I know I will be here a long time: that woman has more life in her than I do.

The longer I lie here the more I believe those curtains will never open. The night shift will end, new nurses and doctors will arrive and Dave and I will still be here. Me lying on a blood-soaked bed and Dave numb from hours sat on a grey plastic chair. The contractions are clawing at my stomach; my writhing is now accompanied by groans, and the sick bowl is filling up. Once again, I'm fighting my body and its desire to reject the child inside me. Maybe the pain wouldn't be as bad if I just gave in to Mother Nature's way of telling me it's over, but I can't, I'm not ready to let go. I vomit, Dave presses the call button again and two pairs of feet appear – a pair of black Converse trainers and some brown leather boots. The curtain is pulled open and I see Rach and Fran, my friend from Weigh and Pray who's also here in Cambridge whilst her husband trains to be a vicar.

The experience of miscarriage has always been a private one – well, as private as it can be with doctors and nurses shining torches up you and inspecting parts of your body you can barely look at yourself. It's a moment you share with strangers and never talk about again. The experience is so shocking that it's burned into your memory more vividly than the experience of pregnancy itself, but it's one you hide away in the secret place, tucked away behind insecure thoughts and ugly feelings about certain people. But as soon as Rach and Fran stepped into our blue-curtained world, my miscarriage was no longer a secret. I had witnesses.

Rach and Fran fussed over me; they talked to Dave when I couldn't. Where Dave and I had submitted ourselves to the fate of our situation, Rach and Fran reacted. When a nurse asked me to walk to the toilet to take a pregnancy test, they passionately pointed out that I couldn't walk and that the nurse's request was unfair. When I writhed and groaned and vomited, they called for help and kept calling until someone came. They fought for me. They cried for me. They got angry for me. They found help for me. They were my witnesses.

The doctor finally came. She told me it was probably too late to save anything; I could have told her that three hours ago. Rach and Fran were asked to step outside, and the blue curtains were pulled shut again, me, Dave, the doctor and a nurse on one side, Rach's black Converse trainers and Fran's brown leather boots on the other. The doctor tells me what she's going to do and then starts asking me questions in an attempt to distract me. I oblige, sharing her hope that talking about what I do with my days might actually stop me thinking about the fact that she's armed with forceps. I tell her I'm studying theology and that I'm doing some voluntary community work, and 'S****! That hurts!' She stops briefly, then tries again but the pain is too great, my reaction rising from the deep and yelling out across to the top of the curtain and into the chaos of the A&E ward.

'I'm afraid I've not managed to get everything out, so I'm going to try one more time, OK?'

I nod. The doctor's head disappears and she starts to ask what Dave does. I tell her he's training to be a vicar. She stops to look over at him, offering the usual reaction of surprise because of how young he looks and then over to me, a vicar's wife, once again screaming out expletives as she drags what was left inside me out, into the real world. Eventually she finishes, prescribes me some pain relief and tells me I'll be moved to another bed soon. The curtains are opened again, the doctor leaves and the nurse carries the bloody remains past Rach and Fran. They hug me, they cry with me, they ask me how I'm feeling and they laugh with me, describing how loudly I yelled expletives through the curtains and how the nurse thought Rach was my mum. The morphine finally kicks in and my body begins to relax.

We talk and we wait. They ask what the doctor did and I tell them. For the first time I am completely honest and don't gloss over the gory details – they are in this with me now. Their presence here is a visible commitment to walking through this messy, bloodstained journey with us.

As we wait to find out what's going to happen next, Dave fills the time pointing out to Rach and Fran how funny I am when I'm on morphine, but I don't mind. I just rest my eyes and listen to them chatting and laughing until another pair of feet appear under the curtains and another nurse comes to talk to me.

'We're going to keep you in overnight, just to keep an eye on you.'

'OK,' I respond, exhausted but kind of glad I was given permission to delay my return home and the life that comes with it.

'We'll come back to get you when we find an available bed for you.'

'OK. Ummm, I was wondering if there was anyone who could help me get cleaned up a bit?' I carefully lift the bedsheet to show the nurse what I'm lying in.

'Oh, yes, right, of course, I'll bring some stuff for you,' the nurse replies. All four of us watch her slip quickly back out through the curtains, wondering when we'll see someone again. Rach and Fran decide to take some form of action by heading out to get me supplies, phone chargers and clean clothes for the night.

'Could you get me some more pants as well?' I ask, knowing what I have will just need to be thrown away.

'Of course,' Rach responds. 'What kind of pants?'

'Massive ones,' I reply. 'The kind an old lady would wear.'

'I know exactly the kind of pants you mean!' Rach reassures me. 'Really comfy but very unattractive.'

'Exactly!' I reply, smiling. After hugs and a few extra requests for Dave, including chocolate and something to drink, Rach and Fran head off leaving us to wait. Me lying there, half-conscious, enjoying the effects of the morphine, and Dave sat next to me, holding my hand. Eventually a nurse and some porters arrive to move me to a ward. I try to explain to the nurse I can't move into a wheelchair until I'm cleaned up, having been left lying in the experience of a miscarriage for the past four hours. She quickly passes me some clothes and some disposable NHS pants along with some nappy-like pads before stepping out and closing the curtain behind her for a couple of minutes to let me sort myself out before being transported to the ward.

I am wheeled into my own swanky room. Dave and I comment on the positive side of getting a nice private room, rather like those moments when you find a parking space on a busy day. It's so much easier to instantly claim God's presence in the trivial than engage with or question his involvement in any deeper life or death moments. I'm hooked up to drips and more morphine, then Rach and Fran arrive, carrying bags of supplies and old lady pants. A new nurse arrives in the room to tell everyone they need to leave but I don't want to be left alone, not for the night, not after a day like today. 'Can my husband stay here with me?' I ask.

'No, you're not allowed anyone to stay,' she replies.

'But, please,' I start crying. 'Please, I don't want to be alone – there's plenty of space here and I'm in my own room.'

'I can just stay in this chair,' Dave adds.

'I'm sorry, but you're not allowed. You're all going to have to leave in the next ten minutes,' the nurse responds, then walks out the room.

'Let's go talk to her,' Fran says, and her and Rach head out to speak to the nurse. I can hear them begging her to change her mind, fighting for me, describing the trauma I've been through. These women are brave and strong and I think the nurse eventually realizes this and agrees to let Dave stay. A mattress, pillows and a blanket are placed on the floor next to my bed; a small victory, but one we never would have won without our advocates.

Fran and Rach leave us with tears, hugs and repeated requests to contact them if we need anything. Then Dave and I settle down to rest, him on a mattress on the floor next to my bed, my right arm hanging down and holding his hand. With nothing to say we just hold hands and try to sleep. My night is a mixture of flashbacks and waking in pain to call the nurse for more morphine. I've no idea if Dave is managing to sleep or if his night, like mine, is filled with the shock of the past twelve hours. At least I can numb my thoughts with morphine.

The morning greets us with tea, toast and promises of a visit by a consultant. Apparently, I will have to stay in hospital a bit longer because of the amount of pain relief I've taken. I doze and Dave contacts people, breaking the same news and facing the awkward responses to what we know is a helpless situation.

After our third cup of tea, a trio of consultants appear in my room with a thick file of notes. Few words are exchanged. I just keep staring at the amount of notes in my hospital file as they tell me that there's nothing more they can do. Why it took three highly qualified medical professionals to break this news to me, I don't know; maybe they think it's safer to travel in groups when delivering difficult news.

The day passes by with a limited choice of NHS sandwich fillings, more tea and my slow return to consciousness as the morphine wears off. Just before I'm discharged, Rach appears at the door again. 'I'm sorry, I couldn't stay away. I just wanted to see how you're doing.' I smile at her and we hug, Dave packs up our stuff as I tell her the uneventful news delivered by my army of medical professionals. Forms are signed, advice is given and the nurses move me into a wheelchair. Dave and Rach clumsily manage to wheel me into the lift, then Dave heads outside to get the car. Rach and I wait in the empty hospital foyer, the two of us looking through the glass-fronted hospital building and into the darkness of a late Sunday evening.

'We were going to call her Emiliana,' I tell Rach. 'We thought she was a girl.' The words echo in the empty, high-ceilinged corridor. It felt silly saying it out loud, but I wanted Rach to know; she was a witness. She knew Emiliana had lived as well, that Emiliana wasn't just someone Dave and I had made up. She was real.

'Oh, mate. I'm so sorry.'

'Thanks . . . Thanks for coming to the hospital too. No one's ever seen me miscarry before, apart from Dave and a load of doctors and nurses, but you know what I mean.'

'I just wish I could have done more.'

'Honestly, Rach, I can't think of anything else you could have done. Just you two being there and seeing what happened – well, it made it real.'

The headlights of the car swing round, briefly shining on us as Dave parks up. Rach takes the brakes off the wheelchair and pushes me forward to the car, into the darkness that waits outside.

I spend the next few days in bed or on the sofa cradling a hot water bottle and trying to push flashbacks of A&E out of my mind by watching trashy telly and sleeping. This morning, instead of turning the telly on straight away, I grab one of Dave's books from the pile on our desk in the corner of the living room. I flick through the introduction and begin reading the first chapter.

It describes how Jesus ate with outcasts, invited undesirables into his inner circle and welcomed those with bad reputations, bringing their stories into the community. It was this act of solidarity that gave authority to these previously insignificant lives. Although I'm still cringing at what Rach and Fran saw, their presence brought a legitimacy to my story that I'd never experienced until now. The look on their faces told me that miscarriage is as bad as I thought it was. This won't bring my baby back, but now it's been called out for what it is, I'm beginning to feel hopeful that this isn't the end of me.

Death

I look around the room and I instantly want to trash it. I want to shake off the time, energy and thoughts I've wasted on the mundane, all the stuff we've collected and the stupid, futile ideas and plans we had. I want to rip them from my skin, their vanity illuminated by the stark, final news of death.

Nothing.

Matters.

Any more.

Nothing.

The Best Cup of Tea I've Ever Tasted

~

'I've never cried at a funeral.'

'Really?'

'Yeah. To be honest, the only funerals I've been to were for elderly relatives. Of course I was sad they'd died, but they'd also lived long lives and most of them had been really sick for a long time before they died, so it was kind of a blessing they weren't suffering any more.'

We're sat in our usual positions: me on the sofa, Louise in the chair opposite. The room is warm and cosy and, as usual, it smells really good. I must remember to ask Louise what she uses to make the room smell so nice. Louise also looks lovely, as usual, with her soft blonde hair and glowing skin. She always looks so healthy; she's probably one of those people who never has a cold because she's been taking echinacea for years. I glance up at the fresh flowers in the vase on the windowsill behind her. They look like they've been gathered from a beautiful meadow and left to find their own place within the china jug, rather than being organized into any strict pattern.

'But that's what funerals are for,' Louise continues. 'If you don't cry at a funeral, then when can you cry?'

'Afterwards?' I ask tentatively. 'I thought it wasn't appropriate to cry at a funeral. I've never seen anyone else cry. Also, a lot of the time the family hosting the funeral have told us not to wear black because they wanted it to be a celebration.'

'I've been to funerals like that as well, but when you lose someone you need to grieve; you need to let yourself be sad.'

I look over at the tissue box, sat on the small wooden coffee table between our seats. 'But if I let myself be sad then I'm worried I'll lose control,' I confess, my gaze fixed on the box of tissues.

'Explain what you mean by that.'

'I'm scared that if I start crying, I'll never stop.'

'That won't happen,' she says, confidently.

'Are you sure?'

'Yes.' Louise nods her head, earnestly. 'You will eventually stop crying. Rarely does anyone lose control of their emotions when they're sad, apart from when they're under the influence of drugs or alcohol.'

'So, if I feel like crying then I should just cry?' I must sound like a child, but everything Louise is telling me is completely rocking my white, middle-class world.

'Yes, that's how you grieve.'

'But what about when I'm alone? Won't that make me depressed? I've had depression before; I'm worried it might make me depressed if I cry when I'm alone, plus it seems like a really sad thing to do, sadder than crying with other people, if you get what I mean?'

'Lizzie, crying can't make you depressed all by itself. In fact, it's the opposite. Numbing your emotions is way more likely to lead to depression.'

'What about if I cry when I'm by myself, though, isn't that more dangerous? Is that more likely to lead to depression?'

'Crying by yourself isn't a bad thing – you know that, right?'

'Well, I wasn't sure, really. I . . . I . . . I didn't know if it was OK. You know, whether I should let myself or not.' I grab a tissue from the rose-covered box.

'Lizzie,' Louise leans forward. 'You do know the only way you can move through this and feel joy again is if you let yourself cry? That's how you grieve. It's hard work, but you have to make the decision to let yourself be sad.'

'OK.' I grab a couple more tissues. 'It's just so tiring.'

'I know,' she responds in the beautiful, caring, reassuring way that makes me love her even more. 'Now, is it OK if we talk about your aunt's funeral for a bit, and how you're going to cope with it?'

'Yes, yes that's fine.'

'When is it?'

'Thursday.'

'How are you feeling about going?'

'Well, it's all so sudden and it's so sad. She died before her time and I think that makes it sadder.'

'Yes, yes, it does.'

'Plus, I'm all over the place. I'm sad because of the miscarriage and because of my aunt and I'm so confused because I don't know who I'm sad for at which time. It's all mixed up.' I lean forward and grab a couple more tissues, for the snot and the tears.

'Do you know what, I don't think you need to work out who you're sad about at which moment, you just need to let yourself be sad. Can I give you some homework?'

I crumple up the soggy tissue in my hand along with the others. 'I suppose so.'

'When you feel like crying, you need to just cry, wherever it is, whether you're with people or by yourself; if you're sad, just let yourself cry, don't hold it in. Is that OK?'

'Well, things are going to get pretty messy,' I say, looking back to the box of tissues. 'But if what you say is true, if crying is the only thing that will help me feel happy again, then I'll do it.'

'It might get messy, but it will be so worth it.'

'Thanks.' I hesitate, wondering whether to tell Louise what I'm thinking. I look over to her; she's so clever she probably knows what I'm thinking anyway. 'You know you were saying about how when we don't cry it makes us feel numb?'

'Yes.'

'Well, do you think that's why a cup of tea tastes so good after you've had a good cry? Almost like, in that moment, you've been fully human, fully alive, rather than numbing how you're feeling?'

'Maybe it is,' Louise replies, smiling.

'I know it sounds strange, but I think crying must affect your taste buds or something because tea tastes amazing after a good cry.'

'As hard as it is to express how we feel, it's the only way to experience the fullness of life, including how good a cup of tea tastes!' She smiles gently again. 'Is it OK if we stop here for today?'

'Yes, of course.' I wish I could stay with Louise forever and she could speak her wisdom over me, but I know she has other people to talk to; I can't keep her to myself. I stand up and walk over to give her a hug. I'm not sure if it's appropriate, but we've shared so much over the past few months I can't think of any better way to say goodbye. I leave the warm, fragrant room with that feeling of peace after you've cried and talked honestly with someone. I'm not sad; in fact, I feel a tiny bit more alive. I unlock my bike, strap on my helmet and cycle into town to meet Sheila, Rach and tiny Rach for coffee, with a new purpose. I have a job to do and I'm going to do it well.

It's Thursday and I'm at my aunt's funeral. The vicar is talking about something beautiful, about hope and a place where there are no more tears and no more sadness, a wonderful home where there is true rest – and my cheeks are wet with tears. We are sat behind my uncle, my cousin and her family. My brother, his wife, Lucy, me, Dave, Mum and Dad are staring up at the vicar in the pulpit. His words wash over me, soothing my soul as the tears fall, fall, fall. I think of Louise; I think of how proud she would be of me right now. I'm one of the few who isn't holding it together, one of the few in a packed church who looks a mess. I look down to the photo of my aunt on the front of the service booklet. Tears fall faster. I have nothing to absorb them with. My hand, already saturated with the salt water flowing from my eyes, slips across my face. I'm trying not to make a scene. I fear that constantly lifting my hand to my eyes to wipe tears will attract attention, that people will think I'm making a fuss. I'm only her niece. I can't look sadder than my cousin or my uncle – people might think I'm being melodramatic. I place my hands on my lap and just let the tears flow, a constant stream running down my face and my neck. I try to stop, but then I remember what Louise said, and I try to relax into my sadness – it's not pretty, but I don't care any more. I'm fighting my own battle of life and death here, and I'm determined to live.

At the end of the service we all file out and into the church hall. I queue up for a suspiciously over-brewed cup of tea served up in a classic eighties' porcelain cup. It tastes amazing.

23

Fear and Faith

'I'm pregnant.'

'Oh.'

Dave watches me as I break the news to my mum over the phone; we talk for a bit but there's nothing much to say.

'So?' Dave asks as soon as I hang up.

'She sounded kind of shocked and then worried,' I tell him. 'There wasn't really much she could say, really. It's not like we haven't been here before.' I take a sip of my cup of tea and lean back into the sofa.

'I know, but it's still good news.' Dave puts his arm around me and pulls me towards him.

'I'm just so scared,' I say into his jumper. 'Every twinge, every time I feel something in my tummy, I think it's happening again.'

'I'm scared too.' He squeezes me. 'There's not much we can do for now, except pray and wait.'

'Other people can pray; God doesn't listen to me.'

We fall back into anxious pregnancy mode easily. I ring the hospital to book an early scan for next week. I tell Red Tent and tiny Rach.

Every day I inject my tummy with Heparin to prevent blood clots and take a progesterone pessary to release more pregnancy hormones into my body. I don't like either; they're both awkward and painful, but in different ways. I don't even know if they make any difference; they didn't last time.

I'm about to head off to see Louise, but I know I can't cycle there and back without going to the toilet and I'm too scared to go. Ever since I peed on the pregnancy test and saw it was positive, I've been too scared to go to the toilet. I put on my coat and grab my handbag and keys; turning the door handle I realize I'm holding my legs together and doing that kind of desperate dance you see kids do before they're going to wet themselves. 'Oh man!' I'm going to have to go, there's no way I can hold it in, not on a twenty-minute bike ride.

I pull my trousers down and sit there looking at the magnolia wall in front of me. I need to look but I can't; I don't want to look. Once I've emptied my bladder, which took a really long time, I look down really quickly, my heart beating in my throat. No, it's OK, there's no blood.

'You need to find a way to help you feel more in control,' Louise tells me. Today she's wearing a baby-blue jumper and it makes her hair look more blonde and her skin even more glowy. 'You've been through a lot of trauma; you weren't prepared for the last miscarriage – everything was out of control, so it might help if you put together a hospital bag just in case.'

'What, like the one women have in case they go into labour?'

'Yes, but this will be your emergency miscarriage bag, just in case you have to go to hospital. It doesn't mean you're going to need it. But just having something there, ready and packed with the things you might need, might help you feel more in control.'

When I get home, I go upstairs straight away to pack my hospital bag. I grab an old rucksack from the top shelf of the wardrobe and think back to the last miscarriage and what I needed. Pants, I need spare pants. I don't want to wear those paper ones or, worse, the nappy pants they gave me last time. Pyjamas, a top, body spray. I found an almost empty tube of toothpaste in a washbag and put that in, as well as some nice moisturiser from a gift set Dave's sister gave me for Christmas, and some lip balm. I zip everything up and leave it in the corner of the bedroom. I pause to look at it. 'Please God, please, I don't want to use this bag. Not until nine months' time, anyway.'

'So, judging by your dates you should be about seven weeks pregnant. Is that correct?'

'Yes,' I reply to the sonographer.

'OK, then, shall we have a look?'

I glance over to Dave and the hospital bag sat on the floor by his chair. I squeeze his hand and look up at the ceiling tiles.

'Here we are!' she declares.

'What!' I turn my head to look at the screen.

'Here's your baby!'

'Oh wow, look at that!' Dave's voice comes out really high and we both look at each other in surprise. 'So, does it look healthy?' he asks in a really deep voice, emphasizing his manliness.

'Oh, yes, it's a healthy size and it's got a really strong heartbeat, look.' She presses some keys on the computer and zooms in to show us. Still, after all the scans I've had I have no idea what I'm looking at, but apparently it's good, so that's great.

'So the last time we had a scan the baby was quite small and the heartbeat was weak, but you're saying this one is OK, that it's a good size and the heartbeat is good?' I ask her.

'Yes, it's a really healthy size – in fact, it looks like it could be a few days further along than we thought. I'd probably put you at about eight weeks.' She removes the probe and passes me a huge wad of tissues. 'Don't worry,' she reassures us. 'This is really good news!'

When I come out from behind the curtain after getting dressed again, the sonographer hands Dave the scan photos. 'Here you are – here's some photos of your baby. You need to go to reception and ask to be booked in for a scan in a couple of weeks.'

'OK. Thanks, bye,' I say, as we walk out, Dave staring at the photos in his right hand, his left hand carrying the hospital bag.

I can't look at the scan photos, they scare me. I told Dave to put them somewhere out of sight. I'm not sure if he's looking at them when I'm not around, but despite receiving the best news we could have imagined, I just don't trust it. I'm encouraged, but I'm not relaxed; the stakes are higher now. We've seen it, we've seen a heartbeat. Every night, as I lie on my side, which is apparently the best position to help the pessary go where it's meant to go, Dave and I pray. We pray for the baby. The prayers are short but at least we're praying, even with the hospital bag still sat in the corner.

'Dave! It's happening,' I scream from the downstairs toilet.

'What? Let me in!'

I unlock the door.

'I think I'm miscarrying.'

'What do you mean? How do you know?'

'It feels like last time, my stomach is really painful and I think I've seen a spot of blood. I can't do this again! I can't do this!'

'What do we do?'

'Get the number for the Early Pregnancy Unit off the fridge and ring it!' He runs back to the kitchen and I move to the sofa and curl up, my legs and arms protecting my tummy. I thought it might be different this time, because of the heartbeat.

'They said you have to wait until the pain and bleeding get worse and then call them.'

'I knew it. I should have just cried down the phone again.'

Ten minutes later there's a knock at the door; Dave answers. I'm sat in the lounge and can't really hear who it is. Black hair with a streak of pink running through it, chunky orange necklace – Rach walks into the room. 'Oh, mate! I got your message. What's happening?' She sits down next to me on the sofa as I describe what I'm feeling. She suggests going to the hospital, but we tell her there's no point. For now, we need to wait, so we drink tea and Rach feeds me chocolate.

Messages keep beeping through on my phone from the rest of my Red Tent ladies. Tiny Rach said she's coming round in a bit once her daughter is asleep, so we continue to drink tea and wait. Dave and Rach watch every movement I make, all three of us willing nothing to happen. Tiny Rach arrives and suggests we pray. Rach and tiny Rach pray for us, our heads bent low, desperate for an answer. I know they long for this baby to live as much as I do.

Two days later and I'm OK, there's no more blood and I just need to wait one more week until the next scan. I know I need to stop being afraid of my pregnancy, but I can't. It's impossible. The only way I could feel super-chill about this pregnancy is if I was dead inside. But I'm not. I'm a living, breathing, sweaty, stressy mess and now I have to go to church. I really wish I wasn't training to be a vicar's wife. I don't care if this is a learning opportunity, I'd rather be sat on the sofa watching box sets and eating Doritos than going to church. But Dave is preaching and I promised I'd go. Today he's preaching on healing. I believe healing is possible. I'm just not sure I believe it's possible in my life.

I don't know how he manages it, but somehow Dave preaches a really good sermon. Once he's finished his talk, he then invites people in the church to come forward and ask for healing. There are so many people walking up to the front of church that Dave asks the vicar, the curate and me to join him at the front to pray. He also hands me a small bottle of oil to anoint those who want it with the sign of the cross on their foreheads.

Until we came here, I didn't really know anything about anointing, but Jane does it all the time at Red Tent and I love it. I feel the sensation of the oil slowly soaking into my skin, of absorbing the prayers of healing and wholeness spoken over me.

Dave invites the youth group forward first and we pray for them one by one, then anoint them with oil as a symbol that Jesus claims them as his own. Once they've all been prayed for, Dave asks them to stay up the front and join us in praying for people. So now I'm here, right at the front of church, holding a bottle of oil and standing between two impressionable teenage prayer buddies. A lady from the congregation walks up to us; she describes her years of suffering with depression then holds out her hands and asks for prayer. I can't believe someone is asking me to pray for them. Me? I feel sorry for her; she should have gone to someone else. I also feel responsible for the two teenagers stood either side of me. Are they expecting me to know what I'm doing? What if it doesn't work? What if nothing happens? According to Dave's sermon, anyone can pray for healing, so I have no choice but to lay my hands on her shoulders and begin to pray.

As my hand rests on this woman the doubts I'm carrying with me dissolve, replaced by the overwhelming desire to bless her. The two teenagers either side of me are amazing, they're really going for it; the innocence of their faith means they don't hold back or moderate their petitions. I follow their lead. I begin to pray boldly, lifted by the expectancy of my praying companions. I pray for this lady to be healed. I'm focused on her and her need for God, but with every petition towards the God of healing, faith increases for my own situation. I'm so conscious of the life inside me, and as I pray for hope, I know I'm asking for myself as well. I mark the shape of the cross with oil on her forehead, and the traces of her faith remain on my fingers, soaking into my skin, making it soft again.

'I think I've been healed!' The guy next to us opens his eyes and starts moving his shoulder around. 'My shoulder doesn't hurt any more!' He lifts his arm up and down and circles it around. 'This is amazing!' He hugs the cluster of people praying for him and rushes off to tell his wife.

'We were not expecting a miracle.'

I read the heading on the sheet of paper Jane has handed me. After yesterday, and our morning of praying for healing in church, I'm now relaxing on sofas at Esther's house, snuggled between Sheila and Rach and watching Hugo, her house rabbit, hop around the room, bowing his head in anticipation of a little head scratch from each of us; he reminds me of Professor Hopalong. I wish our Cambridge landlord would have let us bring him with us. As we talk and laugh and share stories, I struggle to be fully present. My mind rushes between anxiety and the memory of yesterday at church. I'm scared of what could happen, I'm scared of being in pain, but I'm also scared of hoping for a miracle.

'Let's pray,' Jane says. We open the folded sheet of A4 handed to us and begin to read the first few lines together.

A LITTLE LITURGY OF NEW BEGINNINGS
Pray with us, God who is our loving parent[1]
Take our hands in yours
And place our feet upon the rock of your faithfulness
Pray with us Jesus Christ
Enter the depth of our souls
And know the cry of our hearts on this journey
Pray for us Holy Spirit
Find the words for our longings and cover us gently
With your warm, bright wings[2]
WE WERE NOT EXPECTING A MIRACLE
Heavenly Father, we're too afraid to hope for a miracle
We may have hoped for miracles in the lives of others, but
not for ourselves[3]
Yet Lord, Red Tent is a miracle for each one of us
A channel of your grace, a place of healing and love.
Thank you for laughter and tears, for sharing and trust,
For the knowledge of your presence every step of the way.[4]
O Lord, we want to see your miracles.
Help us to hope again;
Give us the courage to ask for miracles in our own lives,
Forgive us and help us to trust in your goodness,[5]
Thank you for laughter and tears, for sharing and trust,
For the knowledge of your presence with us every step of
the way.[6]

'Let's take a few moments to thank God for each other,' says
Jane.

We pray with our whole hearts. It's so much easier to pray
miracles for everyone else in the room than it is for myself.
Instead of squeezing life out of every second before my next
scan, I know I need to step back and remember there is more

to my story than this moment. If I don't stop to breathe in the life and beauty around me, then I'm worried this baby and whatever happens to it will define my future, as well as these past two weeks, and I don't want that. There's more to me than this, surely?

I've sat in so many church buildings and heard people talk about prayer and miracles and healing. So many people have prayed for us, we've even had a couple pray for us who apparently have a 100 per cent success rate of praying for people to have babies. I know people who have been healed just like that guy at church and I also know people who haven't. I've heard a lot of preachers talk about healing, but I've not heard many embrace the tension between healing and unanswered prayer. Some provide quick answers that sound a bit like a cop-out, declaring you don't have enough faith, or your sin or your family's sin got in the way. But I don't think God works like that. God's not a genie or a fairy godmother, only granting wishes when the conditions are perfect. God is far more complex than that. I don't totally understand him, I don't know how he works, but I know Christians are meant to have hope. I'm just confused as to what I should hope for. Is it in God? Is it in healing? Is it in having a baby? I feel pregnant, I feel hopeful, but I still have my hospital bag.

Later that evening, I'm lying on the sofa trying not to worry, and my phone rings.

'Can Tibby and I come over to visit you?' asks tiny Rach.

'Yeah, of course!'

Half an hour later Rach arrives; we wrestle the pushchair up the step and through our front door. Tibby doesn't have time to say 'hi' to me because, as soon as she's out of the pushchair, she's off crawling into the kitchen to play with the buttons on the washing machine.

'Coffee?'

'Coffee would be amazing! So, I hope you don't mind but I told my spiritual director about you. I asked her to pray for you and she's just sent me a message with some thoughts that came to her whilst she was praying. You know, things she thinks God has to say to you. Now, you don't have to do anything with them; I just wanted to share them with you, is that OK?'

'Totally! I'm always up for hearing any wisdom someone might have.' I carry the coffee through to the lounge and Rach carries Tibby.

'OK.' Rach pulls her notebook out of her handbag and flicks through the pages to find her notes, 'So . . . first of all she was reminded of this verse, 1 John 4:18.' She looks down to read from her notebook: 'There is no fear in love. But perfect love drives out fear, because fear has to do with punishment. The one who fears is not made perfect in love.' She looks up. 'I think we can both agree that's pretty relevant for right now.'

'Uh-huh,' I nod.

She looks over to Tibby who's playing with the coasters on our coffee table, bashing them against each other, then putting them in her mouth to suck on. 'Oh, Tibby!' She grabs the soggy coaster out of her mouth.

'It's fine, don't worry about it.'

Tibby looks over to me and puts her arms out.

'I think she wants you to pick her up,' Rach tells me. 'Are you OK with that?'

I pause to think: normally I'd never hold a child, it makes me feel too vulnerable, but Tibby's different.

'It's OK, I think I'd like to hold her.' I lean down to pick her up and she sits on my lap, a coaster in each hand. Rach smiles.

'So, there were a couple of other things she said,' Rach checks her notes. 'She believes God says "Do not be ashamed of your past."' She looks at me, to check I'm OK.

'Yep, I think there's definitely something in that,' I say, hugging Tibby closer, my mind suddenly filled with empty cafés, pregnancies, loss and the pain of not measuring up.

'She also said you should read Psalm 139.'

'Oh.' I was hoping for some words about healing or new life or confirmation that the baby was going to be alright, not a psalm. I've not read Psalm 139 for ages because there's this bit in it that talks about God 'knitting us together in our mother's womb' and I just don't know what to do with that.

Later that night I decide to look up Psalm 139. I search it for promises of healing and there aren't any. I read again and again, but instead of miracles, it just talks about God's knowledge of me, of my thoughts and my fears and of his constant presence wherever I go. I sit there wondering what this has to do with my situation and read through the psalm one more time.

'I think God's most concerned with how I relate to him,' I write in my journal. 'He wants me to know him as he knows me. It's not because my pregnancy isn't important, but I need to remember my life and God are far bigger than this moment I'm living in right now.'

24

It Happens

~

I'm trying not to get my hopes up, but I have to say I'm feeling quietly confident. I'm feeling good; people are saying I'm starting to look pregnant – this could be it; this could be the one. We park up at the hospital, walk past the swanky new maternity ward and into the Early Pregnancy Unit where we find our seats in the waiting room, staring at the same posters, flicking through the same magazines, and having the same conversation about whether you're still awarded the free cinema ticket for taking a chlamydia test if the results are positive. I can feel my bare legs sticking to the fake leather seats; a breeze rattles through the beige office blinds; I'm starting to feel more nervous. I glance around at the couples sat quietly around the waiting room, holding hands and chatting in hushed voices. I wonder what their stories are. I wonder why they're here. Are they scared too?

I grab Dave's hand. 'What if it isn't good news?' I whisper to him. He looks at me and squeezes my hand.

'We don't know that yet, hon, just try to stay positive.' We sit holding hands, staring at a poster about domestic abuse and listening to the nurses running up and down the corridor.

'Elizabeth Lowrie?'

We walk towards the nurse, hands still tightly locked together; the sweaty heat from outside isn't enough to separate us in this moment. The sonographer leads us into her darkened room; I head towards the blue curtain drawn across half the room, ready to get undressed, when she stops me.

'My records here say you should be at ten weeks so we should be able to see what we need to with an external scan on your tummy. Come and lie down on the bed here and we'll give it a go first.'

Surprised and a little bit relieved she's not going straight in with the internal scan, I lie down on the bed, grab hold of Dave's hand again and start talking at her. I tell her that it's the first time we've got to a ten-week scan without miscarrying and how good the eight-week scan was, how strong the heartbeat was and how happy the doctor was at the results. She nods encouragingly, making positive sounds as she presses the probe on my tummy and glancing at the screen in front of her. I keep talking as she scans, my words of how far we've come feeding the strength of the heartbeat inside me. She looks up from her screen. 'I'm not getting a very clear picture; do you mind if we try an internal scan?'

'No, that's fine.' The sonographer passes me tissues to wipe the jelly off my tummy before I change behind the blue curtain and appear with a larger tissue thing wrapped around my waist. I repeat the ritual of lying down and holding Dave's hand. The sonographer puts the probe inside me and we wait. I've stopped talking; there are only so many times I can tell her how good the first scan was and she doesn't seem to want to talk. She's not said anything since she started scanning. She keeps clicking on her screen, not ready to show us what she's found. The silence continues. Either she loves suspense or something isn't right

here. The baby's dead, the baby's dead, the baby's dead. I decide
to repeat those words over and over to myself, hoping that by
saying the worst, it won't happen. She's still scanning and studying the screen, moving the probe around inside me, placing it
at all sorts of funny angles. The baby's dead, the baby's dead,
the baby's dead. I say it to gain control, to be one step ahead, to
deal with the pain before it happens. I can't look at Dave, I just
keep chanting, seeking refuge in the words running through
me. The sonographer removes the probe and wheels her chair
round to look at us.

'I'm really sorry, but your baby's died.' Something rises within
me like a wave and suddenly nothing else matters. My reality crashes head-first into all the petty things I've ever worried
about or wanted, smashing them into tiny pieces. Nothing else
matters. This is, this was, everything. I make a sound I didn't
know I could make. I'm crying, but in a way I've never experienced. It comes from deep within, ripping through my insides,
my whole body invested in this expression, it's so physical. I'm
wailing, I'm actually wailing; tears are merely a by-product of
what my whole being is trying to express. I look to Dave, who's
weeping by the side of the bed. What have we done to deserve
this? The sonographer waits for me to calm down before talking. She shows us images and explains what she's found. She
talks about options and operations and drugs and hands us
leaflets, inviting us to wait in the counselling room after I've
got dressed. We move from the darkness of the sonogram room
into the pale off-white glow of the counselling room. Sitting,
holding hands, crying, there are no words for times like these. I
can't cope with what I'm feeling, so words are beyond me right
now. The tears slow down. The shock remains, but we have to
make a decision before we leave, and reluctantly start looking
at the documents handed to us. I'm struggling to read, or at

least I can see words but my eyes are just scanning over them, unable to register anything I'm seeing. A nurse comes in to see if we've decided.

'What would you recommend?' Dave asks.

'I'd go with the medically managed miscarriage.'

'I suppose we'll have that, then,' I respond, unwilling and unable to invest myself in this decision. More leaflets are handed out and we're sent home with instructions, pills and a date to return and get this baby out of me.

'This is s***!' Sheila says looking over at me, her left hand cupped over her face, protecting her eyes from the sun.

'Yep,' I reply. Sheila and Elis arrived about half an hour ago. They came as soon as they received my message. Elis is supposed to be at a seminar on grief but he said he didn't care, he'd rather be here. I can hear the birds chatting away in the branches of the tree that leans over us, its leaves rustling in the soft breeze running through the warmth of an early afternoon in June. Sheila and I are lying beneath the tree, sunlight and shade speckled over our faces. I can hear Dave and Elis chatting outside the garden shed to the right of us; for some reason they're getting the barbecue out. Is Dave really thinking of having a barbecue? Isn't that inappropriate? Aren't barbecues meant to be fun? No amount of barbecued meat, no matter how tasty, is going to help us right now.

'This is s***!' Sheila repeats again.

'Uh-huh.' I should still be crying, inconsolable. But I feel quite calm. It might have something to do with the wailing that came out of me in the hospital. 'Maybe I'm just not meant to have children; maybe it's just not going to happen.'

'You don't know that.'

'Well, it feels that way.'

'I know. I'm sorry.' Sheila passes me the bag of Doritos sat between our sunbeds. 'So when are you going back in?'

'In three days.' I stuff a handful of crisps into my mouth. 'They've given me a pill to stop the pregnancy hormones, then when I go back in they'll give me another pill to start the miscarriage. I just don't want it to start at home. I can't do that again. I don't want to end up in A&E. I've just got to get through the next three days.'

'Well, we can pray about that.'

'I suppose so.'

The others start arriving about 7. Dave, Sheila, Elis and I have eaten our barbecue dinner and are now sat inside. The patio doors are left open, inviting the cool early evening air into the lounge. Rach arrives first with a great bagful of crisps and chocolate. 'I didn't know what to do, so I just ran round the supermarket throwing things into a basket.' Then Bee, Esther and Ben, Jane and tiny Rach. Bee brings chips, and Rach brings magazines. They listen as I talk, growing more distant from my story every time I tell it, my words breaking each of us one by one, with tears and tissues shared around the room.

'Is it OK if we pray?' Jane asks.

'I suppose so.' I don't know what prayer can do at this point but I know for certain that I'm not in control of what's going on, so I might as well hand my situation over to someone who might be able to do something about it. The red sunset fills the sky, leaving a pink glow hovering over this holy huddle gathered around us. Heads are bowed, hands lifted up to the heavens and words are shared from a deep place. I think I'm praying; I know I'm with them in this moment and I know the friends filling this room will carry me if I fail to make it to Jesus' feet. Words fall from their mouths, broken, salt-stained words, spoken from the heart and interspersed with expletives – yes, that's right, Jane swore. They believe God is here; they rant, they question, they make demands from him as sadness and anger is spoken into this sunset-stained room.

Three days later I'm lying on a hospital bed in a ward with five other women. The nurse has just given me a pessary to start the contractions. Why is it every gynaecological experience involves people putting hands up you? As if the reason I'm here isn't shameful enough, I've now had a nurse greet me by putting her hand up my bottom.

I can hear the others through the curtained walls, chatting to partners or nurses. It's strange because most of them don't sound bothered, it's all very matter of fact. Maybe that's what helps them cope.

'Hi, Elizabeth. Right, you've had the pessary so you should start to get contractions. These will make you need to go to the toilet and will probably give you diarrhoea. I need you to use the toilet directly opposite this ward. Whenever you go to the toilet, you have to use one of these disposable bedpans to collect everything that comes out of you, even if it's just diarrhoea. You have to collect everything, write your name on the bedpan with the pen provided in the toilet, and ring the bell to call the nurse. You will need to keep doing this until we can confirm all pregnancy matter has left your body. Do you understand?'

'Yes.'

'Good. There's a drinks machine in the corridor and you need to try to stay standing and walk around; this will help speed things up, and hopefully you will be home soon.'

'OK.'

Ten minutes later I'm kneeling on the floor with my face pushed into the bed, wailing.

'I'm calling the nurse,' Dave rushes out, quickly bringing a nurse with him.

'Elizabeth, you need to stand up.'

'I can't! I'm in too much pain; I'm going to throw up.' My head is lifted up and a bedpan placed under my chin just in time.

'Can you stand up now?'

'No. It's just too painful.'

'I'll get you some paracetamol.' What the . . .! What is it with hospitals and paracetamol? If I just needed a paracetamol, I'd be at home. I obediently take the paracetamol, knowing it won't touch the pain dragging through my body.

We wait an acceptable amount of time with Dave rubbing my back and my face planted in the mattress again before calling the nurse.

'You need to be standing up.'

'I can't.'

'Has the paracetamol not helped?'

'No.' Obviously.

'Oh, normally people don't need much pain relief.' Surely she's lying. 'I'll see if I can get you some morphine.'

'Thanks.'

The nurse comes back with a syringe and squirts morphine in my mouth as I kneel on the floor. Finally, some relief.

'Right, you need to stand up and start walking around.' Reluctantly I move my very sleepy body and stand upright.

'I'm sorry, I was just in so much pain. I'm surprised no one else has needed pain relief, they're all really quiet.'

'Yeah, well, none of them were as far along as you were. Most of them are here for terminations.'

I keep pacing up and down the hospital ward, until the diarrhoea arrives. Ashamed, I write my name next to it, call the nurse and head back to the ward.

'Would you like a drink?' Dave asks awkwardly, both of us uncomfortable with his helplessness in this hellish experience.

'Yeah.'

'What would you like?'

'Surprise me.' With the drinks choices limited by the NHS, Dave comes back with Ovaltine, which tastes amazing. I watch a nurse walk past the ward and quickly lie down on the bed to enjoy my drink.

'You need to be standing up!'

My trips to the toilet become more frequent. Each time I stand up and turn round to face the bedpan, scared to look but desperate to see. I write my name, call the nurse and return to Dave.

I watch the other women walking back and forth to the toilet and the nurse going in after them. Eventually they begin to leave, one by one. I watch, wondering if I'll ever get to escape this hellish ward and the angry nurse telling me to stand up all the time.

'Let's go for a walk.' Dave puts his arm through mine, I hobble down the corridor and he shows me the drinks machine serving the Ovaltine. We both get a drink and head back to the ward, but we never get to drink them. My breathing gets heavier and the pain in my stomach increases, Dave standing next to me rubbing my back, trying to help me breathe deeper, calmly coaching me, breathing with me.

'I have to go to the toilet!' I rush into the small room and I feel it leave my body; it feels huge and I feel empty. I sit there for a while but eventually I know I have to get up. Slowly I stand up and turn to face it. Bloody and messy, ugly and sad, but there, filling the bedpan. I write my name by it, ring the bell and leave.

At home, Dave leads me to the sofa, lays a blanket over me and sits next to me on the edge of the sofa, stroking my hair. 'John rang, and he said he's going to pop over in a bit for a chat.' John is great, a vicar who's normal and familiar with struggle.

'Okay.' Exhausted, and glad I can finally lie down, I close my eyes. I hear the doorbell and voices floating down the corridor as I rest.

'Hey, hon.' Dave's back in the lounge, sat next to me, stroking my hair again. 'Has he gone?'

'Yeah.'

'What did he say?'

'He talked about what it was like when his son went to prison and then he said something that was really helpful and I think it's because it came from him.'

'What did he say?'

'There's s*** with kids and s*** without them.'

25

Who Told You That You Were Naked?

You belong.

Just because you don't have kids doesn't mean you don't belong.

God says you have value.

Jesus hung out with people who didn't fit.

He would have hung out with you.

Your losses don't make you less significant.

Your childlessness doesn't mean your life is worth less.

You know this.

You know this.

You know this.

I'm currently crouched down, hiding in the bike sheds behind the back wall of the college chapel. My head tells me I belong in that crowd of people chatting and having fun, but I can't move, my feet are stuck here, glued to the concrete floor. I was determined to show my face and see people. I've needed these past few weeks at home to recover, but I can't stay there forever. Dave was sceptical when I told him I was going to come to college today, but I wanted to be here. I want to be part of this community.

I intentionally arrived late. I cycled in through the metal gates, turned right into the car park and then left between the back wall of the chapel and the high, ancient red-brick wall surrounding the college grounds. I squeezed my bike into the bike shed, removed my helmet, locked my bike up and headed towards the quad and the sound of laughter. But as soon as I turned the corner around the side of the chapel, I saw them. Everyone. Students, spouses and kids moving as one around the quad on a family treasure hunt. I know it's ridiculous. I'm not a 13-year-old girl any more, I'm a 6ft grown-up trying to cram my oversized frame behind a bicycle, but I had no choice – 'I was afraid . . . so I hid'.[1]

This isn't the first time I've hidden. Over the past few months I've spent a lot of my time hiding in the toilets, so whilst the bike shed is a lot harder to hide in, it has expanded my repertoire of hiding places. Sheila and I have been slowly gathering a list of venues and occasions we think it's acceptable to avoid. The list includes baby showers, all-age church services, kids' birthday parties and Mother's Day, especially church on Mother's Day. I don't want to be the kind of person who chooses to opt out of life and community – I hate missing out – but as I wade deeper into this dark season of loss, I can't escape this voice that keeps rising up from within me telling me I don't belong.

My legs are cramping so I slowly stand up; besides, I know I can't stay here all afternoon. I want to just grab my bike and go home, but I know I'll just feel worse; the extrovert in me won't be able to withstand missing out. I wait a bit longer until the last voice goes into the chapel and I shimmy out from between the bikes to join them.

Two days later, I'm lying on the sofa waiting for Sheila to come and keep me company whilst Dave's at his lectures. Some days are better than others, and yesterday was a bad day. I should be an expert at living with loss by now, but my grief continues to take me by surprise; it keeps rising up out of nowhere and knocking me down again. Some days my sadness makes me so distressed it triggers a fit, and then I'm right back at square one. Sheila keeps telling me I need to be kind to myself, but I'm not very good at it, and she knows it; that's why she's practically living at our house – to make sure I take it easy. She's taking her role very seriously, which is just one of the many reasons why I love her; it's also way more fun.

'Right, I brought crisps and some Ryan Gosling films because, well, I love him.' Sheila comes straight into the kitchen, lays the crisps and DVDs on the worktop and puts the kettle on. 'Shall we have a coffee?'

'Yeah, that would be great.' Just the fact Sheila has come to look after me sets me off and tears start to fall down my face. 'Oh man, this wasn't meant to happen straight away; you only asked me if I wanted coffee.'

'It's OK, you're meant to be sad.' We hug, I cry, then I make the coffee because Sheila doesn't know how to use our fancy brewing equipment yet, and we resume our usual places on the sofa with my soft blanket draped over us.

'Before Ryan, I've been thinking about how learning to share our stories has been so significant for us.' Sheila turns to look at me face-on. 'We should write a blog.' She grabs her phone. 'I've been looking at some infertility blogs recently and, well, they're terrible!' She holds up her phone to show me. 'They're either really angry and bitter or they just talk about how life is so amazing now they have a baby.'

'Google "recurrent miscarriage blogs",' I tell her. We find a few and scroll through the stories, all of them written once the author had their 'rainbow baby'. 'Oh man, these are awful.

What if your life doesn't look like that? Not everyone's story ends that way.'

'I know,' Sheila adds, 'and where's the vulnerability? They're not writing about what it feels like in the moment, they're writing after it's all over.'

'Google "Christian infertility blogs".'

'Argh! I think these are worse, the titles are terrible.' She reads some out. She's right.

'They're all just encouraging this idea that you can only get your happy ending if you have a baby.' I open the bag of crisps, pour them into a bowl and place the bowl between us on the sofa. 'It's so unhealthy.'

'It's scary,' says Sheila 'They're encouraging this obsession with getting pregnant and we both know that's just not helpful.' She grabs a handful of crisps. 'This is why we *need* to write a blog, Lizzie! We've learned so much at Red Tent and we can share it with people and we can share our stories.'

'If we do a blog, then I think the guys should write stuff too.'

'Yes! That's a great idea! Ooo, I'm getting excited now! Let's write down what we'd include in a blog,' Sheila says, rooting around her bag for her notebook and pen.

Blog
- it will be honest – written from the middle – not when we're all thin with babies
- different voices, including the guys
- little liturgies – ask Jane if we can share the liturgies she's put together for us
- talk about Red Tent
- recipes – we need Jane's flapjack recipe, Sheila's pistachio loaf and my cheese bread
- no Christian clichés

- no images of babies or cots
- get Dave to create the website

'Also, whilst we're talking about sharing our stories more publicly, I think we need to talk to Spice,' Sheila says. 'I think Red Tent should host Spice one night and we should share what we've gone through.'

'Really?'

'Yes, I really think we need to do it, Lizzie. Not just for us, but for them. We should tell them about Red Tent and how it's helped us and encourage them to be more open about what's going on in their lives. Also, they might know someone who's struggling with infertility and maybe we can help them understand what it's like so they can help other people.'

'I suppose so. I mean, I think everyone should have a Red Tent.'

'Of course they should! I think they also need to hear our stories, Lizzie.' Sheila grabs my arm. 'They need to know what's happened to us. Our stories belong in Spice, just as much as anyone else's.'

'You're right . . . I think it would be healing for us too.'

'Exactly! Right, I'm going to talk to Jane and Rach about it.'

When I arrive at the college today, I lock my bike up in the bike shed and walk straight towards the quad and into the chapel, celebrating a secret victory in my soul.

After the service, Dave and I head to the dining hall, sharing food and the long trestle table with friends. Whilst Dave talks to one of his tutors about theology, I chat with one of the trainee vicars sat next to me about his essay deadlines and summer placements. He's going to a big church in London and Dave and I are going to Cornwall for a month. Sheila and Elis are going to Singapore – which is way more exotic – but I'm still looking forward to the Cornish coastline and cream teas.

As we eat our apple crumble and custard, he pauses, leaves his spoon to slide into the custard and turns his face to look at me.

'Erm . . . Lizzie, I heard about what happened. I'm really sorry.' He offers one of those apologetic smiles I've been getting a lot of recently and goes back to his crumble.

'Thanks.'

'I was thinking about you guys.' He keeps talking as he eats. I keep my eyes fixed on my pudding, hoping I won't start crying. 'I was putting the kids to bed last night. I thought about you guys and how sad it is, you know, what happened.'

'Thanks.' We continue eating in silence. I know he was trying to help. I know he was brave to talk to me, when so many people who know are so unsure of what to say that they keep their distance. But something about what he said made me feel uncomfortable. It is sad. He's right. But I don't want people to think that when they look at me. I don't want them to think my life is sad. What's happened is sad, yes, but I don't want the sadness of my story to define me. It's like all those blog posts Sheila and I were looking at the other day: their authors waiting for the joyful climax of their stories before they shared what happened previously because it was too sad, or the others who are so focused on achieving the only happy ending they could imagine. I want my story to go on; I don't want it to stop when I lose a child or even if I have a child. This story I'm living now is just a sub-story, it's part of something way bigger. I guess that's why Jesus hung out with people who had sad stories, to show them they were more than their sadness.

Sharing our stories from the messy middle of life sounds amazing and brave and it's something I want to do, but as I walk through the stone archway entrance the following week, across the quad towards the Principal's Lodge and head up the wide-carpeted staircase to a large kitchen filled with teapots and female voices, I'm beginning to seriously regret agreeing to take this leap into vulnerability.

'Oh, my goodness, I can't believe we're doing this!' Sheila bounds over to me and grabs my arm.

'I know!' I look around at the women I've spent so long avoiding and panic rises up, making my heart beat faster.

'I'm so proud of you ladies!' says Rach, as she hugs us enthusiastically. We all grab a cupcake from the kitchen, smiling hello as we walk past people, then head into the lounge where Jane, Esther and Erin are waiting for us.

'Lizzie, I think you should go first,' says Esther.

'Mmmm,' Sheila adds.

'Yeah,' agrees Rach.

'Definitely,' says Anna.

'OK,' I respond. 'I feel really nervous, though. I think I'm just going to have to read from my sheet.'

'That's fine,' says Jane. At 8 o'clock Rach brings everyone through. Some of the female trainee vicars have joined us as well, which is great because I think they're all awesome and maybe one day, when I'm grown up, I might become one of them. Jane lights a candle, of course; Rach explains a bit about Red Tent, and then she hands over to me.

'I'm afraid I feel a bit nervous about this, so I'm going to read you what I've written.' A room full of women nod in unison. I can feel my face already going red. I pick up my sheet and begin to read it.

'I would imagine most of us, if not all of us here, have cried in the toilet at some point in our lives. I feel like crying in the toilet sums up my experience over the last five years. There's the crying when your period starts and you really thought you could be pregnant this time, there's crying when you see blood and you were pregnant, there's crying when someone tells you

they're expecting a baby, and there's crying when you're surrounded by mothers and mums-to-be and you're mourning the
life you long for. In that crying is also anger with yourself for
being such a horrible person and struggling to celebrate with
your friends. Crying in the toilet also illustrates the loneliness
and isolation of how you feel; no one knows, sometimes not
even your husband.

'If I'm honest, this feeling of isolation became more acute
when I arrived here, at the college – although this is no reflection on the amazing friendships I made when I arrived. It was
my reaction to how I was coping with life and the loneliness
of feeling very much in the minority. It got so bad that last
summer, when I had my fourth miscarriage, we tried to leave
Cambridge, but due to a number of factors, including being
told we couldn't leave, we are still here. I know God was in
this, and I had to learn to face the life I had and find a way of
moving forward. Having children could not be *the* solution to
making my life better. The provision of Red Tent starting this
year has really changed my experience of being part of the community here, and has been a real answer to prayer emotion-
ally, spiritually and practically. After my fifth miscarriage a few
months ago and my sixth miscarriage recently, we were cared
for, people made meals and visited us, and Sheila watched films
with me. I was no longer left crying in the toilet; Dave and I
were no longer left to deal with our sadness in secret; it was out
in the open, and it made such an incredible difference.

'Something that can come out of facing a trial alone, is that
you can end up focusing all your energy on fighting the circumstances, praying for it to be over and hoping you will be rescued
quickly. I can't say I no longer ask God to relieve me from the
pain I can feel. But what I have learned is that, through sharing
the pain and the struggle with the ladies in Red Tent, life can

be found within those experiences rather than just trying to escape them as quickly as possible. God can be found in the darkest and most painful times, as can hope.

'Red Tent has shown me that the pain I feel can be redeemed, that God's glory can come out of it, not merely when this experience is resolved in whatever way, but whilst I am still in it. I can still laugh and enjoy good food and good company whilst struggling.

'Hope has become part of what we talk about. In January we had a "dare to dream" day. When Rach started talking about it a few months before, I couldn't imagine doing it. It's very hard to hope for something you have longed for so much, but that has been taken away from you many times. It's hard to pray when you've prayed repeatedly for your baby to be OK and you've lost it. In protecting yourself, you think it's easier to just not ask for a family, or not hope it will happen, so that you're not disappointed. But Red Tent has enabled me to hope again, and I've come to understand the need for hope; as Christians we're called to be people of hope. In hope there is life and energy; without hope we're not really living. It's not been easy, but Red Tent has helped me to hope again and shown me the importance of having hope.

'Over the past few months I've had to learn how to grieve. I grew up thinking the less crying you do, the better you're coping with your grief, but I've realized that's not healthy. The grief you can feel is not just for the life that has died, but for the loss of a dream you've had since you were little, and the grief that you can't fulfil a role that, as a woman, you were designed to have. I have learned from my counsellor that it is good to cry when you are grieving, and that there is energy and life in expressing how you feel. By hiding away when you're struggling, and not expressing your emotions, you're making yourself numb, and you're not truly living as a human being. I was scared that, if I expressed how I really felt, I would lose control and always be sad, but there is a bottom to grief and you can come out of it. Red Tent has allowed me to grieve and to express how I'm feeling. This might sound as though it could be really depressing but, actually, it is life-giving because you're not pretending any more.

'We went to a talk given by a bishop earlier this year, and he was speaking about how British society today sees the church as hypocritical and untrustworthy. He then went on to talk about how the only way the church can combat this attitude is through honesty. Red Tent has taught me how to be honest, and I hope that when we move to our next church, I can model that honesty and help to provide a safe place for others to share their good and bad times. I acknowledge there needs to be wisdom in when to be honest; I know there are times when I've overshared. But I do think this is a challenge for us as Christians: to show our humanity to those within and outside the church and to allow Jesus to shine through our brokenness.

'There's this Celtic idea of a "thin place"; where the boundary between heaven and earth is more permeable and thinner; it could be a place, a state of being or a season. For me, Red Tent is a thin place, where God can be found through the joy and the pain, where I can vent frustration or sadness at a situation as well as rejoice, which means nothing is hidden from God. The awareness of our brokenness has enabled me to find comfort in Jesus' humanity; the experience of people crying on your behalf has been humbling and has shown me God's heart and compassion for my pain. It has helped me to appreciate the spirituality of the psalmists and to model it in my own spiritual life. In finding this thin place, it has helped me to live differently, and the times we've spent together have been some of the best moments God has had to offer me since I've been here.'

My heart rate is still dangerously high, but for the first time since I started speaking, I make actual eye contact with others in the room, and if I am reading their faces right, this has worked; we have connected and I think they understand. The evening blossoms into a night of heartfelt sharing, and more tears are shed in the room that night than just our own. It isn't easy, and I think we make some of the women uncomfortable by our vulnerability, but it feels good as well. It feels healing.

I don't know if anything will come from this evening, but I don't care – it feels right, like this needs to be done; these women need to hear our stories and we need to share them. It feels like we are all part of redefining what this community could look like, like we've taken a step closer to becoming the kind of community Jesus talked about.

'So? Have you read it?' I'm sat on my bed, my back propped up with pillows and Dave's laptop sinking into the duvet covering my body. It's been two weeks since Sheila and Elis flew to Singapore for his placement, and there's no way we can last another two weeks before seeing each other again.

'Oh, my goodness, Lizzie, I read it in two days.'

'I think I've underlined the entire book!'

'Me too! It's like she knows us.'

'I know! It's amazing, isn't it? Everything she's written just explains what's been happening at Red Tent.'

'Exactly! It's vulnerability! We were learning to be vulnerable and according to Brené – sorry, *Saint* Brené as she will now be known – it's vulnerability that helps us own our stories and be OK with not being OK, which is exactly what's happened to us.' Sheila pauses and looks at her watch. 'Oh, Lizzie, it's nearly midnight here. I'm going to have to log out and get some sleep. I just had to talk to you about Brené!'

'It's alright – when you guys are back from Singapore we'll have plenty of time to talk about all of this.'

'I can't wait!'

I know it's strange to say a book can change your life, but as soon as I picked up *Daring Greatly*[2] I couldn't stop reading it. Dave has told me he doesn't need to read it because I talk about it so much. I can't help it, though; it's like this book was written for me at this moment. All the hiding and running away and loneliness of feeling like I don't fit is, according to St Brené, because of shame.

Shame has never been a word I've used; it wasn't part of my vocabulary. I thought it was an extreme emotion reserved for murderers, not middle-class girls. I also thought that shame didn't exist in a life of faith. But it does. I might be a new creation in Christ[3] and all that jazz, but that hasn't stopped my life from being consumed by shame. Not because God has shamed me, but because I'm human. I'm as human as Adam and Eve hiding in the garden.

I'm ashamed I don't have children.

I'm ashamed of my body and how it's let me down.

I'm ashamed of how painful I find it to be around other women who are mothers.

I know in God's world I belong, but now it's time to believe it. It's time for my bruised, battered and tender heart to absorb the truth that I am worthy of love and belonging. It's time to come out of hiding, it's time to own the story I carry within me because it's all I have; it's who I am.

26

Bittersweet

~

(This is the first blog post I wrote.)

In an attempt to describe the past few week's events, 'bittersweet' is the only word that even comes close. Let's start with Sunday and a powerful church service where my husband, Dave, preached. You could feel God's presence. We prayed for and anointed church members; people were healed, we prayed for freedom from addictions and illness and for a renewed understanding of God's love in people's lives. What made this even more beautiful was that each adult praying was paired with a member of the youth group; these teenagers were amazing and so full of faith as they prayed. Two days later we go to the hospital for an early morning scan to see our developing baby at ten weeks.

Sadly we never saw this.

Our baby had died at eight weeks and one day. The rapidly beating heartbeat and developing body we saw two weeks ago was just a memory and we were faced with a lifeless dark shape on the scan photo.

As we were ushered into a private room to grieve, I couldn't believe that this was actually my life. Surely life cannot be this painful? How is it possible to lose six babies? I'm not careless. I'm not reckless. I've not been taking drugs and bungee jumping.

Quite the opposite; I'd stopped drinking caffeine and alcohol, was taking a variety of vitamins, as well as injecting myself each day to stop my blood clotting, and taking extra progesterone (in the form of a pessary, a word that sounds far nicer than it actually is). How could we have seen and experienced so much life and hope in the past few days but then come face-to-face with death in such a shocking way? We prayed to the same God for the life of our baby as for the people at church that Sunday. The only word that came to mind was 'bittersweet'; I had to allow both to exist; now wasn't the time for finding the answer as to why this had happened to us. The nurses explained our options. My fear of having to go through another six hours in A&E was at the forefront of my mind, but they promised they would care for us. I couldn't read the information through the tears running down my face, but fortunately Dave was able to read out the details of how a medically managed miscarriage works, and we agreed to return three days later to start the process.

What are you meant to do when you're waiting to miscarry? How do you kill time? Well, we just filled our house with people. Amazing, beautiful people. We ate a lot of crisps, chips and chocolate (basically food beginning with 'c' as long as it was unhealthy). That night our lounge was full of people who wept with us; an unforgettable moment of sweetness in the midst of such a sad time. We spent the next few days eating and sitting on the sofa with friends, waiting for the medication to work its way through my body. On the Friday we arrived at the hospital where I would stay until I had miscarried. As I walked in, I thought of my dear friend who had lost three children and was due to give birth any moment. I walked into the ward next to the birth centre, once again acknowledging the presence of another bittersweet moment, knowing she was likely to be next door celebrating new life as I mourned the loss of life. That day was shared with two other women experiencing the same loss. That ward was a hidden place, where three lives that never saw this world were lost; a stark contrast to the joy of sharing and celebrating the birth of new life across the corridor.

I don't want to push an illustration too far, but I do feel like I've got all the bitter, nasty bits of life at the moment, whilst those around me have got all the sweet bits. But I don't want that to make me into a bitter person. In acknowledging the existence of both, I hope this will keep me soft. I've learned from experience not to pressure myself into having to be the first person in line to hold the new baby and change its nappy. If it's too painful then it's OK to step back. Acknowledging there are sweet moments in people's lives doesn't mean I have to be the life and soul of the party; I just need to let those moments happen. There are always those annoying people who say you need to count your blessings when things are difficult. In this time, I do acknowledge the sweetness of the friends and family we have and their love and compassion as well as the amazing food they've brought us. But I will not deny the pain and sadness we feel right now. I love my husband, my family and my friends, but that does not make this time any less painful. Instead, it shows me once more that life can be bittersweet, and that's OK. For now, I will rest in that. There will be a time to wrestle with God and get angry and work out how to live beyond a day at a time. But right now, I'm not in that place, and I think God's OK with that. Jesus was a man of great suffering as well as great joy, and that's enough for me right now.

27

Fist Fighting with God

~

(Dave's first blog post.)

Four weeks ago, we found out our sixth baby had died. Two weeks before there had been a much better scan; we saw a tiny baby and a tiny heartbeat and we were briefly very happy. I say 'briefly' because we had been there before and the heartbeat, somewhere along the way, had stopped, and so it happened again. At some point in time, as we carried on our lives and allowed hope to grow, that tiny heartbeat stopped. We prayed for our baby. Our friends prayed for our baby. People we don't even know prayed for our baby. So why does the passionately loving, all-powerful God do nothing?

There are neat little answers to that question and each and every one of them makes me want to punch whoever says it in the face. I don't, of course; I force a smile, make a non-committal sound and move on. I know that people mean well with these sentiments, but they have all the diplomacy of an atomic bomb. When you enter the arena of grief, leave your simple answers behind. Comfort when you're hurting looks like our friends who gathered around our house the other night to cry and to pray with us. Fresh from trauma it is hard to cry and even harder to pray. Like Job, all you can do is sit in silence, and so those tears became our tears and those prayers our prayers (Job 2:12,13). I am so grateful for our friends and family, that when God made everything, from extraordinary solar systems to intricate biology, he saw a lonely man and knew that it was not good.

Job did not get the comfort we got; his wife told him to 'Curse God and die' (Job 2:9). You don't get that on sympathy cards, but it is, for me, the way I want to react. It's the atheist taunt; it's my high school chemistry teacher, every stand-up comedian on TV and that violent thought: 'God's not here, he's not anywhere, it's just pain and then you die.' I never have, or could have, gone all the way to agreeing with that taunt, but I have gone a long way towards it by distancing God from the situation, by simply ignoring the inconvenience of his presence in our pain. This time, however, he would not let me do that.

A few weeks ago, within the space of a couple of days, three people who didn't know each other, and one who didn't know about the pregnancy, told us that they had been praying for us and felt that Psalm 139 was important. Immediately I scoured that song for anything that would say everything would be alright. It's not there. The only assurance is that in the highs and the lows, in absolutely everything, God would be there. In my wife's pain, in the baby's death, God was there. God is being pastorally insensitive; he gave a grieving couple a passage about knitting babies together in the womb! Did he fail to knit? Did he choose not to? Did he give up? And so now is where I give an amazing insight which ties it all together and makes everything right. Sorry, I don't have one of those. What I have is God coming to us in our most painful times and confronting us with even more uncomfortable truths. To be honest, I like this about God. I avoid the difficult bits of the Bible; most of us do, as it's easier that way, but that's not God's way; he would much rather we have a fist fight with him (Gen. 32:22–32).

When we get as close to God as that, his pure light exposes some ugly stuff in us (Ps. 139:23–24). It certainly exposed an uncomfortable truth in me. With each miscarriage the desire to have children grew stronger in me, to the point where the thought of never having children I now find pretty devastating, even shameful. If we got to our old age and had told loads of people about Jesus but had no kids, I realized I would feel somehow empty, somehow a failure.

What if God never answers this prayer?

Am I really living for God, for his people and his new reality if everything I pray for is for now? Am I truly longing for those distant shores if I set up home here and ask for everything now? Am I actually not like the younger son who wants his inheritance now, who couldn't care less about God (Luke 15:11–31)? God exposed the uncomfortable truth that I'm living for now and not for him, and I imagine that, if I give him time, he'll loosen my grip on all these nice and present things.

This doesn't make everything alright; it doesn't answer anything, really. I don't believe for a second that God allowed our baby to die so I could get some spiritual insight. When Jacob met God, they wrestled till dawn, and he left limping. From that moment God's people were named as those who fight with God . . . God's people walk with a limp. I have always imagined a spiritual person as monk-like; peaceful, serene and full of profound answers. I am discovering that following God actually has very little to do with that or with neat answers; it looks a lot more like two men meeting in the middle of the night to fight until dawn.

28

The Sea

I can see the folder sat there. It's got an important-looking letter attached to it, and it's more than one page long. I can see my name at the top; it's just there; the nurse's left arm is touching it as she types something into the computer. If I could just reach over and look at it, I might be able to understand what happened. Tucked away in that folder are the test results from our baby.

Without giving anything away, the nurse takes us into one of the counselling rooms. Apparently, she's got to ring the consultant because there's something they need to tell us.

We're sitting on grey plastic chairs in a tiny room with a window that doesn't open and those ugly office blinds. 'What do you think could be wrong?' I ask Dave.

'I have no idea, hon. We're just going to have to wait.'

'Well, this is just great; we're going away tomorrow for your placement, and we're sat here waiting for more bad news; this is a great start to the summer.'

'At least it sounds like they might have found something; maybe it will help.'

'Maybe.'

We play around on our phones for about an hour and a half. I take pictures of Dave looking bored, and eventually the consultant arrives.

'Sorry for keeping you waiting.' She's got the file. 'Right, I need to speak to you about the results from the tests we ran after your miscarriage.'

'OK,' I reply.

'So, from the tests we learned that your baby was a girl. We also discovered your baby had extra genetic material from chromosome 13, meaning she had something called Patau syndrome. In some ways it's similar to Down's syndrome, which is also a chromosomal abnormality. But the difference with Patau's syndrome is that the baby rarely survives to birth, and if it does, it's unlikely to live for longer than a few days.' I notice Dave record details of what the consultant said in his phone, knowing he's going to Google it all later.

'Is it hereditary?' Dave asks.

'No, the good thing is it isn't hereditary; it's just very bad luck. I'm going to refer you for genetic counselling, just to rule anything else out, but other than that, there's no further tests we can do at the moment. Do you have any more questions?'

'So she was never going to survive?' I ask.

'No, I'm sorry.' She stands up, offering her hand to shake ours. 'Right, I'm afraid I need to go. You should receive a letter with an appointment for genetic counselling in the next couple of months.'

'Thanks,' Dave replies.

Before heading home we go to a farm shop for a cappuccino and a cheese scone. It's kind of become our tradition after a hospital visit, partly because we're not ready to go home and face normal life and partly because we both deserve a treat and something to soften the shock of whatever news we leave the hospital with. Dave grabs a table outside covered in dapples of shade from a huge oak tree behind it, and I go inside to order.

'Hon, don't look up Patau syndrome,' Dave tells me when I return with two of the biggest cheese scones I've ever seen.

'Why?'

'I've just done it and it's not nice, you don't need to see it.'

'Oh, don't you think I should know?' I cut the scone open and spread butter onto each side, watching it melt into the warm cheesy goodness.

'No, I don't think you need to know any more than what the consultant told us. Even if you managed to give birth, she would never have survived.'

'OK.' I focus on my cheese scone. 'We had a girl. We've never known whether any of the other babies were boys or girls.'

'I know. It makes it more real doesn't it? We had a girl.'

The next day the car is packed and we're off to Cornwall. I was looking forward to this but now I've no idea how to feel. We're spending a month in Polzeath for Dave's placement. He'll be working with a church for surfers that's also a café. For the first two weeks we're staying with a family we've never met, and the next two weeks we're staying in a holiday cottage in Rock, which is apparently very fancy.

'So, I've told the lady who we're staying with about what happened,' Dave says.

'Oh.'

'Yeah, I just ran out of plausible excuses, but she was really nice about it; she said she'd had a couple of miscarriages herself. I also told her you're still not feeling back to normal, so you might not be around to help as much.'

'OK.'

When we finally arrive (Cornwall is so far away!), we're greeted by chaos and love. A family of six, two dogs and a cat.

We eat curry, find out a bit more about each other, then go to bed, ready to meet everyone else the next day. I'm scared. I'm not myself and I don't know how to meet new people right now. I just want to hide from everyone and be near the sea. I want to hear it roar, to watch the waves roll over each other, rising up, glassy blue and crashing down again, curls of white rolling onto the shore. I want to taste the salt water on my lips and feel it in my hair, sticky and salty, making it curl more tightly, bleaching it in the sun.

The first two days I don't leave the house, my body and my mind consumed by fits. I sleep and hide in the bedroom. Occasionally I hear their teenage son, moving around the house, but I just stay out of his way.

On the third day Dave takes me to the café to meet everyone. The Tubestation is a Methodist chapel converted into a café and decorated with bleached wood, white and turquoise. Inside there's now a skate ramp where the stage used to be and surfboards with the name of each of Jesus' disciples painted on them, hanging from the wooden, boat-shaped ceiling. I can see how Dave has already bonded with this place that takes him back to his youth. Standing on the worn wooden floor dusted with sand, amongst a café filled with barefoot customers in board shorts, the Tubestation looks like it's always been here, long before it was a Methodist church.

I've already planned out my day, and it starts with a flat white. I sit on a picnic bench outside and feel my skin relax into the warmth of the sun as I listen to the waves and the laughter coming from the beach below, and drink my coffee. Fuelled by my morning caffeine hit, I head to the beach. I feel guilty not helping out because I know, in another lifetime, I'd be there behind the counter making coffees and baking cakes, but I'm not that person right now. I sit down on my towel and soak up the warmth of a truly British summer heatwave beating onto my skin. I close my eyes for a moment and listen to the waves and the children playing. I wish I couldn't hear them.

Dave has one day off each week, although everyone is so chill, I really don't think they'd be bothered if Dave decided to take more time off. We're hoping to use our days to explore a bit of north Cornwall whilst we're here, so today we're driving into Rock. Some of the guys recommended a pub with an open terrace looking out to the sea, and I like the idea of sitting with a glass of wine and feeling the sun on my face as I look out into the blue. The pub is buzzing with people, and we eventually find a seat in the corner of the terrace and sit with a glass of white wine and a Doom Bar, watching the water sparkle and dance in the sun.

Then I notice her, a couple of tables down. I watch her. I watch her parents interact with her, showing her the menu then ordering their drinks. I watch them chatting away, my gaze hidden by my sunglasses. I watch them put sun cream on her; I watch her say something funny, making both parents laugh out loud.

'Look,' I direct Dave's eyes and we both watch this family enjoying their holiday with their daughter, their daughter with Down's syndrome. Our daughter could have been like her. That could have been us. I would have loved her so much. I would have loved her regardless of her disability.

The Tubestation church meets outside in the summer, people gathering around the musicians, some sat on the grass, on benches or standing in groups. I feel like I'm half in the congregation and half outside it, not quite sure where my story fits, but certain I don't want to miss out on the music. I stand at the back and notice the dad of the family we're staying with watching from a distance. We've had a few chats about God, and he still seems unsure about faith stuff. I nod to acknowledge him, the two of us on the sidelines; he nods back, smiles, then looks down to his coffee cup. In the middle of the congregation is a guy who used to be the town drug dealer before he became a Christian. A huge guy with tattoos, a ponytail and skin weathered by decades of catching waves, he's currently turning his campervan into a holiday home. One of the café staff members is sat down on the grass, swaying along to the music. She's working part-time in the café this summer; she's a really talented artist who's just become a Christian. Then right at the front, preaching barefoot, is the guy who helped us set up Dave's placement; he's a freegan Baptist pastor who switches off his engine and coasts the Cornish roads to save petrol.

'This is great!' Dave tells me, excitedly. 'It reminds me of when Jesus preached to the crowds. There are people sat right at the front totally absorbed in what's happening, some are sat on the grass watching, then there's those on the edges, mingling, chatting, sometimes listening. I wish church was always like this. I wish I could preach barefoot.'

On our last night in Cornwall, we drive over to Falmouth to hang out with the guys from the Tube who are joining another church for a barbecue on the beach, followed by some worship. The car windows are down, and the warm breeze is blowing my hair off my face as I look out the window enjoying the vibrant greens and blues of the Cornish countryside.

'Do you think we could just stay here?' I ask Dave.

'Unfortunately, no.'

'Oh, OK. But can we come back?'

'Definitely.'

'Maybe you could get a job at the Tube?'

'We could, but I don't think this is where we're called to be, not right now.'

We join the crowd of people sitting on a patchwork of blankets and towels stretching across the sand. In my hand is a sheet filled with song lyrics, God songs, printed words of praise calling me to join them. In front of me the strings of guitar, banjo and violin start to play, and voices begin to join with them, songs of praise drifting up into the warm, salty air. Instead of lifting my eyes up, I look down to my feet and slide my toes into the sand, feeling its coolness and watching the soft grains peppered with pieces of broken shell slide over the top of each foot. I want to sing, but there are no words of praise to be found within me, so I let the rhythm of the guitar and the waves of gathered voices carry mine with them. I want to sing and join in the music, but I don't know if I can bring my heart with me. I think about God briefly, wondering if he knows what I'm feeling, and then I remember: he's God, of course he knows.

The music softens; the singing is replaced with words of prayer and praise. I listen politely but know I cannot join them, for my prayers come from a different place. I close my eyes, allowing my weary body to be carried by these hearts full of faith and hope and deep, deep joy. The guitar and banjo continue to play, then the violin joins them, dancing over the chorus of another song of worship to the creator God. I long to stay here forever, my soul lifted by the trio of stringed instruments and the gentle rhythm of the glistening tide on its eternal journey, but I know I need to tend to my own heart and the place I find myself in right now.

I get up slowly and quietly, turning to walk away from the group, gently resting my hand on Dave's shoulder, reassuring him I'm OK. I leave my new friends sat on the sand singing folk songs and God songs, the string medley washing around me as I walk to the water's edge. On my journey towards the tide, I notice a beautiful sea-weathered shell, soft lines curving over it, dusky pink fading to white. I bend down to pick it up, brushing the damp sand away to inspect its pattern more closely. I stroke its smooth surface, tracing the lines with my finger before placing it safely into the pocket of my long, turquoise, patterned skirt. Then I find a mussel shell, unharmed by the power of the sea it came from, its vibrant blue and black lines shouting out amongst the pastel yellows and pale blues of the seaside. I bend down again to collect it, salt water creeping up and curling over my toes.

I continue my journey along the growing tideline with the music gently following me as I search for more shells, studying each one before carefully storing it in my skirt pocket, rejoicing in each new discovery, knowing that soon they will be hidden again, covered by the depths of the sea and the secrets it holds. Walking along the freshly drenched sand, rescuing shells from the encroaching tide, I think about our baby daughter and how beautiful she would have been and how much I would have loved her. I imagine holding her, watching her play, watching her smile, then holding her once again, my heart spilling over with love for her.

I dust the sand off one last shell glistening in the dusky pink light of the most perfect sunset, and place it in my pocket. I feel the weight of my skirt hanging off my hips, the lightweight fabric carrying a priceless treasure. I slide my hand into my pocket, salty fingertips searching through my carefully curated collection of shells, each one a reminder of the eternal journey of the sea, rising then retreating once again to reveal the beauty of life hidden within it. I lift my eyes up from the golden path beneath my feet and look out across the glittering ocean, the warm light of the sunset reflected onto my face. I love the sea; I love its presence, its power and its depth, holding more salt water than I could ever cry.

29

Grace

Dear Grace

I feel like I know you so well, but I never got to meet you, which makes me so sad. I feel as though we were so close, and then you left so quickly I never even got to say goodbye. I want to tell you that I miss you so much and that your dad misses you too. We were so excited about meeting you and caring for you. I want you to know that your daddy and I loved you so much; there was nothing that could ever change how much we love you. We saw your heart beating, and we were filled with joy to know you were alive. I am so, so sad I will never know you on this earth. I would so love to change what has happened and go back to the times when you were with me. I know I complained, but I would have done anything to keep you safe. The injections, and all the medication I took was, in part, a way of showing how precious you are. I am so sad that we are separated, but I know I must trust that you are now with God and with your other brothers and sisters in heaven, and I can't wait to see you there and play with you and hold you.

Today we found out you were very sick before you died, that you had an extra chromosome, and it meant it would have been difficult for you to survive, but I want you to know that we would have cared for you and loved you so much. It wouldn't have mattered what you looked like or what you could or couldn't do, we would have told you how precious you are and how loved you are each day.

I wish so much that you were still with us here.

I miss you very much. Please know Daddy and I love you, and we will always love you until the end of our days here on earth.

Mummy xxxx

30

The Rose

~

'Can you stand up? Yeah, I thought so. You're wonky.'

'Sorry?'

'You're wonky. The way you stand is lopsided.'

'Oh.'

'It's OK, it's quite common, actually. But I think this might be one of the reasons why you're in so much pain – you're leaning to the right. Can you lie down on the bed for me now, please? My hands are always a bit cold, so I'm sorry if it's a bit uncomfortable.' The osteopath's hands move under my back and begin to manipulate the base of my spine. 'Yeah, I thought so, you've got a trapped nerve down your left side. It's pretty bad. That's why you're feeling pain down in your feet. Is there anything that's happened that could have made you feel particularly tense?'

'Um.' Where do I start? I'm not sure if this lovely, young, neat lady is quite ready for my story. 'Yeah, I can think of a few things,' I reply. 'I had a medically managed miscarriage, which was horrendous. Then, for about two months after that I was still in a lot of pain. It wasn't until we got back from a month in Cornwall that I was referred to the hospital because I couldn't stand for more than a couple of minutes – it was too painful. It turned out I had an infection.'

'Oh, I'm sorry to hear that. It's likely that if you've been in a lot of pain for a while this could have caused the trapped nerve. Has the infection cleared now?'

'Yes, thankfully. First of all, they gave me all these drugs. My husband ended up having to make a spreadsheet so I knew when to take each drug because I needed to take some before food, some after, you know what it's like . . .' I trail off.

'Uh-huh.' She's still doing something to my back and I'm not sure if she's really listening, but I've started talking now, so she's got no choice.

'Then I had a scan and they realized it wasn't just an infection, so I had to have an operation to remove what was left and then two weeks later I couldn't walk or sleep because of the pain down my left leg.'

'Oh, that sounds bad.' She stops and looks at me. 'I'm sorry this has happened.'

'Thanks.' I look at her as she returns to working on my back. I bet she's never had back problems; she probably spends her evenings exercising and doing stretches and eating broccoli. 'I've put on a bit of weight with everything that's happened, as well,' I say apologetically, wishing I looked more like her.

The nights are the worst. I can't sleep; the pain runs from my bottom to my toes; it pulses through me, reminding me that there are so many more unexplored sources of pain I have yet to experience. Lying in bed, listening to Dave sleep just fuels my anger at this ridiculous addition to my struggle. 'Uggghhh-hhhh! I can't stay here!' I throw the covers off me, not bothered about waking Dave up because, well, I don't care. My left hand feels around my bedside table until it finally reaches my glasses. I put them on and awkwardly walk out of the bedroom and downstairs as the pain shoots up my leg with each step.

'Arghhhhhh!' Walking in circles around the living room, I spit the 'f' word from my mouth into the silent, sleeping house.

'Hey, hon.' Dave appears in the doorway of the lounge.

'I'm sorry, I didn't mean to wake you. Um, did you hear what I was saying?'

'Yeah, some of it.' He walks towards me, puts his arm around me and leads me to the sofa. We sit down, fresh pain rushing down my left leg with every move.

A tirade of fs fire themselves out my mouth in rage.

'Can you describe what it feels like?' And then in a moment, I remember I'm not alone and I remember why I love him. I describe what it feels like from the base of my spine to the tips of my toes, and he listens as the sun rises to welcome another day.

We sleepily make coffee and breakfast before Dave goes off to college; maybe he'll be on time today? I make a second cup of coffee and take it into the lounge with my new Brené Brown book. I'm working through her back catalogue now. The current chapter I'm reading is about joy. Apparently, Brené believes gratitude is the pathway to joy.[1]

If this nugget of wisdom had come from an annoying Christian with the ability to talk and smile at the same time, then I would have politely ignored it and walked away, but this is St Brené! I think back to the other book I've just read about a woman who decided to write down 1,000 things she's thankful for and how it changed her life.[2] I want my life to change: I want to experience joy, I want to feel it, I'm hungry for it; I want to experience the carefree feeling that laughter brings with it as well as the deeper, contented freedom of joy. From what I can tell, happiness is weaker than joy; it's more fragile and circumstantial, whilst joy seems more robust. My lovely, tall friend Cath talks about joy all the time, even more so since she was diagnosed with breast cancer. She's not faking the joy thing, either. I know she means it, and I know it's joy, along with hope and ginger,[3] that's sustained her throughout her chemo, because, as she keeps telling me, 'I will not allow my heart to be robbed of joy because of my circumstances.' Cath's awesome.

I go to the dining room and search our shelves for the book about gratitude. When I find it, I scan through the numbered list of 1,000 gifts recorded at the back of the book. If I'm honest, I find the author a bit intimidating, but I'm sick of swearing and crying and being angry all the time, so maybe I can try to write down a couple of things I'm grateful for each day and see what happens.

I grab my notebook from the bookshelf in the dining room and a pen from the pot next to the CD player and write 'Monday, 4th February'. I underline the date then write: 1. I stop to think about what I'm thankful for, and the phone rings. 'Hello, is this Elizabeth Lowrie?'

'Yes.'

'This is the Recurrent Miscarriage Clinic.' Why are they ringing me? They never ring me; it's normally me harassing them.

'Oh, hello.'

'I'm just ringing to inform you we've discharged you.'

'What do you mean, you've discharged me?'

'Well, we know why you miscarried and so the next time you're pregnant we'll test the baby for Down's syndrome, and if the test indicates this could be likely, you can terminate the pregnancy.'

'What! Having an abortion is not the solution to recurrent miscarriage.'

'Well, this is what's written here on your notes and the clinic has closed your case. Just come in when you're pregnant and we'll do the test.'

'I'm sorry, but firstly, my last baby didn't have Down's, it had Patau syndrome, and it was highly unlikely she would have survived birth. My husband and I have had genetic counselling and there is no genetic issue on either side that indicates we're more at risk of having a child with Down's syndrome. Plus, even if we did, I wouldn't abort the child. I would keep it.'

'Oh.'

'And why is abortion the solution to six miscarriages? The other five didn't have Patau syndrome, so are you telling me the only option I have is abortion? Is there really nothing else you can do to help me?'

'I'm sorry, I'm not in the position to comment. All I can tell you is that you've been discharged from the Recurrent Miscarriage Clinic.'

'What if I don't want to be discharged?'

'Well, it's not up to you.'

'Oh, great! So I've had six miscarriages and now I'm discharged because you believe the solution is to have an abortion?'

'Once again, I'm not in the position to comment on the other miscarriages. I can only inform you of the clinic's decision following your most recent miscarriage.'

'So there's nothing you can do to help me?'

'No.'

'Well, goodbye, then.'

'Goodbye.'

I slam my notebook shut and storm out of the dining room.

The next morning I'm sitting on two cushions on a dining room chair to soften the pain in my butt. Eating my breakfast from such a great height just means I spill more of my porridge down my top. I gaze out of the bay window to the tiny front garden and the busy road beyond it. I don't want to feel like this. I need some joy in my life.

I grab my notebook from the bookshelf behind me and a pen from the painted flower pot next to the rows of CDs we never play any more. I write the date on a fresh page and pause; I don't know how to do this. I can't think of anything to be grateful for. I lean forward and hide the front page with my arm, like I'm trying to stop the imaginary person sat next to me from seeing my work.

'Tuesday, 5th February.'

'Cup of tea.' This is ridiculous. I look around the house.

'House.'

Looking out of the window at our small, unkempt front garden I notice a rosebud, dusky pink and tightly closed.

'Rosebud.'

My phone rings. Relief. I check the caller ID; it's Hannah, my oldest friend. We met when we were 4 which, I'm reluctant to admit, was a very, very, long time ago. 'Heyyy, how are you?'

'Not good.'

'What's happened?'

'It's James. He's in a coma; he's on life support and he can't breathe by himself any more.'

'Oh no! How long do you think he'll be there?'

'I don't know. He may never come out again; that's how mitochondrial disease works; he just gets weaker.'

'Oh, Hannah, I'm so sorry. It's just not fair. He's so young.'

'I know. It's so sad to see him hooked up to all these tubes, he's only 15 months old; he should be playing, not lying in a coma.'

'Oh man, I wish I could come visit you guys. I just can't move very far at the moment, but I promise I'll come soon.'

'It's OK, I know you're not well. It's just, well, you're my oldest friend, and at the moment, it just feels like everyone is trying to avoid me because they don't know what to say. I know what you're going through is different, but at least it feels like you understand.'

'Of course, and yes, I totally know what it's like to be avoided. I don't understand why it happens. I think people are worried they need to say something that will make it all better, but sometimes that's just not possible.'

'Exactly! Sometimes I also feel like my sadness is pushing people away, like they're scared of what might happen.'

'I know exactly what that feels like; I think some people want to help, but they're just worried they'll say the wrong thing. I definitely used to be like that before all the miscarriages.'

'You're right, I was probably the same too. Listen, I've got to go, but thanks so much for talking to me.'

'It's OK, honey, just call whenever. I'm just so sorry this is happening; it's so unfair.'

'Yeah, yeah it is. But then, so is what's happened to you.'

'Yeah, it is. We've just got to stick together. Speak to you soon, lovely.'

'Yeah, you too. Lots of love.'

'Lots of love. Bye.'

Wednesday 6th February
Cup of tea.
House.
Rosebud.
Cinnamon (why not?).

Thursday 7th February
Cup of tea.
Warm house.
Rosebud growing bigger.

Mark has compassionate leave to spend more time with Hannah and James.

James loves watching *Riverdance*.

I was able to sleep on my side last night.

Friday 8th February

Cup of tea.

Warm house.

Rosebud growing a bit more.

Meeting up with Sheila later to have coffee.

Coffee.

Dave – oh man, why did I not write him down earlier?

After writing my gratitude list I head into town to meet Sheila. She thinks I'm crazy, but I just want to get out of the house and have a nice coffee, and the only way to get there is to cycle.

'You made it!' Sheila's locking her bike to a black railing as I approach her.

'Yeah. Um, can you hold the bike? I'm a bit stiff and I'm not sure how to get off.'

'Sure thing.' Sheila holds the handlebars as I put both feet on the ground and slowly try to back out, trying not to lift my leg too high. Pain is shooting through my back and into my leg as I do it but, finally, I'm off and we can go for coffee.

'How are you feeling?'

'I'm OK,' I lie. 'It's slowly getting better but I'm just sick of not being able to do stuff.'

'I know, it sucks! I miss you not being at Spice. I just hang out with Becci so we can be irreverent, but we wish you were with us so we could all be irreverent together.'

'It's alright, I'll be back soon, and we can all be the naughty ones at the back again.' We grab a seat in the corner of our favourite coffee shop, by the window, and order our drinks.

'Are you guys going to church on Mothering Sunday?' Sheila asks.

'No!' I reply. 'We haven't been for the last three years.'

'We didn't go last year either, but Elis is talking about going this year – urgh! He's such a vicar! I just don't think I can face it, though.'

'Well, Dave and I aren't going. He's renamed it anyway. Now he calls it FMD!'

'Ha! That's not very vicar-like! Well, if you guys aren't going, I'm not going to go either, regardless of what Elis decides.' We both take a synchronized sip of our coffees. I'm so grateful to get out of the house and have a proper flat white.

'I can kind of see where Elis is coming from. It doesn't feel right that we're deliberately choosing to avoid church on Mother's Day.' I pause and take another sip of coffee. 'But at the same time, I really hate that every year there's a church service that makes us feel so isolated. I mean, it can't just be us who find it painful – what about all those people who have lost their mums, or never met their mums, or have a difficult relationship with their mums?'

'It's not just us! Anyway, I've talked to Jesus about it and he's cool with it.'

'Oh, really?'

'Yeah, he told me he wouldn't go either.'

'Oh well, that's fine, then, if Jesus says it's OK!' We both look at each other and laugh.

'Oh, my goodness, Lizzie, I have to tell you something. It's completely unrelated to Jesus and Mothering Sunday, but it is hilarious!' Sheila moves her chair closer to me. 'Elis shocked me yesterday. When I arrived home, I saw him, through the front window, hoovering the living room. I took my bike round the side of the house, through the back gate, locked it up and came in through the back door, and the house was silent. I walked into the lounge and he'd gone; the vacuum cleaner was in the corner of the room. I called out to him and he said he was upstairs. I had to take a pile of clean laundry up because he'd not noticed,' we both roll our eyes, 'so I went upstairs to our bedroom, and that's when I saw Elis. Lying on our bed with slices of mango over his bare chest.'

'Oh, my goodness! That *is* hilarious!'

'He doesn't get it,' Sheila says. 'I just don't think about sex all the time; I'm not like him. I mean, what's wrong with a really good cuddle?'

'I know! I really like cuddling.'

'Exactly. Cuddling makes me feel close. I don't need to have a naked husband with mango on his chest to feel close. If anything, that's going to put me off.'

'Did you eat the mango?'

'What? Of course not! I went downstairs and waited for him to put his clothes on. I think he might have eaten it, though.'

'Well, at least he did the hoovering.'

'Yes, there is that. I always like him more when he does housework.'

'Oh, I totally agree. When Dave cleans the house, I never want to argue with him. I might even give him a cuddle.' We both laugh.

After another flat white and an intense discussion of our book *The Joy of Cuddling*, we head back to the bike rack and help each other prise them from between the stacks of old Cambridge bikes and their huge wooden baskets. Sheila jumps on her bike and waits for me. Helmet on, I try to get my leg over the bike frame but I can't; I can't lift my leg that high – it hurts too much.

'Are you OK?' Sheila asks.

'Yeah, um, I'm just struggling to get back on my bike.' I manage to get my leg over the frame, but when I put my feet on the pedals and push down my left leg to start cycling, the pain shoots up through my body again, and my right foot moves from the pedal to the pavement to stop me moving.

'You can't cycle home, can you?'

'No, I don't think I can.'

'It's OK. Let's call a taxi.'

'Really?'

'Yes, and I'm coming with you. I'll get Elis to come and pick me up later; besides, it saves me from going home to find him covered with another tropical fruit.'

Saturday 9th March
Cup of tea.
Warm house.
Time to laugh with Sheila.
Lie-in.
Cuddle with Dave. It was just a cuddle; I'm in no fit state to be doing anything else.
Rosebud petals beginning to unravel.

Sunday 10th March
Cup of tea.
Warm house.
Hot-water bottle.
Brunch with Sheila and Elis instead of church.
Sheila and Elis.

Dave did the hoovering (nothing else happened).
Rosebud petals opening up.

Monday 11th March
Cup of tea.
Warm house.
Less pain.
Cappuccino on the train.
Seat facing forward on the train.
Opportunity to visit James and see Hannah and Mark.
James's smile.
Referral to St Mary's Recurrent Miscarriage Clinic in
London – apparently, it's the best one in the country.
The NHS.
Rosebud beginning to open.

Tuesday 12th March
Cup of tea.
Warm house.
Dave's scrambled eggs.
Cappuccino on the train.
Seat facing forward on the train.
Appointment at St Mary's Hospital.
Being listened to by a consultant who seems to understand
what I've gone through.
A date for a laparoscopy to help with further investigations.
Free health care.
Time to talk with Dave.
Good friends.
Comfy sofa.
The rose has opened up and it's beautiful.

31

Babies' Coffins

$\sim$

I don't think babies' coffins should exist.

It's not right.

Today we say goodbye to James Daniel Lawson, aged 19 months.

This is the first time I've ever seen a baby's coffin. It's probably the first time the other 250 people gathered here have seen a baby's coffin as well. The priest, confidently carrying us through our goodbyes, stops mid-sentence, trying not to cry.

Sunlight cascades down from the huge windows above us and rests on the silent rows of mourners. Pictures and statues of saints hang on the white-painted walls, with the image of Mary as both a new mum and a mourner displayed in different art forms around us. There's Jesus, hanging on the cross, blood running from the thorns on his head and the wounds on his body, his gaze looking down to the tiny white coffin below. We listen to words of hope, we sing about this big God and about a future inheritance, and we pray for James's family, for comfort and healing. And yet the air is heavy with questions and doubts. I imagine most of them are aimed at God, and rightly so.

I can't stop looking at the toddler-sized casket delicately placed at the front of the church. The priest is praying, but I can't close my eyes; I can't look away. I think about the other tiny lives I know that have been lost, of our six babies, of Esther's babies and Anna's and so many others I've never met. Some who never got to breathe fresh air. Some so small they could be laid to rest in a matchbox. It also makes me think about those children who never got to exist, but who live in the hearts and hopes and dreams of those who longed for them. Grief cannot be measured by the size of the box that holds your loss.

At the end of the service the congregation shuffle out of the church row by row, heads bowed, offering quiet words of thanks to the priest for the service, sharing hugs and condolences. I don't understand; why is everyone saying the service was beautiful and lovely? It was heartbreaking.

Dave and I stand on the gravel path outside the church to wait for Mum and Dad. I watch the black cars drive past us on their way to the burial, and the rest of us head to the reception or wake or whatever you call it; basically, the bit you know has to happen, but no one knows why or what to do there.

The large red-carpeted function room is filled with people eating spring rolls and trying to make conversation. I see my old school friends over the other side of the room holding glasses of wine and catching up, whilst their partners stand together, hands in their pockets, awkwardly trying to make conversation. I know I should talk to them, but the discounted FatFace dress I was so proud of looks faded and scruffy against their polished outfits and shiny hair.

'Come on,' Dave says, 'let's go say hello.'

Reluctantly, I let him lead me over to friends I haven't seen in years. We hug, we say how great it is to see each other, wonder how long it's been since the last time we were together and then begin to attempt a stunted conversation about why we're all here.

'It's just so sad.'

We all nod in agreement.

'I mean, I can't imagine what it must feel like; I was thinking about it when I put the kids to bed last night, and I don't know what I'd do if I lost one of them.'

'I think it's amazing how Hannah and Mark have coped, though; they're so strong.'

Everyone in the circle makes that 'hmmm' sound, slowly nodding their heads once more whilst looking down at the floor in agreement.

'I know, they're incredible. The hard thing is knowing what to say or how to help; I just worry I'll say the wrong thing.'

'At least I was able to make a cake; that's something I know I *can* do.'

We all look over to the dessert table in front of the huge glass doors displaying the endless green of a golf course, the white paper banqueting roll hidden beneath the home-made gifts of cakes and puddings.

The bright, early spring sunlight slowly fades as the afternoon passes by, handing over responsibility to the scalloped wall lights fixed to the magnolia backdrop surrounding us. Dave and I move around the room chatting to distant relatives, old neighbours, Hannah's Spanish exchange student and people who remember me when I was young, but I have no idea who they are. The pressure to explain, rationalize or find something positive to say in the aftermath of this tragedy hangs heavy over each conversation. 'He's in a better place now,' 'There's one more angel in heaven.' They sound like my dad when he refers to Manchester United as MU: 'You know as much about football as these people know about the afterlife, Dad.' I know I used to say all this stuff too; I loved being able to hand out answers and reasons why something difficult had happened and what God had to do with it. I thought that's what you were meant to do.

Now I live in a world with miscarriages and cancer and babies' coffins and it feels like I've been given fresh eyes. I'm living on the other side of death where clichés go to die. Unlike my dad talking about the offside rule, I'm now aware of how little I know. I'm sick of neat answers and polished responses; I don't think life works that way and I'm beginning to think faith doesn't work that way either.

A week after the funeral, Dave and I are sitting on stackable grey plastic chairs in the Recurrent Miscarriage Clinic at St Mary's Hospital in London. Camped out on one floor of a 1960s tower block, the clinic is a cramped, overheated space filled with makeshift consultation rooms divided by curtains; stacks of paper cover every surface. When my mum came with me to an appointment a couple of months ago in January, she said it felt like a temporary hospital during wartime. Through the cracks in the curtains, you could see people having blood taken – a sight Dave almost fainted at the first time we were here. It's hard to believe we're sitting in the best recurrent miscarriage research clinic in the UK.

'Elizabeth Lowrie?'

We follow the nurse towards the consultant's office, one of the few rooms with actual walls, shake his hand and sit down.

'Right then, Elizabeth.' The consultant looks down at the open file in front of him, then back up to us. 'So, we've done the laparoscopy and the dye test, we've checked for scarring and the shape of your womb and the good news is, you're fine; there's nothing wrong with you.' He pauses, waiting for a response, but neither of us have anything to say. 'As we said right at the beginning, there's currently only a 50 per cent chance of finding out why women experience recurrent miscarriage and you're not in that 50 per cent.'

'Isn't there anything we can do?' Dave asks. 'With the last two pregnancies, Lizzie took progesterone and did those Heparin injections.'

'There was also the aspirin,' I add.

Dave nods, leaning even further forward in his chair, hands balled up into fists, calves tensed.

'Yeah!' He adds, 'There's the baby aspirin as well – should she still take that stuff? Could that still help?'

'No,' the consultant responds. 'Research now indicates the aspirin and progesterone don't reduce the chances of miscarriage and you don't need to take Heparin because there's nothing wrong with your blood. Now, I know I'm not the best example of physical health,' he says, opening his arms wide as though presenting his physique to us. I laugh and he looks at me, shocked. 'Staying in a healthy BMI is really the best thing you could do.' He pauses again, closes our file and pushes it to one side. 'I know this is isn't what you wanted to hear.'

We both sit in silence, unsure how to respond. I feel awkward not saying anything, so I move my gaze to the window behind the consultant's head; I thought it was tinted, but now I realize it's just dirty.

'Look,' he continues, 'I don't know why women who are overweight and addicted to drugs and alcohol can have babies and others, like you two, who would probably make great parents, can't. It's not fair. Medicine doesn't have all the answers, and I don't know why you keep miscarrying.' He kind of shrugs his shoulders apologetically and offers a gentle smile.

'Thank you,' Dave says.

We all stand to shake hands with words of gratitude and best wishes before turning to leave, sad but relieved. Finally, someone admitted they don't have an answer.

32

Redemption

~

I love gospel music; the lyrics allow pain and hope to live side by side without questioning which one is real. Few of those who sang the original gospel songs ever saw freedom and equality, but this didn't stop them from singing about it. Their hope was placed in a world beyond this one, a world when they will be with God and 'he will wipe every tear from their eyes', a world when there will be '"no more death" or mourning or crying or pain'.[1] They sang because they knew their story was part of something bigger, they just hadn't seen it yet.

After singing in the college Gospel Choir for three years, I've decided gospel songs shouldn't be performed. I believe gospel songs should be sung together, not observed then applauded. The depth of praise and pain, the search for hope and truth isn't just a journey to be carried out by the few, with others admiring from the sidelines saying how they could never do something like that. Life is meant to be lived in all its fullness, and this means expressing the good and the bad. Gospel songs were written for people to join in; their repetitive simplicity invites you into them, their lyrics and hope-driven melody captivating your soul.

I'm sick of the answers people try to give you when you're struggling. They tell you everything will be OK and that God has a plan, that there's a reason why you're suffering. They're spectators, not wanting to get their hands dirty or their faith messed up by entering into the disaster zone of your life. They're the people who pay to watch a gospel choir concert. They want to listen to something nice, clap and go home. But I believe in a God of the gospel song, not the God of neat answers. I believe in a God of redemption.

'Redemption' isn't just a word that popped into my head. I read it in a book. A guy called Dallas Willard told me nothing on this earth is irredeemable, and I can't stop thinking about it.[2] 'Redemption' wasn't even a word I ever really used until a couple of months ago. Of course, like any good vicar's wife, I know redemption runs through the Christian faith, and I believe the fact Jesus died and rose from the dead offers me redemption. Until now I always thought redemption was to do with heaven, that Jesus would take us there to a better place even though we didn't deserve it. But now I've decided to search for redemption here on earth, amongst the dirt.

What I love about redemption is that it never denies the presence of pain; in fact, when you think of Jesus' story, his pain is not only acknowledged, it's remembered in churches and songs and jewellery and bread and wine. It sounds morbid, but the end of the story is made more glorious because of what came before. If Jesus just had a cool life, hung out with his friends and talked about heaven, there would be no depth of beauty to his story. Instead, the hope and freedom that came with Jesus' resurrection is made more remarkable and magnificent because of the pain that came before it. So, if this is true, if redemption rises from pain and if redemption is also available to us now, here on earth, then surely this must mean our pain will not be wasted.

The shock of pain changes everything; it crashes into your life uninvited. The destruction it brings with it has the power to impact every decision and every relationship. Pain can fuel a deep anger at the injustice of its behaviour and the way it's destroyed the life you used to have. I know I lost myself in that place for a long time, even though my pain is nowhere near as bad as others; my anger at the injustice of my situation affected everything. I watched as those around me celebrated children when I kept losing them, when others talked about the fulfilment of their work and I had to resign from my job because I couldn't control the epilepsy that wrecked my memory. The doctors' appointments without answers, the diagnoses you don't want to hear, the loss of someone you love and the pain of watching others suffer. These experiences hurt, they are unfair and it's understandable to be angry at the imperfect world we live in.

As well as anger, there's also a helplessness that washes over you until you feel like you're drowning in the doubt that you no longer have any agency in this world. I hate that bit; I often feel trapped in a reality I haven't chosen for myself. I feel passive and powerless in the unknown world of infertility and the mystery of early miscarriage and the constant waiting for hospital appointments, test results and the answers which keep wearing me down. My pain, like any pain, is a distressing reminder that I'm not in control.

Pain forces change; it's probably one of the greatest agents of change in this world. At the moment of impact, all the changes forced upon us by pain seem inherently bad, but what I'm realizing is that the moment pain strikes isn't the most critical point of my life; it's what I decide to do with my pain that will have the greater impact. Even though suffering has dominated my story for so many years, this doesn't mean it needs to stay this way; redemption has the potential to play a far more critical role in my story and my future than my losses ever could.

There are some people in this world who have experienced similar and far greater tragedies than I have, who refuse to let their experience of pain play the most significant role in their life. Instead, they learn from it, they see life with new eyes, they discover beauty in new friendships and new roles and a deeper purpose. For these people, the most important experience of their life becomes the transformation that follows the tragedy. The most significant moment in their lives is the redemption of their pain, not the pain itself.

Some of these people tell marvellous stories of transformation and overcoming adversity and their motivation to help others in pain. I have to confess I find a lot of these types of stories intimidating. Firstly, I don't trust anyone who talks about how they're healed and whole and transformed two months after a tragedy; it's just not possible. The journey back from suffering is long and uncomfortable and regularly doubles back on itself. Secondly, I struggle with stories of healing and restoration that are told from a place of completion, when the sufferer has found their happy ending by the time they're 40.

I know I sound really cynical and there are some truly inspiring stories out there, but the stories I'm interested in are the ones that are incomplete. They read like gospel songs, somewhere between the now and not yet, lived out as part of a much bigger story.

Over the past few months I have been amazed at how Hannah and Mark have dealt with their loss. They have gracefully and naturally become so articulate in grief, talking openly with Emma, their 4-year-old daughter, about James, and helping her find ways to express her sadness. A few years ago, I would have been shocked at their open approach to death, believing it to be an unsuitable topic of conversation both among adults, but more specifically around children. But now I can only observe and admire their healthy response to this tragedy, especially now they've found ways to help others with similar stories. For the past few months Hannah has been ringing round farm shops, butchers and supermarkets, raising money to put together Christmas hampers for families who will be spending their Christmas at the Royal Alexandra Children's Hospital in Brighton. Hannah, Mark and Emma spent Christmas there last year when James was really sick, and this year Hannah wants to care for the new families staying there over Christmas. It's the most wonderful and practical gift to offer in James's memory, especially because he really loved his food.

Cath no longer shows any evidence of disease, but long before this, when she was in the middle of chemo, she started a blog called Hope Overflowing.[3] Only Cath could start a blog with that title and it not be annoying. I think if I'd been diagnosed with an aggressive form of breast cancer at 29, one month after I'd given birth to my first child, I'd have called it 'Hope Drought', or 'Lack of Hope', or 'What's the point?' But Cath, in her wonderful way, wanted to tell a different story of hope and perseverance and what it is to be 'struck down, but not destroyed',[4] because, as she says, 'Even in the darkest moments, pain is not all there is to life, there is still blessing to be found.'

As well as blogging, Cath is now a Boobette! Volunteering for CoppaFeel![5] a charity set up by a young woman with breast cancer, Cath speaks at schools and events about having breast cancer as a young woman and encourages people to check their boobs. She's currently in training for a hike up Machu Picchu to raise money for CoppaFeel! and Joel, her husband, is booked in to run a half-marathon dressed as a giant boob. A lesser man would never volunteer to run just over thirteen miles dressed as a boob, but Joel is one of those guys who doesn't get embarrassed; he's also very fit which helps, as I imagine the weight of a giant breast would be quite substantial.

Coordinated Jo and her husband, Tim, have just adopted a sibling group of four kids. Chantal and her husband, Oli, have started the adoption process. Joy and Rob had a daughter through IVF and are now also exploring adoption.

These aren't success stories, they're stories of redemption. Cath still gets really tired; she's still waiting for more surgery and has to take drugs for the next ten years as well as wrestle with the daily fear that the cancer will return. Hannah, Mark and Emma still miss James, and they always will. Loss is part of their story now; it may rise then retreat and will eventually feel less acute, but they will always grieve their little boy. Tim and Jo are exhausted but very happy as they embrace a life they never imagined: one that has brought healing in many ways.

Redemption isn't about happy endings or seeing life in a glass half-full kind of way. Redemption acknowledges pain, then invites it into a bigger story, giving it purpose.

I believe our blog[6] is helping to redeem my story. We've all been so encouraged by the number of people who have left comments and have shared our posts. A lot of old friends and people we've never even met have got in touch with us to share their own story of infertility or miscarriage and it really is such a privilege to be entrusted with these stories. We've also been nominated for multi-author blog of the year (2014) at the Premier Christian media awards; Sheila's now convinced we're going to meet Brené one day. We've also just hosted an evening for all the trainee vicars and their spouses called #Awkward, to talk openly about the struggle of infertility and the need for vulnerability in our friendships, communities and churches. It started with wine and nibbles, mostly as a bribe to get people there – a Wednesday night talking about infertility isn't exactly an easy sell. The room was packed. We were vulnerable and we got our husbands to be vulnerable too; we laughed, and we had honest conversations about how to support people who are struggling with infertility and miscarriage. Helping other people living in this messy, painful story has given me a new kind of purpose and it's been so much fun to create something with Sheila and Elis.

But still, the best story of redemption I've found is God's story; it's bigger and more beautiful than I ever realized. I used to think the Bible was about victorious people serving God, but now I'm reading everything with new eyes and I see that's not true. The Bible is full of struggle and insecurities and mess-ups. It's about pain and grief and suffering, but somehow it comes together; the threads of illegitimate children, widows and barren women is woven into this story of grace with the most dramatic and beautiful ending that has nothing to do with our success or abilities whilst here on earth.

When the café closed, I couldn't imagine good would ever come from bankruptcy. When I was screaming in pain, begging for morphine, I believed my story had ended at A&E. Stuck in the darkness of grief and despair, I never believed I was part of something bigger. I was lost and alone. Sometimes the isolation of suffering resurfaces and I'm still struggling to work out what happened to me and to Dave and to us as a couple. But just like my friends, I've found that by entering into a bigger story, by entering into God's story, I have discovered a new purpose, a purpose that is much deeper and richer and more beautiful than before.

I'm so impatient – I want to know what's going to happen in my life. I desperately want to see the redemption of my pain played out, but as I look back through the stories of God's people in the Bible, redemption is not a quick thing.

There's this bit I love in Hebrews 11; it lists all these heroes of faith who waited hundreds of years to find their purpose, built arks on dry land, repeatedly marched round walls, walked through water, said 'no' to powerful leaders, were imprisoned, stoned to death and 'sawn in two' (v. 37) – you know, just normal, everyday stuff. They did all these crazy, scary, dangerous things because they believed they were part of a bigger story. They never experienced the neatness of resolution, answers and healing in their lifetime, but they endured these struggles because they were longing for a 'better country – a heavenly one' (v. 16).

Dave and I recently received a letter from a guy in Chester. He apologized that it had taken him five years to write his letter, but he really wanted to share something with us. He explained how he used to hang out in our café all the time and how sad he was when it closed. He then told us he became a Christian in our café, and a few months later he met his future wife there. This letter gives me hope that God is at work redeeming the mess even if it seems to be taking forever. I believe that is where we, the suffering, stand, confident we're part of something bigger, and expectant that this bigger story will bring beauty and redemption and life out of our pain, even if we don't see it now, and maybe even if we never get to see it.

It's almost the end of term and tonight is the gospel choir service at the college; it's also the last time I'll sing in the choir before we move to Liverpool for Dave to continue his training at a local church. The chapel feels more packed than normal. Everyone is squished together along the pews, with the latecomers crammed on the benches filling the balcony at the back of the chapel, and standing around the sides and by the door. There's an excited buzz in the air, an expectancy that we're going to share something special together. I'm really excited too;

I love singing in this choir. Elis is our gospel choirmaster this year and he's picked some great songs.

The bread is broken, the wine is poured and as people stand to receive it, the piano begins to play. Elis hands me the mic with a reassuring smile and I start to sing in a way I've never done before, knowing the words are carrying me somewhere in-between this world and the next.

> Those who have nothing, worn thin and worn down
> Those who are grieving; hearts broken by loss
> Those who are crushed, at the bottom of the pile
> The powerless, the helpless, the hopeless, the lost.[7]

I lift my left hand up to the ceiling as I proclaim the lyrics for myself and this messy, imperfect community I've found myself a part of. For the first time in ages I actually believe what I'm singing, and it's not because my life is sorted and everything is resolved; instead, I'm singing this song as it was meant to be sung. I'm singing about the now and what is to come. I'm singing about the unfinished work of redemption.

I pause and move the mic away from my mouth, allowing my hands to drop down by my side. Elis points at the other musicians to the right of us, guitar, bass, cajón and they all join the piano, the sound rising to fill the cramped chapel. Elis's gaze moves from one side of the stage to the other, catching each of our eyes, drawing each one of us into the song. He then stretches his arms wide, hands open and invites us to join him in singing:

> Hallelujah to the King!
> He declares you are worthy
> Hallelujah to the King!

For he longs to embrace you
Hallelujah to the King!
He will wipe away every tear
Hallelujah to the King!
Hallelujah to the King!

Elis raises his arms up to the rafters of the old wooden chapel, his palms open, encouraging us to keep singing. He then turns to the congregation, arms wide, hands beckoning them to join us in our song of redemption.

Hallelujah to the King!
He declares you are worthy
Hallelujah to the King!
For he longs to embrace you
Hallelujah to the King!
He will wipe away every tear
Hallelujah to the King!
Hallelujah to the King!

Epilogue: The Ending You Always Wanted

2019: Five Years after leaving Cambridge

So here we are at the end. This is the bit when you're expecting me to tell you it all worked out. I now have three kids, a dog, a clean house, my dream job and I'm doing it all effortlessly – oh, and I'm really thin too. But that's not how my story ends, although I do have a dog, and she's very cute.

Recently Dave and I were put in touch with a couple who had experienced early miscarriages. The friend who put us in contact thought it would be helpful for us to connect so we could support them as they navigate loss, life and faith. Dave sent them a message and we shared the blog with them so they could get an idea of our story before meeting us. A couple of days later the husband replied, declining our offer to meet. He said his wife found our story too upsetting. At first, I felt ashamed; her reaction fed the belief that my life wasn't good enough. Then I remembered the years I spent scouring the internet for stories of people like me who had gone on to have children – there were loads of books that told the same story too. The one with the happy ending. But I don't want to write that kind of book. I don't think the only stories worth telling are the ones where the main character gets what they want.

One of my favourite modern-day fairy tales is the story of Harry Potter, and of course, the books are way better than the films; even Dave agrees and he rarely reads fiction – he doesn't see the point in reading stories about things that didn't happen in real life. In the first Harry Potter book, *Harry Potter and the Philosopher's Stone*[1] there's a special mirror that Harry finds hidden away in a secret room. This mirror is magical because it shows you what your heart desires, and when Harry discovers it, we're given a glimpse of his deepest longing: a family. Every time he stands in front of the mirror, he sees a perfect family photo, his parents stood either side of him with their hands on his shoulders, all three of them smiling. Upon discovering the mirror, Harry would sneak away and spend hours sitting in front of it, staring at the image of the family he longed for after the death of his parents when he was a baby. But then one day Dumbledore, the headmaster of Harry's school, discovers him sat in front of the mirror and warns him that many people have lost themselves sitting in front of it; driven mad by their obsession with the life they longed for.

I never realized how consumed I had become by my vision of the good life until it began to unravel. Every loss moved me further away from the life I longed for, and rather than adjust my picture-perfect future to incorporate the changes and challenges I was facing, I simply became further consumed by my definition of what a good life looked like. I was lost and angry at how difficult this journey had become because I had somehow naively presumed that I would just sail effortlessly towards the image I had in my mind of how my life *should* be.

The experience of loss, pain and struggle is disorientating; it changes the way you see the world and your place in it. For me, this was where the anguish of suffering was most acute, for it was not the process of emptying the café, or the physical pain of miscarriage, or living with epilepsy that made life unbearable, but the loss of purpose.

The struggle to find purpose sits at the heart of all suffering. I believed my circumstances defined my purpose because I believed my circumstances were what made my life meaningful. I didn't believe pain served my story; I only saw it as an interruption. Every time I was rushed to A&E, I saw nothing but darkness. All those days and nights when I couldn't stop crying, I saw no future, and I definitely didn't see God. But now, as I reflect back over the past few years, I can see beauty, grace and hope. This may sound strange, but whilst I will always wish I never had to experience the loss of a business, the pain of recurrent miscarriage, or the fear of having another fit, I am so glad for the profound way in which my struggles have changed me.

Over the years, so many people have prayed for and talked about what would make a good ending to my story, and most of these prayers and dreams ended with a child. If we know there's a good ending to a difficult story, then whatever went before seems worth it. And whilst there will always be a longing in my heart to be the mother of a child that Dave and I created, I don't think having a child is the best ending. Getting what I wanted can't be the only positive outcome of my suffering; if this were the case, then what about those who never have a child, or those who never marry but long to, or those who are never healed? I believe there's the potential for a deeper, richer and eternal outcome to come from suffering that has nothing to do with circumstances and that is the transformation of the soul.

The most fruitful, inspirational and influential people I know are those who have suffered greatly. Those who have little are often the most generous, those who know struggle offer deep empathy and encouragement, those who have grieved have a joy that comes from a source beyond themselves, those who are limited by the frailty of their body or their mind manifest an inner strength that inspires those around them. I often talk to Dave about how annoying we could have been if everything had gone to plan. We'd be throwing clichés around all over the place! Dave would talk about our children every time he preached, and I would no doubt still be more focused on fitting in than welcoming those who feel left out. But instead, God has given us a greater empathy and the vocabulary to talk about struggle, and the courage to sit with people in that space, and our lives are so much richer for it.

My biggest struggle with faith and loss has always been around prayer and healing, and my prayer life is still bruised by the disappointment of God's silence in the moments when he ignored my desperate prayers for the lives of our babies as I was losing them. I was kind of hoping by the end of this book I'd have a really clever answer worked out that would make everything OK, but I don't think faith resolves that neatly.

When Jesus healed people, he was always far more concerned with what was going on in the hearts of those he prayed for, than the healing of their bodies. The majority of the stories written about those who were transformed by their encounter with Jesus were not about physical healing. Instead, they were stories written about the transformation of the soul; of lives turned around by the forgiveness, grace and love shown to them by Jesus. There are other stories too; stories of those who had their problems healed but not their souls,[2] and I still see this today, when those who experience physical healing work so hard to leave their experience of suffering and its work of transformation behind them, now that they have what they wanted.

At the beginning of Matthew's Gospel there is a long list of names. Matthew meticulously lists a genealogy starting with

Abraham; the list includes great kings such as David, as well as prostitutes and adulterers, and it ends with Jesus. With Jesus, the genealogies stopped. At the announcement of his birth there are no more lists recording parents or lineage because they didn't matter any more. Jesus' birth means my childlessness no longer matters – not because it's not significant, but because it can no longer define my worth. Jesus didn't come to fix me, he came to invite me into a new story, and it's one that's not only made sense of my suffering but has also given it purpose and turned the pain of a life that doesn't fit into something meaningful.

The best stories, the bigger stories, aren't the ones that end with a mum, dad, two kids, a dog and a nice house; the best stories aren't defined by circumstances. The best stories are the ones where the hero is transformed, where they endure suffering and they press into it and let it change and transform them into someone better, someone more humble and more loving, someone who's definition of the good life is bigger than their own desires. That's redemption.

My faith tells me that in heaven there will be a feast – which is amazing, because I love eating! At this feast those who are known by Jesus will all sit around an enormous table filled with the most wonderful food, and no one will be left out. No one will be alone. No one will be nameless. No one unknown. No one with nowhere to go. As Revelation 21:4 says, there will be '"no more death" or mourning or crying or pain'. We will finally be reunited with Jesus and he will 'wipe every tear from [our] eyes.' This is the ending of my story. This is also what drives the life I have now, because I believe this beautiful vision of the world as God intended it isn't just awaiting us in the next life, but it's available now. It's found in churches like Scum of the Earth and homes offered to kids in the care system and

Christmas dinners handed out to families stuck in hospitals as they care for their sick children. It's also what drives Dave and I forward in our own story and in StoryHouse,[3] the coffee shop and church we run with a wonderful bunch of people in the suburbs of Liverpool – yes, I know, we're crazy, we opened another coffee shop.

The end of the story is what gives purpose to the middle, and I have chosen a happy ending that is way bigger and better than the fairy tale ending I started with. I know my journey towards this vision of the good life will be long and messy and I don't know what will happen, but I know I'm part of something much bigger, something beyond my days on earth. I know I have a role in this story, and I know it will be beautiful.

Resources

Websites

www.saltwaterandhoney.org
For information on Mother's Day Runaways services, including where they are held and resources if you would like to host one, go to: www.saltwaterandhoney.org/contact-us

www.rhythmofhope.co.uk A retreat day for Christian couples struggling with infertility

www.miscarriageassociation.org.uk

www.sayinggoodbye.org

www.gateway-women.com

www.tommys.org

www.fertilitynetworkuk.org

www.homeforgood.org.uk

www.fertilityfest.com
The world's first arts festival dedicated to fertility, infertility, reproductive science and modern families

Books

B. Brown, *The Gifts of Imperfection: Let go of who you think you're supposed to be and embrace who you are* (Center City, MN: Hazelden, 2010).

B. Brown, *Daring Greatly: How the courage to be vulnerable transforms the way we live, love, parent, and lead* (New York: Gotham Books, 2012).

B. Brown, *Rising Strong: How the ability to reset transforms the way we live, love, parent, and lead* (New York: Random House, 2017).

J. Day, *Living the Life Unexpected: 12 weeks to your plan B for a meaningful and fulfilling future without children* (London: Bluebird, 2016).

Viktor Emil Frankl, *Man's Search for Meaning: The classic tribute to hope from the Holocaust* (London: Rider, 2004).

P. Greig, *God on Mute: Engaging the silence of unanswered prayer* (Kingsway Publications, 2007).

S.E. Isaacs, *Angry Conversations with God* (London: Faithwords, 2011).

D. Miller, *A Million Miles in a Thousand Years: What I learned while editing my life* (Nashville, TN: Thomas Nelson, 2009).

S. Niequist, *Bittersweet: Thoughts on change, grace, and learning the hard way* (Grand Rapids, MI: Zondervan, 2010).

A. Sampson, *The Louder Song: Listening for hope in the midst of lament* (Colorado Springs, CO: Navpress, 2019).

M. Sares, *Pure Scum: The left-out, the right-brained, and the grace of God* (Downers Grove, IL: IVP Books, 2010).

Gerald Lawson Sittser, *A Grace Disguised: How the soul grows through loss* (Vereeniging: Christian Art, 2011).

Gerald Lawson Sittser, *A Grace Revealed: How God redeems the story of your life* (Grand Rapids, MI: Zondervan, 2012).

A. Voskamp, *One Thousand Gifts: A dare to live fully right where you are* (Grand Rapids, MI: Zondervan, 2011).

S. Voysey, *The Making of Us: Who we can become when life doesn't go as planned* (Nashville, TN: W Publishing Group, 2019).

L.F. Winner, *Still: Notes on a mid-faith crisis* (New York: Harperone, 2013).

Notes

5 She Will Be Remembered

[1] John 12:1-8.
[2] Matthew 16:24.

6 Secrecy

[1] www.babycentre.co.uk (accessed 5.9.19).

8 Walking on Eggshells

[1] Clare Morgan, https://undertheinfluenceofsix.wordpress.com/2013/06/28/21st-century-mourning-clothes/ (accessed 5.9.19). Used with permission.
[2] Esther Shreeve, *The Gingerbread House* (London: Inspire, 2005).
[3] *Walking on Eggshells*, Jessica Aidley, cited in Esther Shreeve, *The Gingerbread House*. Used with permission.

9 No Perfect People Allowed

[1] Words in italics Nic Findlay, http://unnecessarybeauty.blogspot
com/search?q=beatitudes (accessed 5.9.19). Used with permission

[2] See the woman at the well, John 4.

11 More Tea, Vicar?

[1] https://www.nhs.uk/conditions/ivf/ (accessed 7.9.19).

12 Feasting and Fasting

[1] https://www.fertilityfriends.co.uk/ (accessed 5.9.19).

[2] Psalm 13:1,2; Psalm 143:7.

[3] Psalm 22:1; Psalm 6:3; Psalm 6:6; Psalm 69:1-3; Psalm 88:14.

17 Salt Water and Honey

[1] Romans 12:15.

[2] Dorothy McRae-McMahon, *The Glory of Blood, Sweat and Tears:
Liturgies for Living and Dying* (Melbourne: Joint Board of Christian Education, Australia, 1996), p. 42.

[3] Jane Keiller, unpublished. Used with permission.

[4] Author's own words.

19 Dare to Dream

[1] Isaiah 43:18,19.

[2] Isaiah 43:18,19, MSG.

[3] McRae-McMahon, *The Glory of Blood, Sweat and Tears*, pp. 24, 110.

20 An Authorized Life

[1] My definition.

23 Fear and Faith

[1] Author's own words.
[2] McRae-McMahon, *The Glory of Blood, Sweat and Tears*, p. 69.
[3] Author's own words.
[4] Jane Keiller, unpublished. Used with permission.
[5] Author's own words.
[6] Jane Keiller, unpublished. Used with permission.

25 Who Told You That You Were Naked?

[1] Genesis 3:10.
[2] Brené Brown, *Daring Greatly* (New York: Penguin Random House USA, 2015).
[3] See 2 Corinthians 5:17.

30 The Rose

[1] Brené Brown, *The Gifts of Imperfection*, Chapter 4 (Center City, MN: Hazelden, 2010).
[2] Ann Voskamp, *One Thousand Gifts* (Grand Rapids, MI: Zondervan, 2012).
[3] Cath now runs her own business called Hope and Ginger, where she creates beautiful paper goods and gifts with words to live by and encourage you in your daily life: www.hopeandginger.com (accessed 7.9.19).

32 Redemption

1 Revelation 21:4.
2 Dallas Willard, *The Divine Conspiracy: Rediscovering Our Hidden Life in God* (London: HarperCollins [Fount Paperbacks], 1998).
3 https://hopeoverflowing.wordpress.com (accessed 5.9.19).
4 2 Corinthians 4:9.
5 https://coppafeel.org (accessed 29.8.19).
6 www.saltwaterandhoney.org (accessed 5.9.19).
7 Some lines of the verse were taken from a friend's blog post where she rewrote the beatitudes. Nic Findlay, http://unnecessarybeauty.blogspot.com/search?q=beatitudes. Used with permission (accessed 7.9.19). The other wording of the song in this chapter is my own.

Epilogue: The Ending You Always Wanted

1 J.K. Rowling, *Harry Potter and the Philosopher's Stone* (London: Bloomsbury Publishing, 1997).
2 For example, Luke 17:11-19.
3 www.storyhouse.community (accessed 5.9.19).

saltwater and honey

After facing the pain of miscarriage, Lizzie, her husband and her friends started the Saltwater and Honey blog to help connect with people experiencing the same issues.

In a society and church culture that is not great at knowing what to do with pain, the Saltwater and Honey blog exists to provide a collection of voices that share stories about the struggle of childlessness, infertility miscarriage and faith. Experiences such as these can be painful and leave you feeling isolated, but this blog allows you to know that you are not alone, that it's okay to grieve and your story matters.

The blog has an average of 20,000 visits each year and has become a resource for Christians struggling with childlessness, infertility, miscarriage and faith in the UK and overseas. The blog also provides 'little liturgies', small samples of services and prayers for people to use during times of grief or suffering. These liturgies are also used as a resource for The Miscarriage Association.

www.saltwaterandhoney.org

 **Lizzie Lowrie** is a writer, speaker and co-leader of StoryHouse coffee shop and church in Liverpool. Her collaborative work with the Saltwater and Honey community and the creation of Mother's Day Runaways services seeks to address the struggle of infertity, miscarriage, childlessness and faith.

You can find Lizzie at: Twitter:
@Saltwater_Honey Facebook:
@swhcommunity Website:
saltwaterandhoney.org

A–Z of Prayer

Building strong foundations for daily conversations with God

Matthew Porter

A–Z of Prayer is an accessible introduction that gives practical guidance on how to develop a meaningful prayer life. It presents twenty-six aspects of prayer to help you grow in your relationship with God, explore new devotional styles and deepen your daily conversations with God.

Each topic has a few pages of introduction and insight, an action section for reflection and application and a prayer to help put the action point into practice. There are also references to allow further study.

978-1-78893-062-8

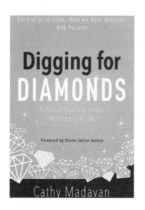

Digging for Diamonds

*Finding treasure in the
messiness of life*

Cathy Madavan

What is hidden always shapes what we can see. In this
book, Cathy Madavan encourages us to dig deeper and discover
more of the life-transforming treasures of our identity, strength,
character and purpose that God has already placed within us –
right where we are.

Cathy explores twelve key facets which point the reader to a
deeper understanding of their unique, God-given raw material
and how God wants to transform them to live a valuable,
purposeful life that will also unearth precious potential in others.

978-1-78078-131-0

Finding Our Voice

*Unsung lives from the Bible
resonating with stories from today*

Jeannie Kendall

The Bible is full of stories of people facing issues that are
still surprisingly relevant today. Within its pages, people have
wrestled with problems such as living with depression, losing a
child, overcoming shame, and searching for meaning. Yet these
are not always the stories of the well-known heroes of faith, but
those of people whose names are not even recorded.

Jeannie Kendall brings these unnamed people to vibrant life.
Their experiences are then mirrored by a relevant testimony
from someone dealing with a similar situation today.

Finding Our Voice masterfully connects the past with the
present day, encouraging us to identify with the characters'
stories, and giving us hope that, whatever the circumstances,
we are all 'known to God'.

978-1-78893-037-6

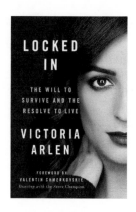

Locked In

*The will to survive and the
resolve to live*

Victoria Arlen

Paralympics champion and *Dancing with the Stars* contestant
Victoria Arlen shares her courageous and miraculous story of
recovery after falling into a mysterious vegetative state.

For two years her mind was dark, but in the third year her mind
broke free, and she was able to think clearly and to hear and
feel everything – but no one knew. When she was 15, against
medical predictions, she was finally able to communicate
through eye blinks and gradually regained her ability to speak,
eat and move her upper body, but faced paralysis from the waist
down. However, she didn't lose her determination, and two
years later won a gold medal for swimming at the London 2012
Paralympics.

Victoria shares her story – the pain, the struggle, the fight to
live and thrive, and most importantly, the faith that carried her
through.

978-1-78893-067-3

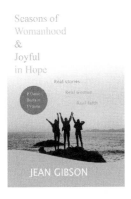

Seasons of Womanhood
and
Joyful in Hope

Real stories, real women, real faith

Jean Gibson

In this omnibus edition, Jean Gibson presents two contemporary collections of inspiring stories from women who have faced the reality of life and proved the sufficiency of God's power in many different circumstances.

Through their personal testimonies, these women reassure us that none of us are alone in our experience and that no situation is beyond hope.

978-1-78893-093-2

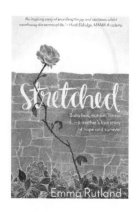

Stretched

*Baby loss, autism, illness – a
mother's true story of hope
and survival*

Emma Rutland

Real, raw and candid, *Stretched* will encourage anyone struggling
with baby loss or parenting challenges.

Emma Rutland shares her very honest account of a faith that
is tested to the limit when faced with the reality of living with
children with special needs and the pain of baby loss.

Stretched is a story of fear and loss, hope and strength, reality and
acceptance and, ultimately, the victory of living an unexpected life
with a faithful God.

978-1-78893-039-0

The
POWER
of a
PROMISE

Nurturing the Seeds of God's Promises
through the Seasons of Life

Jen Baker

The Power of a Promise

*Nurturing the seeds of God's
promises through the seasons
of life*

Jen Baker

God loves to sow promises in our hearts, but they very rarely
come to fruition immediately. Too often the storms of life can rob
us of our hope, and we can give up on these promises. But what if
these dark times were all part of the journey to fulfilled promises –
would that give us hope to persevere?

Using a seed as a metaphor for the journey, Jen Baker shares six
key stages a promise undergoes on its way to fulfilled purpose.
Each stage of the journey is detailed, including what to expect and
how we could respond.

Weaving together biblical reflections and real-life experiences, Jen
inspires us to look at how we can all live fully in the calling God
has uniquely designed for each of us.

978-1-78078-986-6

Authentic

We trust you enjoyed reading this book
from Authentic. If you want to be
informed of any new titles from this author
and other releases you can sign up to the
Authentic newsletter by scanning below:

Online:
authenticmedia.co.uk

Follow us: